What Leaders Are Saying about Women's Bible Journals

"This Bible study has it all—great illustrations, accurate information, simple explanations, and relevant applications! Well done, Lenya Heitzig and Penny Rose. It is with joy that I heartily recommend this Women's Bible Journal."

—Anne Graham Lotz, Bible teacher and author of the best-selling *Just Give Me Jesus*

"I'm touched and blessed by your heart for His kingdom."

—Kay Arthur, Bible teacher and author of many best-selling Bible studies

"This Bible study will take you into a deeper relationship with Christ, bringing about transformation in your life."

—Ruth Bell Graham, speaker, poet, and author of *Footprints of a Pilgrim*

"Lenya's love for the Lord and knowledge of His Word uniquely equips her to help other women discover the pathway to God through these in-depth Bible studies."

—Kay Smith, wife of Chuck Smith (Calvary Chapel)

James

Women's Bible Journal

pathway to
Living Faith

Lenya Heitzig | Penny Pierce Rose

TYNDALE HOUSE PUBLISHERS, INC. • WHEATON, IL

Visit Tyndale's exciting Web site at www.tyndale.com

Pathway to Living Faith: James

Some material and questions written by Kristi DuBay and Sharon Danneels.

Designed by Kelly Bennema

Edited by Mary Horner Collins

Printed in the United States of America

07 06 05 04 03 02
8   7   6   5   4   3   2   1

Contents

There's a bit of explorer in all of us. Like Dorothy, some people may long to go "somewhere over the rainbow" instead of the flatlands of Kansas. Others dream of journeys aboard the starship *Enterprise,* boldly going "where no one has gone before." Though none of us will ever make it to Oz or Deep Space Nine, it is within our reach to take a family vacation to Disneyland or perhaps travel to Paris for a romantic honeymoon. While these vacations take us across the globe for a short time, we can take spiritual journeys that are out of this world and will last a lifetime. Those are the trips worth taking!

Spiritual journeys have something in common with real travel—you have to experience them for yourself. Perusing travel guides about Paris doesn't come close to strolling along the Champs-Elysées. In the same way, reading books about God's grace can't compare with experiencing it in your own heart. Until you have reached a destination yourself, it is just secondhand knowledge—stimulating but not fulfilling.

Have *you* dreamed of taking spiritual journeys but didn't know where to start? The Women's Bible Study Journals are your ticket to exciting adventures in God's Word, helping you become an explorer instead of a bystander. Your journeys will take you on paths through the Bible and lead you into experiences with God that are up close and personal—no more secondhand knowledge! Whether you are doing this study in a small-group setting or alone for personal study, you will be able to bring home your own spiritual mementos from the journey of a lifetime.

On this particular trip we will take a pilgrimage through the book of James, where we are challenged to exhibit *Living Faith.* The main theme of James, believed to have been the first book written in the New Testament, can be stated in an acrostic for BIBLE—Basic Instructions before Leaving Earth. James wants to make sure that his readers (including you!) understand how to live what they believe. As you travel through this wonderful, practical book, ask yourself, *Am I living what I've learned?*

Exploring God's Word can be as vast as a trip around the world, so we need a map to keep us on course. We've plotted the route by dividing each of the twelve lessons into five sections—one study for each weekday. Every day you will follow a pathway that leads you to deeper understanding and application of God's Word. Allow us to familiarize you with the steps you'll take:

Preparation is where each day's journey begins. Start with the prayer designed to lead you into the lesson, then read the relevant promise from Scripture. The story at the beginning of each day's study will help you begin to think about how the theme of the day's study expresses itself in contemporary life. Most of the stories in this book are written from Lenya's point of view; the stories that reflect Penny's life are indicated with a parenthetical note.

Exploration is the next stop. Here you will ask, *What are the facts?* These are the who-what-when-where-how questions that will help you explore the passage verse-by-verse. Unless otherwise indicated, the definitions have been adapted from *Nelson's Illustrated Bible Dictionary.* Parenthetical abbreviations for sources used include *(Unger's)* for *New Unger's Bible Dictionary; (Vine's)* for *Vine's Complete Expository Dictionary of Old and New Testament Words; (Webster's)* for *Merriam-Webster's Collegiate Dictionary.* We have used the New King James Version in this study along with verses selected from the New Living Translation. Feel free to use other Bible translations as well.

Explanation sidebars will help you answer the question, *What does it mean?* Questions that have a related sidebar comment are marked with the symbol 🐾, and the sidebar insight with the same number will help you understand what the passage means through contemporary illustrations, biblical principles, and key definitions. We have gleaned insights from various Bible scholars and have relied on the *PC Study Bible,* which contains many study resources (see bibliography).

Transformation exercises answer the question, *How should this change my life?* Here you will not only personally apply the lessons you have learned but also have the opportunity to reflect on what you've studied. The journal section of each lesson is an important place for you to open your heart and express your thoughts, goals, commitments, and prayers. It becomes a personal record of God's transforming work in your life. When you have completed all twelve lessons, you may want to take a few minutes to read through your journal responses, seeing how God has touched your heart and moved you to action during the weeks that you heard Him speak to you through James. The story at the end of each day's study will again help focus the day's theme.

Contemplation ends the day with inspiring quotes and encouraging insights from seasoned travelers who have learned much from their own life's journeys.

Before starting this study, read the How to Get the Most out of This Study section to find tips and checklists for individuals, groups, and group leaders.

Traveling to exotic places and experiencing new cultures may change your perspective, but exploring God's Word has the power to revolutionize your life. We pray that as you journey through James, you'll discover the joy and power of Living Faith.

In His love,
Lenya Heitzig and Penny Pierce Rose

How to Get the Most out of This Study

This book is ideal for discussion in a small-group setting as well as for individual study. The following suggestions will help you and your group get the most out of your study time.

PERSONAL CHECKLIST

___ *Be determined.* Examine your daily schedule, then set aside a consistent time for this study.

___ *Be prepared.* Gather the materials you'll need: the Bible, your Women's Bible Journal, and a pen.

___ *Be inspired.* Begin each day with prayer, asking the Holy Spirit to be your teacher and to illuminate your mind.

___ *Be complete.* Read the suggested Bible passage and finish the homework each day.

___ *Be persistent.* Answer each question as fully as possible. If you're unable to answer a question, move forward to the next question or read the explanation, which may offer further insight.

___ *Be consistent.* Don't get discouraged. If you miss a day, use the weekend to catch up.

___ *Be honest.* When answering the transformation questions, allow the Lord to search your heart and transform your life. The journal questions will help you write out your thoughts, a form of reflection that has proved helpful to many fellow pilgrims. Take time to reflect honestly about your own feelings, experiences, sins, goals, and responses to God.

___ *Be blessed.* Enjoy your daily study time with God as He speaks to you through His Word.

SMALL-GROUP CHECKLIST

___ *Be prayerful.* Pray before you begin your time together.

___ *Be biblical.* Keep all answers in line with God's Word; avoid personal opinion.

___ *Be confidential.* Keep all sharing within your small group confidential.

___ *Be respectful.* Listen without interrupting. Keep comments on track and to the point so that all can share.

___ *Be discreet.* In some cases, you need not share more than absolutely necessary. Some things are between you and the Lord.

___ *Be kind.* Reply to the comments of others lovingly and courteously.

___ *Be mindful.* Remember your group members in prayer throughout the week.

SMALL-GROUP LEADER CHECKLIST

___ *Be prayerful.* Pray that the Holy Spirit will "guide you into truth" so that your leadership will guide others.

___ *Be faithful.* Prepare by reading the Bible passage and studying the lesson ahead of time, highlighting truths and applying them personally.

___ *Be prompt.* Begin and end the study on time.

___ *Be thorough.* For optimum benefit, allot one hour for small group discussion. This should allow plenty of time to cover all of the questions and exercises for each lesson.

___ *Be selective.* If you have less than an hour, you should carefully choose which questions you will address, and summarize the edited information for your group. In this way, you can focus on the more thought-provoking exploration questions. Be sure to grant enough time to address pertinent transformation exercises, as this is where you and the women will clearly see God at work in your lives.

___ *Be sensitive.* Some of the transformation exercises are very personal and may not be appropriate to discuss in a small group. If you sense that this is the case, feel free to move to another question.

___ *Be flexible.* If the questions in the Women's Bible Journal seem unclear, reword them for your group. Feel free to add your own questions to bring out the meaning of a verse.

___ *Be inclusive.* Encourage each member to participate in the discussion. You may have to draw some out or tone some down so that all have the opportunity to participate.

___ *Be honest.* Don't be afraid to admit that you don't have all the answers! When in doubt encourage ladies to take difficult questions to their church leadership for clarification.

___ *Be focused.* Keep the discussion on tempo and on target. Learn to pace your small group so that you complete a lesson on time. Though participants may get sidetracked, you should redirect the discussion to the passage at hand.

___ *Be patient.* Realize that not all people are at the same place spiritually or socially. Wait for the members of your group to answer the questions rather than jumping in and answering them yourself.

A+ Faith

According to recent polls, virtually everyone (94 percent) in the United States claims to believe in God or a universal Spirit. Most people (84 percent) believe Jesus Christ is God or the Son of God. An overwhelming majority of Americans (93 percent) own a Bible. Yet, sadly, most Americans are as uninformed in matters of faith as the boy who wrote on his test paper that "the epistles were the wives of the apostles; Sodom and Gomorrah were husband and wife; and the stories Jesus taught were called parodies" (instead of parables).

Would you make the grade in the test of faith? Maybe in *Bible Knowledge 101* you could ace the test by answering every question correctly. But an A+ faith is based not only on what we believe but also on how we behave. Many Americans profess faith in God, yet very few practice their faith in daily living. A Roper poll revealed that born-again Christians actually engaged in the following negative behaviors more frequently after conversion than before.

	BEFORE CONVERSION	AFTER CONVERSION
Engaged in illicit sex	2%	5%
Abused drugs	5%	9%
Drove while intoxicated	4%	12%

God wants our talk and our walk to match. How do we improve our faith walk? The book of James was written as an "instruction manual" to help believers attain a *Living Faith* that practices what is preached. In God's book, that's A+ faith!

DAY 1 FAITHFUL TEACHER

preparation

Father, moment by moment, day to day, from my first breath in the morning to my last breath at night, help me to live by faith in You. Amen.

LIVING BY FAITH
For in the gospel a righteousness from God is revealed, a righteousness that is by faith from first to last, just as it is written: "The righteous will live by faith."
Romans 1:17, NIV

explanation

🌸
JAMES
James is widely considered to be the first of Jesus' four younger brothers (see Mark 6:3), not James the apostle. According to church tradition, James was a leader of the church in Jerusalem for nearly thirty years until his martyrdom. He wrote this book around A.D. 50 to teach and encourage Jewish Christians.

exploration

Today we meet James, the man of A+ faith who wrote this letter, and the people to whom he wrote.
Read James 1, then focus on verse 1.

> *James, a bondservant of God and of the Lord Jesus Christ, to the twelve tribes which are scattered abroad: Greetings. James 1:1*

1. Who was the author of this letter? . . . .

. . . .

2. According to Galatians 1:19, how was James related to Jesus?

. . . .

3. Rather than introducing himself as "Christ's half-brother" or "Mary's son," how did James describe himself in verse 1? Who were his masters?

. . . .

. . . .

4. What does James's description of himself reveal about his character?

. . . .

. . . .

5. To whom did James write this letter? What was their situation?

. . . .

. . . .

6. For background, skim Genesis 49:1-28. Who were the founders of the twelve tribes of Israel?

. . . .

. . . .

7. Read Acts 8:1-4, then answer the following questions.

a. Why were the Jewish believers scattered? . . . .

. . . .

b. What was the positive result of the persecution and dispersion?

. . . .

. . . .

transformation

8. We discovered that Jesus had brothers and sisters in His earthly family. Read Matthew 12:46-50 to discover who else is related to Christ.

Journal about how you can be included in Christ's spiritual family and how that makes you feel.

. . . .

. . . .

. . . .

. . . .

. . . .

3

BONDSERVANT
A *bondservant* is a person bound in servitude to another human being as a laborer; one who has no freedom and no rights. Paul, Peter, and Jude also considered themselves bondservants. Even Jesus "made Himself of no reputation, taking the form of a bondservant." (Philippians 2:7).

5

SCATTERED
Scattered literally means "to sow seed." Biblically, it suggests the "scattering" of the spiritual seed of the Word of Life. James wrote to first-century Jewish Christians dispersed throughout the Roman world, living in mostly Gentile communities. He also wrote to all Christians everywhere.

8

HIS FAMILY
Being members of God's family has its privileges. When you are born again, you become an heir to God's heavenly treasures. "Since we are his children, we will share his treasures— for everything God gives to his Son, Christ, is ours, too" (Romans 8:17, NLT).

9

BORN-AGAIN
You can be alive physically but dead spiritually. Until you are born again, you are one of the living dead. "You have been born again. . . . This new life will last forever because it comes from the eternal, living word of God." (1 Peter 1:23, NLT).

SET FREE
Being a bondservant of Christ is liberating! "If you were a slave when the Lord called you, the Lord has now set you free from the awful power of sin. . . . God purchased you at a high price. Don't be enslaved by the world" (1 Corinthians 7:22-23, NLT).

PEN PALS
Far away doesn't have to mean forgotten. Make every effort to keep in touch with friends and loved ones who don't live nearby; you'll comfort their hearts and quench their souls. "Good news from far away is like cold water to the thirsty" (Proverbs 25:25, NLT).

9. Many people wonder whether they have truly been born again into the family of God. Fill in the following chart to discover whether you exhibit the family traits that God's children should display.

SCRIPTURE	FAMILY TRAIT	SELF-EVALUATION
1 John 2:29		
1 John 3:9-10		
1 John 4:7-8		
1 John 5:1		

10. Today we saw that James was a leader and faithful teacher, yet he considered himself a slave to God and Jesus Christ. Check the items below that indicate what things have held you in bondage.

— The perfect house   — Substance abuse
— Child-centered parenting   — Quest for money
— All-consuming hobby   — Other _____

Now journal about how Christ has set you free from that area of bondage.

. . . .

. . . .

. . . .

. . . .

. . . .

11. James addressed his letter to his Jewish brethren "scattered abroad." Take the time now to write a letter to a loved one of yours whom God has placed in a faraway location. Encourage him or her to sow the Good News of the gospel in the place God has planted him or her.

Throughout this letter, James faithfully instructs believers how to pass the test of faith with flying colors. His lesson plan does not include reading, writing, or arithmetic; instead it includes lessons his students must master to prepare for final exams. James persuades us to *act* smart, not just sound smart, so his curriculum contains valuable instruction that requires implementation. Here is his lesson plan:

- James 1: Accounting. Making trials count. "My brethren, count it all joy when you fall into various trials, knowing that the testing of your faith produces patience" (James 1:2-3).
- James 2: Behavioral Science. Exhibiting behavior that reflects our beliefs. "Faith that doesn't show itself by good deeds is no faith at all—it is dead and useless" (James 2:17, NLT).
- James 3: Debate 101. Using our speech to bless others. "Out of the same mouth proceed blessing and cursing. My brethren, these things ought not to be so" (James 3:10).
- James 4: Political Science. Discovering the source of human conflict. "Where do wars and fights come from among you? Do they not come from your desires for pleasure that war in your members?" (James 4:1).
- James 5: Economics. Learning how God's economy differs from ours. "Come now, you rich, weep and howl for your miseries that are coming upon you!" (James 5:1).

Our instructor challenges us to examine the quality of our faith in terms of attitudes and actions. Living Faith will produce real changes in your brain as well as your behavior.

DAY 2 PUT TO THE TEST

preparation

Lord, I know that I can't always be happy, but I can always have Your joy no matter what circumstances come my way. Help me to remember Your joy in the midst of trials. Amen.

JOY
So be truly glad! There is wonderful joy ahead, even though it is necessary for you to endure many trials for a while.
1 Peter 1:6, NLT

Norman Vincent Peale once ran into his friend, George. "Norman, I'm fed up," George said. "I have nothing but problems. I'd give you five thousand dollars to get rid of all of them." Norman replied, "Yesterday I was in a place where no one has any problems. Let me take you there." George agreed. "Good," Norman answered. "Tomorrow afternoon, I'll take you to the cemetery. The only people without problems are dead."

The Bible tells us to expect trials. The book of James does not say *if* you fall into trials but *when* you fall into them. If you are alive, you will definitely experience trials. They come in all shapes and sizes, and there's one tailor-made to fit your individual circumstances. You see, God uses the trials you face to test your faith. Often, understanding which kind of trial you are experiencing will help you when put to the test.

- Cause and Effect Trials: These trials are directly related to our actions or lack thereof. In other words, you reap what you sow.
- Spiritual Trials: This kind of trial comes from simply living the Christian life. It includes being persecuted, avoided, or mocked, as well as experiencing spiritual warfare.
- Mysterious Trials: This is the hardest kind of trial because there is no rational or logical reason for it, at least not from a human point of view.

Today we discover that God has a purpose for every trial and that even trials can produce great joy.

exploration

Yesterday we met James, the half-brother of Jesus, and learned that he wrote this letter to the Jewish believers scattered throughout the world. Now we dig into the text of the letter and discover how to view the trials we encounter.

Review James 1, then focus on verses 2-3.

> **My brethren, count it all joy when you fall into various trials, . . .** James 1:2

1. How did James address the recipients of this letter? . . . .

. . . .

2. What emotion did he advise them to display? . . . .

. . . .

3. What phrase makes you think this emotion is a choice?

. . . .

4. What key word did James use in verse 2 to reveal that trials are inevitable?

. . . .

5. What types of trials did James speak of? . . . .

. . . .

> **. . . knowing that the testing of your faith produces patience.** James 1:3

6. What is one spiritual reason for trials in the life of the believer, according to James?

. . . .

7. How do you think the test of faith produces patience?

. . . .

transformation

8. Jesus accurately assessed His trials by counting them as joy: "Jesus, the author and finisher of our faith, who for the joy that

3

ADDING UP
To *count* means to evaluate. When we face life's trials, we must evaluate them in the light of God's will and eternity. James taught that triumph over trials is a question of mind over matter—change your mind about the trials, and they won't matter!

4

TRIALS
Trials come through temptation or adversity and prove the merit of an individual's faith. Christians encountering adversity experience times when their faith proves either true or false before God. Since many positive things come about through trials, Christians are urged to rejoice at their occurrence.

8

ETERNAL JOY
Trials are not a sign of God's displeasure. Jesus did not suffer the Crucifixion because God the Father was displeased with His Son. It was through the agony of His own soul and through the suffering of the Cross that Jesus received and brought eternal joy.

FRUITFUL FAITH

Living Faith is productive, bringing forth a harvest of spiritual fruit in a believer's life. In the midst of trials, Living Faith will develop joy and patience. "When the Holy Spirit controls our lives, he will produce this kind of fruit in us: love, joy, peace, patience, . . . " (Galatians 5:22, NLT).

REAP AND SOW

Don't blame God for the trials you've brought upon yourself. "A man reaps what he sows. The one who sows to please his sinful nature, from that nature will reap destruction; the one who sows to please the Spirit, from the Spirit will reap eternal life" (Galatians 6:7-8, NIV).

was set before Him endured the cross" (Hebrews 12:2). List some trials you've endured that you once considered deficits. Then write how Living Faith has transformed them into assets.

DEFICIT   ASSETS

_____

(Example: physical weakness) . . . . (Example: spiritual strength)

. . . .

. . . .

. . . .

9. The Old Testament prophet Habakkuk suffered trials that produced the spiritual fruits of patience and joy in his life.

Journal Habakkuk's proclamation into a personal prayer concerning a current trial in your life. "Though the fig tree may not blossom, nor fruit be on the vines; . . . though the flock may be cut off from the fold, and there be no herd in the stalls—yet I will rejoice in the Lord, I will joy in the God of my salvation" (Habakkuk 3:17-18).

. . . .

. . . .

. . . .

10. In the introduction to today's lesson we identified three types of trials: Cause and Effect Trials, Spiritual Trials, and Mysterious Trials. Fill in the chart to describe which type(s) of trial was evident.

SCRIPTURE   TYPE OF TRIAL

_____

Deut. 8:1-3 . . . .

2 Sam. 12:7-14 . . . .

Luke 22:31-32. . . . .

John 9:1-3 . . . .

Journal about your most recent trial. Into which category does it fall, and why?

. . . .

. . . .

. . . .

. . . .

. . . .

A Midwesterner buys a thirty-thousand-dollar Jeep and invites five buddies duck hunting. They load up the Jeep with a dog, guns, and decoys, then head to a nearby frozen lake. In the dead of winter, it's common to park your vehicle on the frozen lake. It's also common (if slightly illegal) to blast a hole in the ice. A construction worker has brought along dynamite to blast a hole in the ice. The Jeep owner lights the fuse and hurls it across the ice.

Remember the vehicle, the guns, and *the dog?* Yes, a black Labrador bred for retrieving (especially things thrown by his owner) sprints across the ice, bent on retrieving the stick-shaped object. The five frantic fellows yell at the dog to drop the dynamite. The bewildered dog runs for cover under the nearest refuge—the brand-new Jeep Grand Cherokee. BOOM! Both dog and brand-new Jeep sink to the bottom of the lake. The Jeep owner had no one to blame but himself for this trial.

Understanding what kind of trial you are experiencing can help you know how to defuse the situation. Like our mighty hunters, if a trial is blowing up in your life as a result of something you've done, then repentance will restore your joy and help you to remain patient until the trial has passed.

MAKING THE GRADE

preparation

Lord, I often pray for "patience—right now!" Yet, I realize that becoming patient is a long and sometimes painful process. Help me demonstrate the fruit of patience in my life. Amen.

PATIENCE

Now may the Lord direct your hearts into the love of God and into the patience of Christ. 2 Thessalonians 3:5

One of the primary goals of parenting is to see our children progress. We long for them to graduate from adolescence to adulthood, completing the necessary stages of maturity. Picture your preschool child, twenty years in the future, off at college. One spring break there's a knock at your door. As you open it, there stands your fully-grown child saying, "Mama, Dada, I want my baba." Your heart sinks with the realization that your offspring has grown older without growing up. Your child has graduated without making the grade.

I recently saw a bumper sticker that read, "I may grow old, but I refuse to grow up." It reminded me of the storybook figure named Peter Pan. He could be the poster child for Stunted Growth Syndrome, a tragic malady plaguing our nation. The symptoms include: refusing to grow up; living in Never Land; believing life's a game of make-believe; and kidnapping mothers against their will.

Stunted Growth Syndrome can be found in Christians who do not progress spiritually. James reveals that trials are good medicine meant to stimulate growth in the Lord. Today we discover that God uses hard times not only to make us stronger but also to make us *complete,* a biblical term for mature. Let's follow Paul's example of seeking maturity: "When I was a child, I spoke as a child, I understood as a child, I thought as a child; but when I became a man, I put away childish things" (1 Corinthians 13:11).

exploration

We've learned that when our faith is tested by trials, we can count it all joy. Now we discover the results of living a life that exhibits patient faith.

Review James 1, then focus on verses 2-4.

> **But let patience have its perfect work, that you may be perfect and complete, lacking nothing.** James 1:4

1. What phrase did James use to convey the idea of allowing trials to run their course?

   . . . .

2. Verse 4 describes three attributes patient faith develops in believers. Fill in the blank with the first attribute. Patient faith will make me p_____.

3. Fill in the following chart to discover where true perfection is found.

SCRIPTURE	PERFECTION FOUND IN
Ps. 18:30	
Col. 1:28	
Col. 4:12	
1 John 4:18	

4. Besides becoming perfect, verse 4 reveals that patient faith will make me c_____.

5. Read 2 Timothy 3:16-17, then answer the following questions.

   a. List the four things for which Scripture is profitable.

   . . . .

   . . . .

   b. How does Scripture affect the man or woman of God?

   . . . .

6. According to verse 4, patient faith means I live my life

   l_____.

explanation

1

LET IT BE
"Let go, let God" is a popular phrase. James said it better, telling believers to "let patience have its perfect work." When you *let go* of your plans and patiently *let God* work out His perfect plan for your life, you are embracing a life of faith.

2

PERFECTION
Since human perfection is impossible for anyone but Jesus, what does James mean by saying we can "be perfect"? The word *perfect* means "full-grown or mature." In God's eyes, patient faith makes us spiritually mature Christians who "behave wisely in a perfect way" (Psalm 101:2).

4

COMPLETION
Complete means "entire" and carries the idea of wholeness. Have you ever felt like there was something missing inside of you? Learning patience in trials makes you completely whole. If you're looking for the missing piece, it's Jesus! "You are complete in Him!" (Colossians 2:10).

PATIENCE
Patience is that calm
and unruffled temper
with which the good
man or woman bears
the evils of life, whether
these evils proceed
from persons or things.
It manifests itself in a
sweet submission to the
providential appoint-
ments of God. Patience
displays fortitude amidst
the duties and conflicts
of life (adapted,
Unger's).

9

PERFECT LORD
The suffering caused
by trials is meant to
make you perfectly
mature. Jesus was also
perfected through
suffering. "For it was
fitting for Him, . . . in
bringing many sons to
glory, to make the
captain of their salvation
[Jesus] perfect through
sufferings" (Hebrews
2:10).

7. Do you think "lacking nothing" means that you can expect everything on your "wish list"? Why or why not?

. . . .

. . . .

transformation

8. Patience isn't passive; it is persistence in spite of struggle, peace in the midst of suffering, and perseverance instead of surrender. With this in mind name a person or situation that makes you impatient.

> Journal a prayer to God by rewriting the following verse and asking Him to grant you patience: "May God, who gives this patience and encouragement, help you live in complete harmony with each other—each with the atti-tude of Christ Jesus toward the other" (Romans 15:5, NLT).

. . . .

. . . .

9. Patient faith will help us become perfect. "Perfect" in this context does not mean without sin; it means spiritually mature. Assess your spiritual maturity by writing a number between 1 and 10 (1 = not mature, 10 = perfectly mature) in the areas described by the apostle Paul in Romans 12:9-15:
   —"Abhor what is evil. Cling to what is good" (v. 9).
   —"Be kindly affectionate, . . . giving preference to one another" (v. 10).
   —"Not lagging in diligence, fervent in spirit, serving the Lord" (v. 11).
   —"Patient in tribulation, continuing steadfastly in prayer" (v. 12).
   —"Distributing to the needs of the saints, given to hospital-ity" (v. 13).
   —"Bless those who persecute you; bless and do not curse" (v. 14).
   —"Rejoice with those who rejoice, and weep with those who weep" (v. 15).

10. Being complete means to be made whole. Jesus is the only one who can fill the void in our lives.

Journal about a time you felt like your life had a gaping hole, then describe how Jesus made you whole again.

. . . .

. . . .

. . . .

. . . .

. . . .

10
WHOLENESS
To *be whole* means to lack nothing—to have everything you need. God sees the big picture and knows the difference between your needs and your greeds. He will "supply all your needs from his glorious riches, . . . given to us in Christ Jesus" (Philippians 4:19, NLT).

It was my (Penny's) first Mother's Day. I just knew my husband, Kerry, would give me the perfect gift since I had been working so hard at being the perfect wife and mother. But come Mother's Day, I didn't find a little box with sparkling jewelry inside or a wonderful new outfit to wear—I found a nice, big filing cabinet. I tried to respond maturely, but I had a hard time muttering, "Thank you." My husband, unaware of my feelings, said, "You've been saying you need to get more organized. Isn't this great?"

Now it was true that I needed to get organized. But instead of a practical gift, I wanted to be showered with lavish gifts. And sometimes that's how it is with God. We think we deserve extravagant gifts or great blessings, only to find ourselves disappointed when we receive a trial instead. Yet God, in His wisdom, knows exactly what we need; He understands that oftentimes only trials will mature us. Since that Mother's Day years ago, Kerry has given me some wonderful presents. Ironically, the gifts of clothes have worn out, some of the jewelry has been misplaced, but I use that filing cabinet every day. And the same is true of God. While He has blessed me abundantly, it's the lessons from the trials I tend to remember. Without the trials, I would never have grown up.

contemplation

The more experience of [God's] goodness and faithfulness we have, the more he is able to test and develop our faith by teaching us long-suffering and the assurance to wait patiently.
Hannah Hurnard

DAY 4 GUIDANCE COUNSELOR

When evangelist Billy Sunday was converted, a fellow believer said to him, "William, there are some simple rules I wish you'd practice so no one can ever write 'backslider' after your name." The friend then gave Mr. Sunday three valuable suggestions: "Every day take fifteen minutes to let God talk to you; allow fifteen minutes to talk to Him; and then spend fifteen minutes telling others about the Savior." Impressed, Billy made up his mind that he would use this wise counsel as the pattern for his life. From that time forward, he set aside at least fifteen minutes each morning to meditate upon God's Word. He would spend the same amount of time in fervent prayer, communicating one-on-one with God. Throughout the day he would talk to anyone who would listen about the Lord. Later, when he became a nationally known evangelist, he attributed the success of his ministry to the fact that his wisdom came directly from heaven.

Billy Sunday's wise counselor pointed him to the *wisest* Counselor of all—God. We all need guidance; we need wisdom beyond our limited human resources. And God desires to be our divine Guidance Counselor. The good news is that we don't need an appointment, and He doesn't charge a fee. The wisdom God offers is free of charge and readily available throughout our lives. We can say with the psalmist, "You will keep on guiding me with your counsel, leading me to a glorious destiny" (Psalm 73:24, NLT).

exploration

James has pointed out that our goal as believers is to become "perfect and complete, lacking nothing" (James 1:4). Now we find that spiritual maturity and wholeness come only from our divine Guidance Counselor.

Review James 1, then focus on verses 5-6.

> *If any of you lacks wisdom, let him ask of God, who gives to all liberally and without reproach, and it will be given to him.* James 1:5

1. Here James points out that a particular lack keeps believers spiritually imperfect or immature. What do believers often lack in the midst of trials?

. . . .

2. To understand biblical wisdom more fully, read 1 Corinthians 2:6-7. What types of worldly wisdom did Paul describe, and why are they unreliable?

. . . .

3. According to James 1:5, how can you access the wisdom of God?

. . . .

4. How did James describe the ways in which God gives wisdom?

. . . .

5. What promise did James give to those who ask for wisdom?

. . . .

> *But let him ask in faith, with no doubting, for he who doubts is like a wave of the sea driven and tossed by the wind.* James 1:6

6. Explain how we should and should not ask God for wisdom.

. . . .

7. What image did James use for a person who doubts, and why is it a good one?

. . . .

. . . .

1

WISDOM
Wisdom is the ability to judge correctly and to follow the best course of action, based on knowledge and understanding. Biblical wisdom is not only practical understanding of matters relating to this life but also accepting divine revelation (adapted, *Nelson's* and *Unger's*).

3

A.S.K.
If you need wisdom, just A.S.K.: "Ask, and it will be given to you; Seek, and you will find; Knock, and it will be opened to you" (Matthew 7:7).

6

FAITH
Faith is "1) a firm conviction, producing a full acknowledgement of God's revelation or truth; 2) a personal surrender to Him; 3) a conduct inspired by such surrender" (*Vine's*). To have faith is to believe God's Word, surrender to Christ's Lordship, and unquestionably obey Him.

transformation

FEAR THE LORD
To *fear the Lord* does not mean being afraid: rather, it is a feeling of reverence and awe based on love for God. It springs not from dread of punishment but from a desire to please Him. "Those who follow the right path fear the Lord" (Proverbs 14:2, NLT).

WISE
How to tell if someone's truly wise? Not by what they *know* but by what they *do* with what they know. Jesus said, "Anyone who listens to my teaching and obeys me is wise. . . . Anyone who hears my teaching and ignores it is foolish" (Matthew 7:24, 26, NLT).

10

DOUBT
Doubt is distrust or uncertainty usually caused by fear. To doubt God reveals a lack of trust in His love or ability. Like oil and water, faith and doubt don't mix. " 'You don't have much faith,' Jesus said. 'Why did you doubt me?' " (Matthew 14:31, NLT).

8. We have learned to ask for the wisdom we lack. Read Job 28:28, then write your own biblical definition of wisdom.

. . . .

. . . .

. . . .

9. Using the word *WISE* as an acrostic, list some trials you are experiencing for which you need God's wisdom.

W (Example: Work is a struggle. I need wisdom to approach my boss.) . . . .

I . . . .

. . . .

S . . . .

. . . .

E . . . .

. . . .

10. James described the two attitudes you can display when asking for wisdom—doubt or faith. Doubt will rock your boat, while faith will be an anchor to your soul. With this in mind, think of your recent prayer requests. Place a "d" in the blank where you have prayed in doubt and an "f" where you have asked by faith.

—— My Past Sins
—— My Salvation
—— My Future
—— My Marriage
—— Salvation of Family
—— My Children
—— My Friendships
—— My World
—— Other_____

Journal a prayer asking God to give you faith where you are experiencing doubt. Start by saying, "Lord, I believe; help my unbelief!" (Mark 9:24).

. . . .

. . . .

. . . .

. . . .

. . . .

Experience has taught me that faith is not a feeling; it's a choice to believe God in spite of doubt or fear. It is not a mystical inner state produced by chanting a mantra, or a hyper-charismatic frenzy where I can "name it and claim it." It is a simple obedience to God in spite of obstacles. Great faith believes God even when circumstances are not favorable or life is a disappointment.

As newlyweds, my husband, Skip, and I both firmly believed that God had called us to start a church in Albuquerque, so by faith we relocated one week after our wedding. Leaving friends, family, and familiar surroundings was harder than we anticipated. We were lonely, homesick, and in culture shock. At first, one of us cried almost every day. We began to doubt God's call on our lives. One day Skip declared, "We're going home." That night God reminded him, "You promised to serve me for one year in New Mexico." It took all the faith we could muster to keep our hands to the plow for another six months. In that short time, our little Bible study grew from five people to nearly one hundred. Today we pastor the largest church in New Mexico with over fifteen thousand in attendance. If we had surrendered to our doubts, we would never have seen God's hand move so miraculously. We discovered that when Doubt asks, "Can God?" Faith says, "God can."

Why do we need wisdom when we are going through trials? Why not ask for strength, or grace, or deliverance? For this reason: . . . Wisdom helps us understand how to use these circumstances for our good and God's glory.
Warren Wiersbe

DAY 5 FLUNKING OUT

"Our heart, reason, history, and the work of Christ convince us that without Him we cannot achieve our goal, that without Him we are doomed by God, and only Christ can save us," wrote Karl Marx. But by 1844, nine years later, he had abandoned any Christian devotion he may once have felt. In fact, his militant atheism and philosophical ideas of the struggle for a classless utopia, free from the numbing effects of religion, established him as one of the most influential figures of the nineteenth century.

Marx had been baptized into the Lutheran church in 1824 at age six and was confirmed at sixteen. However, at the University of Berlin, he fell under the influence of theologian Bruno Bauer, who taught that the Christian gospels were no more than a record of human fantasies arising from people's emotional needs, and that Jesus had not been an historical person. Marx began to doubt the wisdom of God and placed his confidence in the wisdom of men. In fact, his most famous quote revealed his disdain for Christianity, "Religion is the opiate of the people."

Karl Marx is considered by many to be a brilliant philosopher. On college campuses throughout the land, Marxism is still embraced as the answer to humankind's problems. In the world's eyes, Marx's philosophy received an A+. But according to Scripture, Marx flunked out when it came to divine wisdom. "The fool says in his heart, 'There is no God' " (Psalm 14:1, NIV).

exploration

We have found that the truly wise person will ask God for wisdom in the midst of trials, in faith, with no doubting. Today we read James's description of one who has flunked the lessons of faith.

Review James 1, then focus on verses 7-8.

For let not that man suppose that he will receive anything from the Lord; . . . James 1:7

1. Looking back to yesterday's lesson, what person was James referring to here?

   . . . .

2. What can the one who doubts expect to receive from the Lord?

   . . . .

3. Besides doubt, according to Isaiah 59:1-2, why are our prayers unanswered?

   . . . .

. . . he is a double-minded man, unstable in all his ways.
James 1:8

4. In verse 8, James described a doubting person. What is the first adjective he used?

   . . . .

5. What is the second description of one who doubts?

   . . . .

6. Read Ephesians 4:14 to learn more about spiritual instability.

   a. What are we admonished not to be? . . . .

   . . . .

   b. Describe the characteristics of an immature Christian.

   . . . .

   . . . .

   c. What (or who) causes instability in immature believers?

   . . . .

   . . . .

2

NOTHING
God desires to give His children "everything we need for living a godly life" (2 Peter 1:3, NLT). Sadly, some receive nothing because they harbor doubt in their hearts. "All that's required is that you really believe and do not doubt in your heart" (Mark 11:23, NLT).

4

DOUBLE-MINDED
Double-minded literally means "two-spirited," describing one who vacillates between two opinions. The prophet Elijah challenged Israel to be single-minded: "How long are you going to waver between two opinions? If the Lord is God, follow him! But if Baal is God, then follow him!" (1 Kings 18:21, NLT).

6

INSTABILITY
An unstable person is double-minded, fluctuating, irregular, and characterized by an inability to control his or her emotions. The double-minded crowds who followed Jesus sang "Hosanna" one day and the next day shouted, "Crucify Him!" They were easily swayed by their emotions. Are you?

7

ANSWERS
God answers every prayer, but that doesn't mean you receive everything you ask for. If you haven't received your request, either the answer is no or God is asking you to "pray without ceasing, . . . for this is the will of God" (1 Thessalonians 5:17-18).

8

STEADFAST
In contrast to the double-minded person, a single-minded person is steadfast, firm in faith, and determined to remain loyal regardless of the crashing waves or blowing winds. "Continue in the faith, grounded and stead-fast, . . . not moved away from the hope of the gospel" (Colossians 1:23, NLT).

7. We've found that sometimes we receive nothing from God because we ask with a heart of doubt. We cannot always know *why* God answers our prayers the way He does, but we can be confident that He will answer them one way or another.

> With this in mind, journal about some things you've asked of God and how He responded. (Try to think of a time He's said, "Yes," a time He's said, "No," and a time He's said, "Wait.")

REQUEST OF GOD   RESPONSE OF GOD: YES, NO, WAIT

(Example: Heal my illness.)(Example: I must wait until heaven.)

. . . .

. . . .

. . . .

> Now journal about which of the above things you asked for with a heart of doubt. Why do you think you were filled with doubt in this instance? Did God transform your doubt into faith?

. . . .

. . . .

8. We have been warned against being double-minded and vacillating between two opinions. Instead, God wants a steadfast heart that will believe in God's goodness.

> Journal about a situation when you were double-minded in your thinking. What were the varying opinions, and how did you finally decide on a course of action?

. . . .

. . . .

. . . .

9. Double-mindedness brings instability. Put the following phrases in the proper column to help you determine what provides stability and what causes instability in your life (add your own insights to each column):

Want things my way / Trust in God / Trust in myself / Grumble / Focus on circumstances / Pray / Do what the Bible says / Do what the world does / Criticize / Help others / Look up / Look around.

STABILITY	INSTABILITY
. . . .	. . . .
. . . .	. . . .
. . . .	. . . .
. . . .	. . . .

9.
STABLE
Life can be unstable, with winds of change that blow and threaten to sweep us off our feet. In our own strength, we may not be able to stand, but in God's strength, we're immovable. "When my heart is overwhelmed; lead me to the rock that is higher than I" (Psalm 61:2).

A man paid a visit to his local psychologist. When the doctor asked him what had prompted the visit, the man said, "I'm suffering from an inferiority complex."

In the ensuing weeks, the psychologist put his new patient through an intensive battery of tests. Next came the long wait while the test results were tabulated and appropriate correlations were made.

Finally, the doctor called the man and asked him to return to the clinic. "I have some interesting news for you," the doctor began.

"What's that?" asked the man.

"It's no complex," the psychologist said. "You are inferior."

Outraged, the man said, "I want a second opinion!"

"Fine," replied the doctor. "You're ugly too."

The world and its opinions will tear you down. Wall Street makes you feel like you don't have enough money, Madison Avenue convinces you that products will make you happy, and Hollywood tells you that you need a face-lift. By the world's standards, many of us feel that we are inferior. We want a second opinion.

A wise woman will not be swayed by the world's opinions; she realizes that the only opinion that matters is God's. God has only one test He asks you to pass—the test of Living Faith. Will you count it all joy when you fall into trials, grow in patience, seek wisdom from God, and trust Him completely? If you can answer yes to these questions, then you are on the road to achieving A+ faith.

contemplation

Give me, O Lord, a steadfast heart, which no unworthy affection may drag downwards; Give me an unconquered heart, which no tribulation can wear out; Give me an upright heart, which no unworthy purpose may tempt aside.
Thomas Aquinas

In Gold We Trust?

One of the best things about vacations when I (Penny) was a girl was going to the store before the trip. My parents would give my brothers and me a dollar each to buy comic books, hoping we'd stay occupied. My brothers would snatch up *Batman* and *Superman*. Me? I'd head straight for *Archie*.

Remember Archie and the gang? There was Jughead, Archie's ditzy best friend; Reggie, his jealous nemesis; Moose, the dumb jock; and of course, Betty and Veronica, the girls vying for Archie's affection. Veronica was a beautiful brunette, spoiled rotten by her rich daddy. Betty was a bouncy blonde with a great personality.

Who are you like—Betty or Veronica? While I wanted to be like Betty, growing up I was more like Veronica. We weren't mega-rich, but I was a bit spoiled by my daddy. The problem with Veronicas is that they are often brought down a notch because they only trust in their connections or money. In the end, it's the humble Bettys who come out ahead. In Jesus' words, "Those who exalt themselves will be humbled, and those who humble themselves will be exalted" (Matthew 23:12, NLT).

Early in our marriage, my husband and I were brought down by financial trouble. That's when I learned a valuable lesson: God is more concerned with what is in my heavenly bank account than what is in my pocketbook. I learned that trusting in God makes me truly rich while trusting in gold made me miserably poor.

preparation

Lord, I'm so grateful that Your Word is offered freely to everyone—rich and poor, high and low. Help me to listen and to gain insight into the wisdom You offer me today. Amen.

FREE WISDOM
High and low, rich and poor—listen! For my words are wise, and my thoughts are filled with insight. Psalm 49:2-3, NLT

explanation

LOW DOWN
"Lowly brother" refers to believers who are cast down, hold a low social station, or are impoverished. God has a special place in His heart for the poor and downcast. He commanded the Israelites, "If one of your brethren becomes poor, . . . then you shall help him" (Leviticus 25:35).

exploration

We have found that Living Faith not only allows us to victoriously overcome the trials of life, but it also instills joy, patience, and wisdom in the hearts and minds of believers. Now we discover that true Living Faith will view earthly riches from God's heavenly perspective.

Review James 1, then focus on verses 9-11.

> *Let the lowly brother glory in his exaltation, but the rich in his humiliation, because as a flower of the field he will pass away.* James 1:9-10

1. Whom did James address first? . . . .

. . . .

2. What emotion was the lowly person to exhibit?. . . . .

. . . .

3. What phrase reveals that the lowly person's spiritual condition was the reverse of his financial condition?

. . . .

4. Turning to the next group James addresses, in what was the rich person to glory or rejoice?

. . . .

5. What phrase did James use in verse 10 to remind us that this life is temporary?

. . . .

6. Why do you think he reminded rich believers of this?

. . . .

. . . .

> *For no sooner has the sun risen with a burning heat than it withers the grass; its flower falls, and its beautiful appearance perishes. So the rich man also will fade away in his pursuits.* James 1:11

7. Describe the impact of the sun's burning heat on nature.

. . . .

8. James compared the fragility of the natural world with the fragility of human beings. What will happen to rich people in their pursuit of pleasure, luxury, and wealth?

. . . .

. . . .

transformation

9. We have seen that in God's eyes things are not always what they seem. This was exemplified in the life of Christ. Draw a line to show how Christ's position on earth is the opposite of His true spiritual position.

WORLD'S EYES	GOD'S EYES
A poor man	Glorious abode in heaven
Hungry	Highly exalted by God
Cast down by society	Bread of life
No home on earth	Eternally rich

2
GLORY
To *glory in* means to rejoice. Even the most lowly Christian can rejoice because of God's blessings. Regardless of our circumstances, like the psalmist we can say, "My heart shall rejoice in Your salvation. I will sing to the Lord, because He has dealt bountifully with me" (Psalm 13:5-6).

3
GOD'S ECONOMY
"'My thoughts are completely different from yours,' says the Lord. 'And my ways are far beyond anything you could imagine'" (Isaiah 55:8, NLT). In God's economy the poor are rich, the weak are strong, and the lowly are lifted up and exalted.

4
HUMILITY
Humiliation means to be brought low in rank or emotion. God allows humbling experiences in wealthy believers' lives to teach them that genuine happiness and contentment depend not on earthly wealth, but on the true riches of God's grace. "With humility comes wisdom" (Proverbs 11:2, NLT).

EXALTED
Exalted means to be highly regarded or esteemed. Jesus was "despised, and we did not esteem Him" (Isaiah 53:3). Yet in a heavenly vision, Isaiah "saw the Lord sitting on a throne, high and lifted up" (v. 6:1). Jesus, the despised One, was really Jesus, the Most High.

10

GOD DECIDES
You might think your boss decides whether or not you get a promotion. But in reality God is the one who decides. "No one . . . can exalt a man. But it is God who judges: He brings one down, he exalts another" (Psalm 75:6-7, NIV).

11

ETERNAL RICHES
You can't take it with you, but you *can* send treasures to heaven. Paul urged the wealthy "to do good, to be rich in good deeds, and to be generous and willing to share. In this way they will lay up treasure for themselves" (1 Timothy 6:18-19, NIV).

10. James revealed that the lowly believer is really exalted or lifted up. The Bible teaches that Jesus Christ is to be exalted above all.

> Journal Philippians 2:9-11 into a personal declaration, exalting Jesus above everything and confessing Him as *your* Lord. "God also has highly exalted Him and given Him the name which is above every name, that at the name of Jesus every knee should bow, of those in heaven, and of those on earth, and of those under the earth, and that every tongue should confess that Jesus Christ is Lord, to the glory of God the Father."

. . . .

. . . .

. . . .

. . . .

11. In verse 11, James borrowed vivid imagery from Isaiah the prophet to warn the rich of the danger of trusting in themselves and their wealth. Read Isaiah 40:6-8 and answer the following questions.

   a. Describe what "all flesh"—people and their glory— is compared to.

   . . . .

   b. What blows on the grass and flowers? . . . .

   . . . .

   c. What happens as a result? . . . .

   . . . .

   d. What "treasure" will last into eternity?. . . . .

   . . . .

12. We learned today that God will often send humbling circumstances so that believers will rely on God rather than on earthly riches. Fill in the chart to discover how God humbled His people throughout Scripture.

Deut. 8:3 . . . .

2 Chron. 32:24-26. . . . .

Dan. 5:22-28 . . . .

Luke 18:9-14. . . . .

> Now journal about a time when God allowed you to be
> humbled or brought low in one of the ways listed above.
> How did you respond? How did God lift you up?

. . . .

. . . .

. . . .

. . . .

The story is told of a shepherd who, given a position of nobility by a Scottish king, often went to a solitary room in the palace. The king became suspicious and asked to look inside this secret room. To his surprise he saw only a chair, a shepherd's crook, and an old plaid scarf. "What does this mean?" asked the king. The nobleman replied, "I was a humble shepherd when Your Majesty promoted me. I come to this room to look at the crook and the plaid scarf. They remind me of what I used to be, and also that I am nothing but what the grace of the king has made me."

We are all paupers, spiritually speaking, until the King of kings promotes us to a position of honor beside His dear Son. "God raised us up with Christ and seated us with him in the heavenly realms in Christ Jesus" (Ephesians 2:6, NIV). When I forget that and get too big for my britches, I just recall my past as a partying college co-ed by day and a discothèque bartender by night. Images of me hugging the toilet and waking with a hangover serve as stark reminders of how God can radically change a life by exalting the lowly. If God's hand of favor and His bountiful blessings have caused you to develop an inflated perception of yourself, perhaps you should revisit your own humble beginnings and remember that without Christ we're nothing.

contemplation

The call of Christ is always a promotion.
A. W. Tozer

DAY 2 STINKIN' RICH

preparation

Lord, I praise You for the heavenly treasures You have blessed me with on earth—the sweetness of Your love, the fruits of the Spirit, and the hope of eternity with You. Amen.

ETERNAL TREASURES
*Lay up for yourselves treasures in heaven, where neither moth nor rust destroys and where thieves do not break in and steal. For where your treasure is, there your heart will be also.
Matthew 6:20-21*

In a small town in Florida, a woman known as Garbage Mary could be seen dressed in rags, scavenging through garbage cans for food, which she hoarded in her car or her tiny two-room apartment. A recluse with no friends, she bummed cigarettes and ice from strangers. Those who met her believed that she was a destitute old woman.

Eventually Garbage Mary was arrested and institutionalized. When her apartment was searched, officials were amazed to discover bankbooks, stock securities, oil-drilling rights, real-estate documents, and cash strewn everywhere. Garbage Mary was worth more than a million dollars. They also discovered that she was a forty-eight-year-old college graduate who had inherited a great deal of money. While her money collected interest, she collected garbage! Where riches are concerned, how much is enough? For Mary, mounds of riches weren't enough. She refused to access her vast resources to benefit herself or others for fear of losing what she already had. James teaches that riches often bring misery to those that possess them. Some rich folks squander their wealth on "riotous living" like the prodigal son. Others parade their wealth using designer labels and status symbols to buy prestige. Any way you look at it, those who waste their wealth are just stinkin' rich.

exploration

A proper perspective on wealth is a recurring theme in James. We now jump ahead to James 5 to continue our study on this important topic. Here we see that God looks unfavorably upon those who selfishly hoard their riches.

Read James 5, then focus on verses 1-3.

Come now, you rich, weep and howl for your miseries that are coming upon you! Your riches are corrupted, and your garments are moth-eaten. James 5:1-2

1. James used the words "Come now" as an insistent command to pay attention. Whose attention did James want to get?

. . . .

2. What did James tell the rich to do, and why? . . . .

. . . .

3. Describe what happens to riches and garments that are hoarded (verse 2).

. . . .

Your gold and silver are corroded, and their corrosion will be a witness against you and will eat your flesh like fire. James 5:3

4. What did James say will happen to gold and silver that is stockpiled?

. . . .

5. Against whom does the corrosion of gold and silver bear witness? Of what does it bear witness?

. . . .

6. How will corrosion act as the rich person's executioner?

. . . .

You have heaped up treasure in the last days. James 5:3

7. Reword the indictment made by James against the unrighteous rich man.

. . . .

IS IT SIN?
Sin has to do with context. Money, like food and sex, is neutral in and of itself. Eating is necessary; gluttony is sin. Sex within God's guidelines is good; prostitution is aberrant. Riches are not evil, but when abused in ways God did not intend, they become harmful.

10

USE OR LOSE
When it comes to riches, the Bible encourages us to "use it or lose it." Possessions unused are wasted. Grain will rot. Gold will rust. Garments will become moth-eaten. God blesses us with riches and gifts in order to bless others.

11

SAVINGS
Saving is not wrong. However, failing to provide for your household is sinful. "If anyone does not provide for his own, and especially for . . . his household, he has denied the faith" (1 Timothy 5:8).

8. Read Romans 2:5-6. According to these verses, what will a hard, unrepentant heart store up in the day of God's judgment?

. . . .

transformation

9. 1 Timothy 6:9-10 says: "But those who desire to be rich fall into temptation and a snare, and into many foolish and harmful lusts which drown men in destruction and perdition. For the love of money is a root of all kinds of evil, for which some have strayed from the faith in their greediness, and pierced themselves through with many sorrows."

   a. Circle the words above that describe what happens to those who desire to be rich.

   b. Underline the words that describe the love of money and the results of that love.

10. Today we learned that when rich people hoard their earthly wealth, denying its benefits to those in need, they store up the wrath of God on Judgment Day. Read 1 Timothy 6:17-19. List what these verses command us to do with our earthly wealth and how we will benefit from obedience.

COMMAND   BENEFIT OF OBEDIENCE

. . . .

. . . .

. . . .

. . . .

11. 1 Corinthians 4:2 tells us that we must be faithful stewards of what God has given us. In what ways do you spend your money?

   __ Things I don't really need   __ Eating at restaurants
   __ Paying my bills   __ Entertainment
   __ On my vices (i.e. cigarettes)   __ Supporting a missionary
   __ Tithing to the Lord   __ Savings and investments

12. Many people hoard their money because of fear of financial insecurity, or they waste their money on things that do not last simply to impress others.

> Journal about some of the reasons you have stored up wealth or squandered your resources.

. . . .

. . . .

. . . .

. . . .

The book *Malcolm Forbes: The Man Who Had Everything* tells of a motorcycle tour the multimillionaire took through Egypt in 1984. Reflecting on the burial tomb of King Tut, Forbes asked an associate: "Do you think I'll be remembered after I die?" Malcolm Forbes is known for his pithy statement, "He who dies with the most toys wins." In fact, that was his ambition. That's why he collected scores of motorcycles. That's why he would pay over a million dollars for a Faberge egg. That's why he owned castles, hot air balloons, and countless other toys that he can no longer access.

Another book has been written that could have been titled *Jesus Christ: The Man Who GAVE Everything.* God knew that all of the silver and gold in the world couldn't open the pearly gates, so He "purchased our freedom through the blood of his Son, and our sins are forgiven" (Ephesians 1:7, NLT). If Malcolm Forbes had taken a ride through Israel to the empty garden tomb, he might not have asked, "Will I be remembered after I die?" but like the thief on the cross, he would have requested, "Jesus, remember me when you come into your Kingdom" (Luke 23:42, NLT). He who dies with the most toys doesn't win—he just dies. But whoever dies believing in Jesus gains all of eternity.

contemplation

I would not give one moment of heaven for all the joys and riches of the world, even if it lasted for thousands and thousands of years.
Martin Luther

preparation

*Father God, it gives
me great comfort to
know that when the
oppressed and needy
cry out, You always hear
them. I praise You that
in Your sovereign time
You deliver us from the
hands of our enemies.
Amen.*

DELIVERANCE

*For He will deliver the
needy when he cries,
the poor also, and him
who has no helper.
Psalm 72:12*

My husband called and said, "Penny, put on a nice outfit. We're going out to celebrate!" Kerry had started his own architectural company and business had been slow. Then he got a call from a developer who wanted him to design a new subdivision. That meant that we'd be financially secure for the first time in years. We were overjoyed.

In good faith, Kerry spent months visiting the site and supervising the building of several high-end southwestern homes nestled in the foothills of the Sandia Mountains. The developer had said, "As soon as the first house sells, I'll pay you." Naively, we believed him and kept waiting to receive a check. But the first house sold, and then the second, and we didn't get paid. Finally, Kerry confronted the man, who taunted, "You can sue me; I'm not gonna pay you." That's when we realized we'd been had by a smooth-talking con man.

This businessman thought he would get ahead by defrauding honest laborers like us. But time has shown that God's Word is true; the businessman's heaped-up riches have corroded. He has filed bankruptcy several times, and so many people refused to work with him that he left town. His heart has also grown hard. He divorced his wife and severed relationships with personal friends.

Anyone who has been defrauded by a dishonest employer will be encouraged to learn that the wages you're owed call out to God—money talks.

exploration

We have learned that hoarding wealth is a sin, but when we use our possessions for God's glory, those things become treasures and we invest in eternity. James now turns his attention to the ways the unrighteous rich deal with their employees.

Read James 5, then focus on verse 4.

> *Indeed the wages of the laborers who mowed your fields, which you kept back by fraud, cry out; and the cries of the reapers have reached the ears of the Lord of Sabaoth.*
> James 5:4

1. What happened to the wages of the laborers? . . . .

. . . .

2. Describe what the laborers had done to earn their wages.

. . . .

3. How did the money talk?. . . . .

. . . .

4. Whose cries were also heard? . . . .

. . . .

5. Who heard these cries? . . . .

. . . .

6. Read Deuteronomy 24:14-15 and answer the following questions.

   a. What does God command *shall not* be done to the hired servant?

   . . . .

   . . . .

   b. What does God command *shall* be done? Why?

   . . . .

   . . . .

explanation

1

FRAUD
Fraud is the "intentional perversion of the truth to induce another to part with something of value; to deceive or misrepresent" (*Webster's*). Jacob defrauded Esau: "Jacob . . . has deceived me twice, first taking my birthright and now stealing my blessing" (Genesis 27:36, NLT).

2

LABORERS
In a rural farming economy, most laborers depended on daily wages to survive. To withhold pay from a workman was a serious sin in God's eyes. "Woe to him . . . who uses his neighbor's services without wages and gives him nothing for his work" (Jeremiah 22:13).

5

SABAOTH
Sabaoth is derived from the Hebrew word *tsaba*, meaning hosts or armies. The *Lord of Sabaoth* describes God as Commander of the armies of heaven (adapted, *MacArthur Commentary*). God, the mighty warrior, will hear the cries of the downtrodden and oppressed, and He will judge righteously.

7. Today we have seen that God condemns financial fraud. Read Jeremiah 22:13-14 and answer the following questions.

    a. Upon whom did Jeremiah pronounce this "woe"?

. . . .

    b. In what ways had this person committed fraud?

. . . .

    c. How did the person spend his ill-gotten gain?

. . . .

8. Today's text focused on laborers who had not received their due. Has there ever been a time in your life when you were owed money but were denied payment?

> Journal about your experience. How does it make you feel to learn that your lost wages actually "cry out" to God?

. . . .

. . . .

. . . .

. . . .

9. We have been warned against defrauding others of their well-earned pay.

Journal the truths of this proverb into a personal prayer to God:
"Remove falsehood and lies far from me; give me neither poverty nor riches—feed me with the food allotted to me; lest I be full and deny You, and say, 'Who is the Lord?' Or lest I be poor and steal, and profane the name of my God" (Proverbs 30:8-9).

. . . .

. . . .

. . . .

. . . .

. . . .

Most of us would never think of defrauding someone we know. But there are subtle ways of defrauding that you may never have considered: holding back an allowance, underpaying a baby-sitter, or cheating the I.R.S. Ann Landers received this letter about a very creative act of fraud:

Dear Ann Landers:

Aunt 'Emma' was married to a tightwad who was also a little strange. He made a good salary, but they lived frugally because he insisted on putting 20 percent of his paycheck under the mattress. (The man didn't trust banks.) The money, he said, was going to come in handy in their old age.

When Uncle 'Ollie' was sixty, he was stricken with cancer. Toward the end, he made Aunt Em promise, in the presence of his brothers, that she would put the money he had stashed away in his coffin so he could buy his way into heaven if he had to. They all knew he was a little odd, but this was clearly a crazy request. Aunt Em did promise, however, and assured Uncle Ollie's brothers that she was a woman of her word and would do as he asked. The following morning she took the money (about twenty-six thousand dollars) to the bank and deposited it. She then wrote a check and put it in the casket four days later. This is a true story, and our family has laughed about it ever since.

"Don't let the world around you squeeze you into its own mould," the apostle Paul wrote in Romans 12:2 (*Phillips*). Honor God by being honest in all your financial dealings, and God will honor you.

4 BUY NOW,
PAY LATER

In 1923, seven of the world's most successful financiers met
at Chicago's Edgewater Beach Hotel. These guys were rich—
rich—rich!

1. Charles Schwab, the president of the largest steel company
2. Samuel Insull, the president of the largest electric utility
   company
3. Howard Hopson, the president of the largest gas company
4. Arthur Cutten, the great wheat speculator
5. Richard Whitney, the president of the New York Stock
   Exchange
6. Albert Fall, the Secretary of Interior in President Harding's
   Cabinet
7. Jesse Livermore, the greatest "bear" on Wall Street

Financially, these high rollers could have anything money could
buy. Wouldn't you like to change positions with them? Before
deciding, look twenty-five years ahead to 1948:

1. Charles Schwab went bankrupt, living his last years on
   borrowed money.
2. Samuel Insull died penniless in a foreign land, a fugitive
   from justice.
3. Howard Hopson lost his sanity.
4. Arthur Cutten became insolvent and died abroad.
5. Richard Whitney spent time in Sing Sing prison.
6. Albert Fall was pardoned from prison so he could die at
   home—broke.
7. Jesse Livermore committed suicide.

These men lived for the "now" without any regard for "later." If
they'd had a proper perspective on money, perhaps they wouldn't

have lost their fortunes. Solomon counseled, "Don't weary yourself trying to get rich. . . . For riches can disappear as though they had the wings of a bird!" (Proverbs 23:4-5, NLT). James also warns that with a "buy now" mentality, you are sure to "pay later."

exploration

Wealth unjustly gained will bear testimony against those who steal it. James now introduces us to the sin of self-indulgent spending. Read James 5, then focus on verse 5.

> **You have lived on the earth in pleasure and luxury;**
> **you have fattened your hearts as in a day of slaughter.**
> James 5:5

1. Where do the unrighteous rich live, and why do you think James focused on this?

. . . .

2. Read Hebrews 11:13-16 and answer the following questions.

 a. What did these saints understand about life on the earth, and what were they looking for (vv. 13-14)?

 . . . .

 . . . .

 b. Explain why returning to their birthplace wouldn't make them feel at home (v. 15).

 . . . .

 c. Describe their true home (v. 16). . . . .

 . . . .

3. According to James 5:5, how do the unrighteous rich live?

. . . .

4. Describe the end of the hedonist. . . . .

. . . .

explanation

AT HOME
Too at home here on earth? Maybe it's time to renovate your heart and mind. "Store your treasures in heaven. . . . Wherever your treasure is, there your heart and thoughts will also be" (Matthew 6:20-21, NLT). Home is where the heart is.

3

HEDONISTS
Pleasure comes from the same Greek word as *hedonism*, and describes the lustful gratification of the natural/sinful desires. "In the last days . . . men will be . . . lovers of money . . . lovers of pleasure rather than lovers of God" (2 Timothy 3:1-4).

5

SELF-INDULGENT
Scripture never condones self-indulgent living. This lifestyle is inconsistent with the very purposes for which God made us. God views a life of ease and luxury, especially at the expense of others, as foolish and deadly. "She who lives in pleasure is dead while she lives" (1 Timothy 5:6).

HEAVENLY HOME
All things earthly are perishing, but heavenly things will last throughout eternity. "When this earthly tent we live in is taken down—when we die and leave these bodies—we will have a home in heaven, an eternal body made for us by God himself" (2 Corinthians 5:1, NLT).

F.A.T.
Earthly F.A.T. is Foolish Acquisition of Treasures. However, spiritual F.A.T. represents a person who is Faithful, Available, and Teachable. "To you who fear My name . . . you shall go out and grow fat like stall-fed calves" (Malachi 4:2).

5. In Luke 12:16-21, Jesus tells the parable of the rich fool. Underline the self-indulgent statements of the rich fool. Circle God's responses to him.

> "A rich man had a fertile farm that produced fine crops. In fact, his barns were full to overflowing. So he said, 'I know! I'll tear down my barns and build bigger ones. Then I'll have room enough to store everything. And I'll sit back and say to myself, My friend, you have enough stored away for years to come. Now take it easy! Eat, drink, and be merry!' But God said to him, 'You fool! You will die this very night. Then who will get it all?' Yes, a person is a fool to store up earthly wealth but not have a rich relationship with God" (Luke 12:16-21, NLT).

transformation

6. Read Philippians 3:17-21. Contrast those who live for earthly pursuits with those who understand that heaven is their true home.

. . . .

. . . .

7. Using the word *FAT* as an acrostic, describe how people today have fattened themselves with pleasure and luxury.

F . . . .

A . . . .

T . . . .

Journal about the ways you have overindulged in pleasure and luxury. Then write a prayer telling God how you will start a heavenly diet.

. . . .

. . . .

. . . .

. . . .

8. The unrighteous rich will be corrupted by their possessions. The riches that your heavenly Father gives are meant to be a blessing. Fill in the following chart to discover some of the rich blessings God offers.

SCRIPTURE	RICH BLESSINGS
1 Chron. 29:11-12	
Ps. 112:1-3	
Prov. 24:3-4	

8
POSSESSIONS
God loves to give good things, but your possessions should never posses you. "Command those who are rich . . . not to . . . trust in uncertain riches but in the living God, who gives us richly all things to enjoy" (1 Timothy 6:17).

An old man had built a prosperous business through hard work. Childless, he worried about who would be his heir. His three nephews were the most likely candidates. He gathered the young men and said, "I'm giving you each an equal sum of money. Buy something to fill this office from floor to ceiling. Whoever comes up with the best solution to this problem will be my heir."

The nephews hurried to fulfill their task. The first nephew brought a bale of hay that filled the room two-thirds of the way. The second brought in two large bags of goose-down, which filled three-fourths of the room. Then the third nephew walked in, empty-handed. "What did you bring?" the benefactor asked. The nephew replied, "I spent half of my money to feed a hungry child and gave almost all the rest to the church. With what I had left, I bought these matches and this candle." He lit the taper, and light filled every corner of the room! The old man realized that here was the best purchase of all. He freely gave his wise nephew all his possessions.

God bestows financial blessings not so we can live lives of idle luxury, but so we can bless others and help light their way. Jesus said, "Let your light so shine before men, that they may see your good works and glorify your Father in heaven" (Matthew 5:16).

contemplation

If money be not your servant, it will be your master.
Italian Proverb

DAY 5 TIPPING
THE SCALES

preparation

*Jesus, I am grateful for
Your sacrifice on the
cross for my sins. Thank
You for saving me from
the bondage of my flesh
and eternal condemna-
tion. I praise You for my
new life in the Holy
Spirit. Amen.*

NO CONDEMNATION
*There is therefore now
no condemnation to
those who are in Christ
Jesus, who do not walk
according to the flesh,
but according to the
Spirit. Romans 8:1*

The judge glared down from his bench at the prospective juror.
"And why do you not want to serve on this jury?" he asked.

The man replied, "Well, judge, I'm biased. One look at that
man convinced me that he is guilty."

The judge scowled and replied, "That man is not the defendant;
he's the district attorney."

Stacking a jury with those prejudiced against the defendant is
just one way to tip the scales of justice. Other imbalanced tactics
may include enlisting false witnesses, denying the defendant's
right to legal representation, conducting a trial behind closed
doors, or bribing the judge. The crafters of the Declaration of
Independence dreamed of justice for all when they wrote, "We
hold these truths to be self-evident, that all men are created
equal. . . ." Sadly, the rich seem more equal than others within
the jurisprudence system.

Ancient Israel, like the United States, was established with laws
meant to ensure each citizen a fair trial. But the book of James
reveals that society in his day was plagued with corruption just as
ours is today. The wealthy were making the ancient legal system
lopsided through bribery. They hoped their deep pockets would
tip the scales of justice in their favor.

exploration

We have discovered that being self-indulgent with God-given
wealth is sin. Continuing in chapter 5, James addresses another
sin of the wicked rich.

Read James 5, then focus on verse 6.

You have condemned, you have murdered the just; he does not resist you. James 5:6

1. What were the crimes of the overindulged rich? . . . .

. . . .

2. How do you know the "sentence" they passed on the poor was unfair?

. . . .

3. Describe how the poor responded to the unjust rich according to James 5:6.

. . . .

4. The prophet Amos gives us some insight into the corrupt judicial system in Israel in the Old Testament. Read Amos 5:12-15 to learn more.

   a. In what three ways had the judges sinned against the poor (v. 12)?

   . . . .

   b. How did the people respond and why (v. 13)? . . . .

   . . . .

   c. What was God's ideal for the judicial system, and how would the nation benefit (v. 15)?

   . . . .

5. Though Israel's courts were corrupt, God established a system of judicial fairness. Fill in the table below to discover what God expected of judges.

SCRIPTURE	FAIR JUDGE
Exod. 18:21-22	
Lev. 19:15	
Deut. 19:15-19	

explanation

1

CONDEMNED
To *condemn* is a judicial term meaning to declare guilty, convict, or doom. God alone is our Judge, and He demands righteousness. "What does the Lord require of you but to do justly, to love mercy, and to walk humbly with your God?" (Micah 6:8).

2

INJUSTICE
Some Bible commentators say that the rich used the judicial system to condemn the poor. Often they literally murdered to maintain their luxurious lifestyle (as when Jezebel had Naboth murdered to obtain his vineyards). The poor had no resources and thus no way to resist.

4

FAIR PLAY
When God established Israel, He set up a system of fair and impartial courts to protect His people. The judges were commanded to be fair and honest. They were not to be greedy, show partiality, or take bribes. The Jews in James's day would have known this.

6

HYPOCRISY
Hypocrisy, a Greek
word describing an
actor, is "feigning to
be what one is not;
the false appearance
of virtue or religion"
(*Webster's*). "What is
the hope of the hypo-
crite, though he may
gain much, if God
takes away his life?"
(Job 27:8).

7

MURDER
Throughout history,
murder has been
considered the worst
of crimes. God consid-
ers the taking of human
life a capital offense.
Murder is an outrage
because human beings
are created in the image
of God (adapted,
Unger's).

6. We have learned that ancient Israel was plagued by a corrupt judicial system, as was the Roman society in James's day. Jesus condemned hypocritical rulers who exploited others while pretending to be righteous. Fill in the chart to unmask the hypocrisy.

SCRIPTURE	SEEMS RIGHT	ACTS WRONG
Matt. 23:14		
Matt. 23:23		
Matt. 23:25-27		

7. James rebuked the rich for pronouncing a death sentence on the poor, and in effect, murdering them. In the Sermon on the Mount, Jesus revealed that anger is as lethal as murder: "You have heard that the law of Moses says, 'Do not murder. If you commit murder, you are subject to judgment.' But I say, if you are angry with someone, you are subject to judgment!" (Matthew 5:21-22, NLT).

> With this in mind, journal about a time when you were angry enough to wish another person harm. Confess this anger as sin and ask God to forgive you.

. . . .

. . . .

. . . .

. . . .

8. James revealed that the just did not resist the actions of the unjust. Jesus also spoke to this in Matthew 5:39-42. Read the passage, then rewrite in your own words the principles Christ taught.

. . . .

. . . .

Journal about a time you have put these principles to work in your life.

. . . .

. . . .

. . . .

. . . .

. . . .

The judges in James's day were willing to tip the scales in favor of the rich for a price. But justice is never true if it can be sold to the highest bidder. The cries of the poor fell on deaf ears—the jangling of gold coins drowned out the truth. The poor were helpless to resist the inequity of the system.

Jesus knew what it felt like to be the victim of a rigged trial. Caiaphas, the chief priests, and elders (the supreme court of ancient Israel) sought out false witnesses to accuse Jesus. They even resorted to bribery in an attempt to subvert justice. "Judas Iscariot . . . went to the chief priests and said, 'What are you willing to give me if I deliver Him to you?' And they counted out to him thirty pieces of silver" (Matthew 26:14-15). The prophet Isaiah described Jesus like this: "He was led as a lamb to the slaughter. And as a sheep is silent before the shearers, he did not open his mouth" (Isaiah 53:7, NLT). Perhaps James was thinking of his brother, Jesus, when he wrote this passage about the just not resisting the unjust.

But don't be deceived; God will one day even the scales of justice. As believers, we can confidently say with the psalmist, "The Lord loves justice, and he will never abandon the godly. He will keep them safe forever" (Psalm 37:28, NLT).

Triumph over Temptation

*J*ames begins this discourse on temptation by saying, "Blessed is the man who endures temptation." The word *blessed* can be translated "O how happy." I don't know about you, but I do not feel blessed when temptations come my way. In fact, I think I've done something terribly wrong when temptation knocks on my door. But temptation is not a sin; it's what you do in response to temptation that can cause sin. Martin Luther used to say, "You can't stop birds from flying about your head, but you can keep them from building a nest in your hair." Even Jesus was tempted when He sojourned here on earth, but He triumphed over temptation. The writer of Hebrews said that Jesus, our great High Priest, "was in all points tempted as we are, yet without sin" (Hebrews 4:15).

Over twenty years ago, before I was a Christian, I thought getting high was a way to escape reality. After salvation, I was delivered from the desire to smoke marijuana. But a few years ago at a reunion, I smelled a familiar pungent aroma coming from the basement of the home I was visiting. I was shocked at the random thought that ran through my mind, "A joint sounds relaxing; I could get away with it here." My palms began to sweat when I realized I was being tempted. That's when the Lord spoke to my heart, "Lenya, you can triumph over temptation, . . . just flee!" And that's exactly what I did.

1 BLESSED TEMPTATION

preparation

When temptations come my way, Lord, help me to discover the blessing of resisting them and obeying Your Word. Help me to seek You with all my heart. Amen.

BLESSED
Blessed are the undefiled in the way, who walk in the law of the Lord! Blessed are those who keep His testimonies, who seek Him with the whole heart! They also do no iniquity; they walk in His ways. Psalm 119:1-3

explanation

1

BLESSED
A *beatitude* is a declaration of blessedness, meaning spiritual well-being and prosperity, the deep joy of the soul. The blessed have a share in salvation and have entered the kingdom of God. Some scholars render each beatitude as: "O the bliss [or bless-edness] of."

exploration

Through James we have learned that those with Living Faith will count it all joy when facing the trials life brings their way. We have also learned that a right perspective on earthly wealth is evidence of a true Living Faith. Now we discover how to turn temptation into a blessing.

Read James 1:12-18, then focus on verse 12.

> **Blessed is the man who endures temptation; for when he has been approved, he will receive the crown of life which the Lord has promised to those who love Him.**
> James 1:12

1. What beatitude did James pronounce? . . . .

. . . .

2. Fill in the following chart to discover other beatitudes found in Scripture.

SCRIPTURE	BEATITUDE
Ps. 1:1	
Ps. 128:1-2	
Matt. 5:3-10	
John 20:29	

3. Explain what a person must do to receive this blessing according to James 1:12.

. . . .

. . . .

4. What phrase reveals that the one who endures temptation has done well in God's eyes?

. . . .

5. What will this person receive? . . . .

. . . .

6. To whom will the Lord give this gift? . . . .

. . . .

7. How can you be sure you will receive this gift? . . . .

. . . .

transformation

8. There are times we look at temptations as a curse. James tells us to view them as a blessing when we faithfully endure them.

Journal about a situation in which God transformed your curse (temptation) into a blessing. How were you able to resist the temptation? How did God bless you?

. . . .

. . . .

. . . .

. . . .

3
TEMPTATION
Temptation literally means to put to the test, examine, or try. Therefore a temptation either puts something good to the test or entices us to do something evil. Depending upon our response to it, temptation can be helpful or harmful to our spiritual growth.

5
CROWN
A crown shows a person's status or honor. Royalty and high priests in Old Testament times wore crowns signifying their authority. Athletes were crowned with wreaths of leaves. Christians are promised several types of crowns symbolic of our inheritance in heaven.

8
BLESSING
Our blessed Savior became a curse to transform our curse into a blessing. "Christ has redeemed us from the curse of the law, having become a curse for us . . . that the blessing of Abraham might come upon the Gentiles in Christ Jesus" (Galatians 3:13-14).

9

HOLD FAST
Jesus warned that Christians could forfeit their crowns if they aren't careful to persevere in the faith. Focusing on Christ's return helps us cling to what we already possess. "Behold, I am coming quickly! Hold fast what you have, that no one may take your crown" (Revelation 3:11).

11

ENDURANCE
More than physical endurance, we need spiritual endurance in the race of life. "Let us lay aside every weight, and the sin which so easily ensnares us, and let us run with endurance the race that is set before us" (Hebrews 12:1).

9. Scripture promises various crowns to believers. Check which crowns you have obtained from the Lord.

—— Wisdom is a crown of glory (Prov. 4:7-9)

—— Excellent wife is a husband's crown (Prov. 12:4)

—— Grey hair is a crown of glory (Prov. 16:31)

—— Grandchildren are a crowning glory (Prov. 17:6)

—— Temperance brings an imperishable crown (1 Cor. 9:25)

—— Others brought to faith are a crown of rejoicing (1 Thess. 2:19)

—— Crown of righteousness to those who love His appearing (2 Tim. 4:8)

—— Crown of life to those who endure temptation (James 1:12)

10. James did not say "if" you are tempted but "when" you are tempted. Temptation is common to all humanity. With this in mind, fill in the following chart to discover how others have been tempted.

SCRIPTURE	TEMPTATION
Josh. 7:20-21	. . . .
2 Sam. 11:1-3	. . . .
Matt. 4:1-4	. . . .
Acts 8:18-20	. . . .

11. Describe a situation in which you have been greatly tempted.

. . . .

. . . .

. . . .

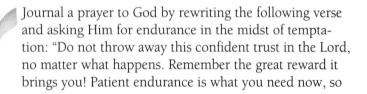

Journal a prayer to God by rewriting the following verse and asking Him for endurance in the midst of temptation: "Do not throw away this confident trust in the Lord, no matter what happens. Remember the great reward it brings you! Patient endurance is what you need now, so you will continue to do God's will. Then you will receive all that He has promised" (Hebrews 10:35-36, NLT).

. . . .

. . . .

. . . .

. . . .

St. Augustine was a famed fourth-century bishop who was one of the great leaders of the early Christian church. His writings have had a strong impact on religious thought throughout the ages. His mother, Saint Monica, was a devout Christian while his father was a pagan. As a young man, Augustine pursued worldly success and pleasure.

At the age of thirty-two, after a life steeped in sexual immorality, Augustine repented and devoted his life to the gospel. Soon after his conversion, he was walking down the street in Milan, Italy when he encountered a prostitute whom he had known intimately. She called to him, but he would not answer. He kept right on walking. "Augustine," she called again. "It is I!" Without slowing down and by the grace of God, he exclaimed, "Yes, but it is no longer I." Even though he was a recent convert, he understood that God would bless him if he resisted temptation. His reply, "It is no longer I," proved that he had a supernatural power available to combat the forces of sin and evil which had dominated his life in the past. He was a changed man. Through patient endurance, Augustine was able to "flee the evil desires of youth, and pursue righteousness, faith, love and peace" (2 Timothy 2:22, NIV). So take heart. God will give you power to face temptations, and He has promised to bless you through them, working all things for good in your life.

contemplation

Holiness is not freedom from temptation, but power to overcome temptation.
G. Campbell Morgan

2 TEMPTATION UNMASKED

Young Jamie wanted a new baseball bat, so he was desperately saving his money. But it wasn't easy. One night his mother overheard his bedtime prayer: "God, help me save my money for a bat. And please don't let the ice cream man come down the street!"

What areas tempt you? Shopping malls? TV shows? All-you-can-eat buffets? Affection? Temptations can be described as good desires run amok. Sarah and Abraham's temptation began with a good desire to have a child. This was in God's will for them, but they went about it the wrong way. Sarah encouraged Abraham to use her servant Hagar as a surrogate mother. Hagar conceived Ishmael, but God declared that Ishmael was *not* the son of promise—Sarah's own son, Isaac, would be God's chosen heir. In this case (and most others), giving in to temptation carried long-lasting consequences. Ishmael was a ruthless bully to Isaac, and his ancestors antagonize Israel to this day.

In drawing a distinction between trials and temptations, James unmasks the temptor. Trials usually come from the outside; temptations frequently happen on the inside. God may send trials, but temptations are authored by Satan and encouraged by our own fallen nature. If we aren't careful, the testings on the outside may become temptations on the inside. When our outside circumstances are difficult, we may find ourselves inwardly complaining against God, questioning His love, and resisting His will. That's when Satan provides us with an "opportunity" to escape the difficulty—this opportunity is temptation.

exploration

James has encouraged us to patiently endure the temptations we encounter. Now he unmasks the source of temptation.

Review James 1:12-18, then focus on verses 13-14.

> **Let no one say when he is tempted, "I am tempted by God"; for God cannot be tempted by evil, nor does He Himself tempt anyone.** James 1:13

1. Who should we *never* blame when we are tempted?

. . . .

2. Why do you think James made this point so forcefully?

. . . .

3. Look up Genesis 3:11-13. Summarize whom Adam and Eve each blamed for their sin, and why.

. . . .

. . . .

4. Identify two reasons James gave as to why we should never accuse God of tempting us to sin.

. . . .

> **But each one is tempted when he is drawn away by his own desires and enticed.** James 1:14

5. What phrase reveals that no one is exempt from temptation?

. . . .

6. If God does not tempt, then how is a person tempted?

. . . .

7. What phrase reveals that we are often tempted from within?

. . . .

8. What word reveals that external forces often tempt us?

. . . .

BLAME SHIFTING
Since the Fall in the Garden, we have played the blame game when yielding to temptation: Eve blamed the serpent and Adam blamed Eve. During James's time, Jewish philosophers theorized that God was to blame for having "created" us with the propensity to sin.

4

BLAMELESS
It stands to reason that if God can't be tempted by evil, then He cannot and will not tempt others. God hates sin; therefore He would never promote what is repugnant to his nature. "God is light and there is no darkness in Him at all" (1 John 1:5, NLT).

8

PREDATOR
Drawn away means to bait a trap. *Enticed* refers to baiting a hook. As a predator, Satan knows how to catch his prey. "Watch out for attacks from the Devil. . . . He prowls around like a roaring lion, looking for some victim to devour" (1 Peter 5:8, NLT).

9

SOLACE
God is *not* to be
blamed for tempting
you; He *is* to be blessed
for praying for you in
temptation. Jesus told
Peter, "Simon, Simon!
Indeed, Satan has asked
for you, that he may sift
you as wheat. But I have
prayed for you, that
your faith should not
fail" (Luke 22:31-32).

10

SAFETY
While God does not
tempt us, he does set
parameters for the
temptations that come
our way. Satan wasn't
allowed to tempt Job
above what he could
endure. "Satan . . .
said, 'Does Job fear
God for nothing? Have
You [God] not made a
hedge around him?'"
(Job 1:9-10).

9. James warned us against blaming God for the temptation to sin. When you're enticed by sin, whom do *you* blame?

—— The devil

—— My upbringing

—— Myself

—— My husband

—— My boss

—— My hormones

—— My kids

—— God

If you've been blaming others for the sin in your life, then it's time to take personal responsibility. Journal a prayer admitting that you are a sinner who still needs a Savior.

. . . .

. . . .

. . . .

. . . .

10. Our evil desires and outward enticements tempt us. Read 1 Corinthians 10:13 to discover more about the dynamics of temptation.

a. Are you the only one who is tempted? How do you know?

. . . .

. . . .

b. How do you know that the temptations you face are not insurmountable?

. . . .

c. What makes temptation bearable?

. . . .

11. Temptations are often the result of satanic warfare. Fill in the chart below to discover Satan's predatory tactics.

SCRIPTURE   SATAN'S TACTICS

Matt. 4:3 . . . .

John 8:44 . . . .

Rev. 12:9 . . . .

Rev. 12:10 . . . .

SATAN
Other names for Satan include "the devil," meaning slanderer or false accuser; "the tempter"; "Beelzebub"; "the wicked one"; "the ruler of this world"; "the god of this age"; "the prince of the power of the air"; and "the accuser of our brethren."

What do advertisers and our adversary have in common? They push the right buttons so we'll succumb to the weakness of the flesh. Ad executive Jerry Della Femina said, "Advertising deals in open sores: Fear. Greed. Anger. Hostility. . . . We play on all the emotions and on all the problems, from not getting ahead to the desire to be one of the crowd. Everyone has a button. If enough people have the same button, you have a successful ad and a successful product." But advertising can be deceptive. The right toothpaste won't give you sex appeal, and driving a European car doesn't mean you're successful.

We are all susceptible to temptation in three areas: bodily appetites, beautiful things, and boastful pride. John called these "the lust of the flesh, the lust of the eyes, and the pride of life" (1 John 2:16). Like a successful advertising executive, Satan takes advantage of our lusts. And like a concert pianist, Satan knows how to get us to sing his tune. On a piano, when the sustain peddle is pressed while a specific note is struck, the coordinating strings will recognize the note and vibrate in harmony. That's what Satan does; he sings out a sinful tune and hopes our coordinating fleshly desires will sing along. To stop the vibration on a piano, you take your foot off the pedal. To resist temptation, you unmask the real temptor, then "get up and pray. Otherwise temptation will overpower you" (Luke 22:46, NLT).

contemplation

The devil tempts that he may ruin; God tests that he may crown.
Saint Ambrose

DAY 3 DEADLY TEMPTATION

preparation

Father, You have power over sin and death. Give us strength to let go of temptation and look to you. Amen.

WRONG WAY
There is a way that seems right to a man, but in the end it leads to death. Proverbs 14:12, NIV

Have you heard about a rather tricky method used by monkey hunters? Trappers take a small cage out into the jungle with a tasty bunch of bananas locked inside. Now a monkey comes along and spots the bananas. The unsuspecting primate reaches his greedy paw through the narrow rungs of the cage and grabs a banana. But he can't get the paw back out. And no matter how hard he tries—twisting his hand back and forth—he can't pull his hand through the rungs while hanging on to the banana. The trappers merely have to grab the unrelenting monkey. Now if you were standing there in the jungle, watching all of this happen, and wanted to save the monkey, you might yell in exasperation, "Drop the banana!"

Satan employs the same clever strategy on unsuspecting Christians. He takes advantage of the appetites of our flesh, hoping we will grasp the enticing temptations he puts in our path. If we refuse to release the alluring bait, we will be unable to escape Satan's trap. Our evil desires cry out, "Don't let go! Hang on to this pleasure for as long as it will last!" If you are clinging to sinful practices that are destroying your testimony and preventing you from growing in grace, "Drop the temptation!" Get out of Satan's trap before it's too late.

exploration

James has unmasked our true enemy who tempts us. Now he continues to explain the power of our own sinful desires.

Review James 1:12-18, then focus on verse 15.

> **Then, when desire has conceived, it gives birth to sin; and sin, when it is full-grown, brings forth death.**
> James 1:15

1. Remembering yesterday's lesson, explain what happens when we give in to our desires.

. . . .

. . . .

2. What earthy physical metaphor did James use to depict the process of yielding to sinful desire?

. . . .

. . . .

3. What phrase lets you know that sin develops over time?

. . . .

. . . .

4. What is the end result of this process?. . . . .

. . . .

5. We have found that sin is a process that begins with the conception of evil desires and ends in death. Read Acts 5:1-11 and answer the following questions.

a. Explain what Ananias and Sapphira conceived in their hearts (vv. 1-4).

. . . .

. . . .

b. What happened to Ananias as a result (vv. 5-6)?

. . . .

. . . .

c. Explain how Sapphira allowed the conspiracy to grow (vv. 7-10).

. . . .

. . . .

explanation

1

DESIRE
Desire literally means "lust"—a longing for what is forbidden or an intense craving or need. Desires can be deadly. Before you yield to desires, consider where they may lead you. "The righteousness of the upright delivers them, but the unfaithful are trapped by evil desires" (Proverbs 11:6, NIV).

2

CONCEIVED
To *conceive* means to take into one's being. Physical conception occurs by taking in male seed; intellectual conception comes by taking in thoughts; emotional conception begins with taking in a desire for good or evil. "They trust in empty words and speak lies; they conceive evil and bring forth iniquity" (Isaiah 59:4).

4

STILLBORN
James uses the imagery of childbirth to depict the birth of sin. Desire is the "mother" who conceives a child, "sin." Giving birth to a child is a painful experience that is transformed into joy; giving birth to sin is a seemingly pleasurable experience transformed into grief and death.

transformation

6

STEP-BY-STEP
Sin is a four-step
process resulting in
death: 1) *Desire:* We
experience a strong
compulsion to have
or do something we
should not; 2) *Deceit:*
We justify our desire;
3) *Design:* We con-
sciously plan to satisfy
our desire; 4) *Disobey:*
We disregard God's
Word to gratify our
sinful urge.

7

FULL-GROWN
Sinful behavior can
make us adult-sized
sinners while godly
behavior will make us
full-grown saints. "We
should no longer be
children, tossed to and
fro, . . . but, speaking
the truth in love, may
grow up in all things
into Him who is the
head—Christ" (Ephe-
sians 4:14-15).

6. We have learned that good desires can be fulfilled in wrong ways, making us susceptible to the attacks of Satan. List some good desires you have that could be fulfilled the wrong way.

GOOD DESIRES	WRONG FULFILLMENT
[To be accepted by others]	[Succumbing to peer pressure]
. . . .	. . . .
. . . .	. . . .
. . . .	. . . .
. . . .	. . . .

Journal about how one of the good desires, fulfilled the wrong way, gave birth to trouble in your life.

. . . .

. . . .

. . . .

. . . .

7. James revealed that sin has a maturation process. Complete the exercise to show how different desires and temptations become full-grown sins. This may take some creative thinking, but try it.

BIRTH OF SIN	CHILDHOOD	ADOLESCENCE	ADULTHOOD
Illegal drugs	*Occasional partying*	*Weekly habit*	*Complete addiction*
Pornography . . . .
Anger. . . . .
Materialism . . . .

8. We know that the birth of sinful desires will ultimately lead to death. If you are reaping the consequences of your sinful desires, take heart! God promises new life to those who repent.

Journal a prayer by rewriting the following Scripture and asking God to give you new life in Christ: "I have been crucified with Christ; it is no longer I who live, but Christ lives in me; and the life which I now live in the flesh I live by faith in the Son of God, who loved me and gave Himself for me" (Galatians 2:20).

. . . .

. . . .

. . . .

. . . .

NEW LIFE
As surely as sin gives birth to death, repentance gives birth to new life. Resurrection is just a prayer away. "Those who become Christians become new persons. They are not the same anymore, for the old life is gone. A new life has begun!" (2 Corinthians 5:17, NLT).

News stories of the rich and famous often read like tombstones in a graveyard. They carve in our memories people who have followed the tragic cycle of sin that leads to death, people such as Jimi Hendrix, Janis Joplin, and Jim Morrison—the forefathers of rock and roll who literally partied themselves to death. More recently, we have read about Kurt Cobain who, even with all the trappings of fame and fortune, committed suicide.

But it's not just the rich and famous whose lifestyles can lead to an early grave. I (Penny) grew up with a promising young man I'll call Chad. He was tall, blonde, and handsome, and was always the life of the party. It started out innocently enough: he'd sneak liquor from his parents' cabinet. Later, he and his buddies began to host keggers on a weekly basis, relying on fake IDs to get them the beer. After high school, Chad became a fixture at the local bar scene.

As we grew up, most of our gang got married, had families, and put our partying days behind us. But not Chad. He ended up a severe alcoholic. The last time I saw him, he reeked of tobacco and bourbon even though it was early in the day. A short while later, I heard that in a state of drunken despondence, Chad had shot and killed himself. Ignoring the warning James gives us about sin really can have deadly consequences.

contemplation

Sin may open bright as the morning, but it will end dark as night.
Thomas De Witt Talmage

DAY 4   TEMPTED TO DOUBT

preparation

Lord, thank You for Your faithfulness even when we doubt. We praise You that when darkness seems so strong, Your never changing love and goodness are always stronger. Amen.

FAITHFULNESS

Through the Lord's mercies we are not consumed, because His compassions fail not. They are new every morning; Great is Your faithfulness.
Lamentations 3:22-23

September 11, 2001 was a day that made Americans doubt. After hijackers turned commercial airplanes into missiles, Americans doubted the nation's security. They doubted that President Bush was up to the task. They doubted whether they could ever trust an immigrant again. And some of them began to doubt God.

Skeptics asked, "Where was Jesus on September 11?" He was on Flight 93 inspiring the passengers to recite the Lord's Prayer before taking action to thwart their captors' plans. He was helping over fifty thousand people (94 percent) escape before the World Trade Center collapsed. He was in the smoke-filled Pentagon accompanying those who walked through the valley of the shadow of death. He was with Father Mychal Judge who offered last rites to the mortally wounded.

The question is not where was God on September 11, but where was Satan? *He* was there, too: in the terrorist training camps, in the hearts of the hijackers, and inspiring Osama bin Laden to religiously promote his demonic agenda. The Bible tells us that "the Devil . . . was a murderer from the beginning and has always hated the truth" (John 8:44, NLT).

When we are tempted to doubt God, James reminds us that evil begins with the "Evil One," while God is the One who can bring good out of evil.

exploration

We've seen that our evil desires can lead to tragic consequences. Today James brings us back to the goodness of God.

Review James 1:12-18, then focus on verses 16-17.

Do not be deceived, my beloved brethren. James 1:16

1. What did James implore his readers to do? . . . .

. . . .

2. How do you know James truly cared for the people to whom he wrote?

. . . .

. . . .

Every good gift and every perfect gift is from above, and comes down from the Father of lights, with whom there is no variation or shadow of turning. James 1:17

3. What things are from above? . . . .

. . . .

4. From whom do these gifts come? . . . .

. . . .

5. How do you think this knowledge helps prevent us from accusing God when we face temptation?

. . . .

. . . .

6. God is described as the Father of lights. This description refers to Genesis 1:14-19 and Psalm 136:7-9. What do you learn about God from these Scriptures?

. . . .

. . . .

7. What portion of James 1:17 lets you know that God is unchanging?

. . . .

---

explanation

1

DECEPTION
Deceive means "to cheat or beguile; that which gives a false impression, whether by appearance, statement or influence" (*Vine's*). James implores us not to be deceived into thinking that God is responsible for our temptations.

3

EVERY GIFT
"Every" means *every*. Therefore, every gift that God gives, without exception, is beneficial to His children. "If you sinful people know how to give good gifts to your children, how much more will your heavenly Father give good gifts to those who ask him" (Matthew 7:11, NLT).

7

UNCHANGING
In a world of change, from the seasons to the latest fashions, it's comforting to know that God is a constant. "I am the Lord, and I do not change" (Malachi 3:6, NLT). God cannot change for the worse because He's flawless. He can't get any better because He's the best.

BE A BEREAN
Before you believe what others say about God, make sure the Bible agrees with what they've said. "The people of Berea . . . searched the Scriptures day after day to check up on Paul and Silas, to see if they were really teaching the truth" (Acts 17:11, NLT).

9
·FAITHFUL
Faithfulness implies dependability, loyalty, and stability. It is difficult to depend on someone who is erratic or switches allegiance. It is hard to find stability in a relationship with someone who is always changing. You can depend on God to be loyal and steadfast.

8. James strongly commanded, "Do not be deceived." Unfortunately, there are many misconceptions about God. Check the boxes below to indicate how you have been deceived about God in the past.

—— There are some things God can't do.

—— There are some things God doesn't see.

—— There are some times God doesn't care.

—— There are some people God won't forgive.

—— There are some places God won't go.

Journal about which of the above deceptive ideas ensnared you the most and caused you to doubt God's goodness. How did God correct your unrealistic view of Him? What Scripture reinforced the truth about God?

. . . .

. . . .

. . . .

. . . .

. . . .

9. The following hymn was inspired by this passage in James and Lamentations 3:22-23. Read or sing it out loud as you spend time worshipping our unchanging God.

Great is Thy Faithfulness, Oh God my Father,
There is no shadow of turning with Thee;
Thou changest not, Thy compassions they fail not;
As Thou hast been Thou forever will be.
Great is Thy faithfulness, Great is Thy faithfulness,
Morning by morning new mercies I see.
All I have needed Thy hand hath provided;
Great is Thy faithfulness, Lord unto me.

(Thomas O. Chisholm)

10. God is the giver of every good and perfect gift. Make a list of some of the good things (gifts) He has given to you (home, health, happiness, etc.):

. . . .

Journal your own psalm of praise to God, thanking Him for His goodness.

. . . .

. . . .

. . . .

. . . .

It's hard to believe that *everything* in our lives is a good and perfect gift from the Father of lights. In addition to the obvious blessings we have, all of us can look back to something tragic from our past and respond by doubting God or blaming others. It's easy to do. Yet James's teaching implies that what happens here below has its origin in heaven above. Paul shed light into the dilemma of the seemingly bad being actually good when he wrote, "We know that all things work together for good to those who love God, to those who are the called according to His purpose" (Romans 8:28). Somehow, in some miraculous way, God promises to transform "bad things" into "beautiful things" in His children's lives. But in between the bad-into-beautiful is time—time when we can doubt God's motives or His ultimate intentions.

For me, I could simultaneously doubt God and blame my father for my problems: "Why did God allow me to be born to parents who would split?" Before I was a Christian, the divorce broke me, turning me into a partyer to hide the pain. But once I was born-again, the divorce made me a reconciler, sensitive to the pain of others. Amazingly, God used my past to define my future. My greatest joy is counseling and praying for fractured families to be reconciled to God and each other. As I have seen relationships restored, I thank God for His good and perfect gifts!

contemplation

God's gifts put man's best dreams to shame.
Elizabeth Barrett Browning

DAY 5 TEMPTATION TRANSFORMED

During the Victorian era, an English paper factory boasted that it made the finest stationery in the world. One day an American businessman toured the factory and inquired, "What is the secret ingredient for making such fine stationery?" The supervisor showed him a huge pile of dirty old rags and told him that the rag content was the key to producing the highest quality paper. The skeptical man thought he was being misled in order to keep the secret ingredient a secret. Sometime later he received a package of fine writing paper embossed with his initials. An enclosed note simply read: "Dirty rags transformed."

God's view of us is similar to the factory supervisor's view of the dirty rags. He sees beyond who we are and looks instead at who we can become. He looked at Peter, the rough fisherman who was tempted to deny Jesus, and saw a man who could become the rock on which His church was built. He saw Chuck Colson, a man tempted by power and position, and saw a man who could build Prison Fellowship Ministries into an organization that preaches the gospel to thousands of incarcerated prisoners throughout the world. He looks at *you* and looks past the things that tempt you to see the person you can become. He says: "Give your life to me. I will transform you." And when you turn your heart over to Him, your life will become a rags-to-riches story.

exploration

James has reminded us not to doubt that God is a faithful giver of good gifts. We discover today that God will continue his transforming work in our lives.

Review James 1:12-18, then focus on verse 18.

Of His own will He brought us forth by the word of truth,
that we might be a kind of firstfruits of His creatures.
James 1:18

1. James repeats the analogy of birth. Explain who is being "born." How?

. . . .

2. How do you know that this birth is in God's plan? . . . .

. . . .

3. Explain what the Word of Truth is. . . . .

. . . .

4. God's Word is very important to believers; it is the basis of faith. Look up the following Scriptures to discover what the Word of God does.

SCRIPTURE	WHAT THE WORD DOES
Isa. 40:8. . . . .
Rom. 10:17 . . . .
1 Thess. 2:13. . . . .
2 Tim. 3:16 . . . .

5. It is significant that the believers James was addressing were called "firstfruits." Look up Romans 1:16. Why do you suppose the Jewish believers were referred to as "firstfruits"?

. . . .

. . . .

transformation

6. James reminded believers that they had been born again through the Word of Truth. Read 1 Peter 1:22-23 and answer the following questions:

1

TWO BIRTHS
God designed two types of birth: 1) the flesh, born through human parents, and 2) the spirit, born-again through God's Word implanting new life. Jesus said, "Humans can reproduce only human life, but the Holy Spirit gives new life from heaven" (John 3:6, NLT).

2

GOD'S WILL
God's will is His specific design, intent, or purpose; His acting with a specific objective (adapted, *Nelson's*, *Vine's*, and *Strong's*). Here, God's will is His desire for humanity to experience new birth. "[God is] not willing that any should perish but that all should come to repentance" (2 Peter 3:9).

5

FIRSTFRUITS
In Old Testament times, the Israelites offered their "firstfruits," the first and best of their crops, to God. In the New Testament, "firstfruits" refers to the first converts in a place, the Christians of that age, or of Christ, who first rose from the dead (adapted, *Bible Encyclopedia*).

6

LIFE
In biology one criterion for being categorized as alive is to be capable of procreation. Life springs from life. God's Word—the Bible—is living and breathes new life into those who believe its message. "The word of God is full of living power" (Hebrews 4:12, NLT).

FREE WILL
God's will is that we follow His perfect plan found in Scripture. Yet, in His love, God has given us free will to make choices, even if our choices oppose His will. But how much better to pray, "I want your will, not mine" (Luke 22:42, NLT).

GOSPEL
Gospel literally means "good news." The gospel is the story of the saving work of God in His Son, Jesus Christ, and a call to faith and new life in Him. Jesus is more than a messenger of the gospel; He is the living embodiment of the gospel.

a. Describe the characteristics those who have been born again display.

. . . .

b. What type of seed does God implant for our new birth?

. . . .

c. What do you learn about the Word of God from this passage?

. . . .

7. Today we learned that God's will is for us to be born again. Fill in the chart to discover other aspects of God's will for us.

SCRIPTURE	GOD'S WILL
John 1:12-13	
1 Thess. 4:3-5	
1 Thess. 5:18	
1 Pet. 2:15	

8. The Jewish believers were the "firstfruits," or first crop, of people to embrace the gospel message and become born again. From them, God's spiritual seed was spread throughout the world. With this in mind, work through the following exercise.

Step One: Journal about your "firstfruits"—the first people from whom you heard the gospel message.

. . . .

. . . .

Step Two: Write about when and how the message took root in your own heart so that you believed the Word of Truth.

. . . .

. . . .

Step Three: List some people in your acquaintance who have not heard about the new birth Christ offers.

. . . .

. . . .

Step Four: Journal a prayer asking God to give you the boldness to be "firstfruits" to them as you plant the seed of God's Word in their lives.

. . . .

. . . .

. . . .

A rabbi desired his wisdom to live on after he died, and he wondered whom he could trust to carry on his work. He decided to test the honesty of his pupils. Calling them all together, he posed a question: "What would you do if you were walking along and found a purse full of money lying in the road?"

The first disciple answered, "I'd return it to its owner." The rabbi thought to himself, *His answer comes so quickly; I must wonder if he really means it.*

"I'd keep the money if nobody saw me find it," said another. *He has a frank tongue, but a wicked heart,* the rabbi told himself.

"Well, Rabbi," said a third disciple. "I believe I'd be tempted to keep it. So I would pray to God that He would give me the strength to resist such temptation and do the right thing." *Aha,* thought the rabbi, *here is the man I would trust!*

Like the rabbi, God is looking for people He can trust. He wants to know if we'll be able to carry on the work of spreading new life through the gospel message. He allows temptations to test us to see what's in our hearts—have we truly been born again? He wants to know how we'll handle difficult situations—will we glorify Him by resisting or grieve Him by succumbing? When your temptation is transformed into triumph, God knows you are trustworthy to carry his life-giving message to others.

contemplation

He who made us also remade us.
Saint Augustine

Mirror, Mirror, in the Word

The most famous mirror was a mirror that could speak. We all know Grimm's fairy tale of Snow White, whose wicked stepmother would gaze into her magical mirror and ask, "Mirror, mirror on the wall, who's the fairest one of all?" The mirror, which could not lie, answered, "Thou, O Queen, art the fairest one of all," and the queen was content, because she knew the mirror spoke the truth.

As time passed, Snow White grew more beautiful. By the time she was seven, she was even lovelier than the queen herself. Once again the queen asked, "Mirror, mirror on the wall, who's the fairest one of all?" The mirror answered, "O Lady Queen, though fair ye be, Snow White is fairer still than thee." The queen was horrified, and from that moment envy and pride grew in her heart like rank weeds.

All mirrors have one thing in common: they don't lie. Whether we have bad hair or a beautiful smile, mirrors faithfully reflect the truth. James teaches us that God's Word is a supernatural mirror that can look beneath the surface to expose the heart. Instead of asking, "Am I the fairest in the land?" we should be discovering, "Am I faithful in word and deed?" God's mirror reveals the inconsistencies between religious activity that is useful or useless. This week, gaze into God's looking glass and ask yourself: Do I hear God's Word? And am I doing what I hear and see?

DAY 1
Do You Hear?

DAY 2
Do You Do?

DAY 3
Do You See?

DAY 4
Do You Speak?

DAY 5
Do You Go?

DAY 1 — DO YOU HEAR?

preparation

Father, I want to be righteous in Your sight. Teach me how to pluck out any "weeds" in my heart and plant Your Word deep so I can act in a way that pleases You. Amen.

APPEARANCES
For the Lord does not see as man sees; for man looks at the outward appearance, but the Lord looks at the heart.
1 Samuel 16:7

explanation

BELOVED
Beloved comes from the Greek word agape, used of God's unconditional love for Christ, His Son. James loved the early church the same way God loves His Son. "Beloved, if God so loved us, we also ought to love one another" (1 John 4:11).

exploration

In his instruction manual on Living Faith, James has taught believers how to pass the tests of trials, riches, and temptations. Now he asks us to pass the test of responding faithfully to God's Word. Read James 1, then focus on verses 19-20.

> *So then, my beloved brethren, let every man be swift to hear, slow to speak, slow to wrath . . .* James 1:19

1. How did James address the recipients of the letter so they would know he spoke out of love and concern for them?

. . . .

2. What phrase did James use to show that no one was exempt from his instruction?

. . . .

3. What must every person "be swift" to do? . . . .

. . . .

4. What was the first thing James said to be "slow" to do?

. . . .

5. Rewrite in your own words the meaning of the phrase "slow to wrath."

. . . .

6. Fill in the following chart to discover how to become slow to wrath.

SCRIPTURE	SLOW TO WRATH
Ps. 37:8	
Prov. 15:1	
Prov. 29:8	
Rom. 12:19	
Eph. 4:26	

> *. . . for the wrath of man does not produce the righteousness of God.* James 1:20

7. What phrase lets you know that our human wrath is fruitless?

. . . .

8. What can never result from human anger? . . . .

. . . .

transformation

9. James considered the church "beloved" family members and friends. As an older brother, he offered some loving advice. Fill in the chart to discover further advice, given by the apostle Paul, to those beloved by God.

SCRIPTURE	INSTRUCTION TO THE BELOVED
1 Cor. 10:14	
2 Cor. 7:1	
Phil. 2:12	
Col. 3:12	

3
DO YOU HEAR?
"Be swift to hear" is preceded by the phrase "so then," referring back to verse 18 and the "word of truth." Jesus' followers must listen to God's infallible Word and evaluate every idea, philosophy, or piece of advice against it.

8
GOD'S WAY
Our anger can never bring about God's righteousness, for God's ways are not our ways. His righteousness is seen in His holy and just actions. Even God's wrath, so different from ours, is an expression of His holy love and the personal manifestation of His moral character in judgment against sin.

9
LOVING ADVICE
James proved his love by telling them hard truths. The truth is that behavior betrays birth: Those born of God have good behavior; those born of the flesh behave poorly. "He who does good is of God, but he who does evil has not seen God" (3 John 11).

10

DULL HEARING
Your spiritual ears may need cleaning so the world's clamor doesn't drown out the wisdom of God's Word. "The hearts of this people have grown dull. Their ears are hard of hearing, . . . lest they should understand with their hearts and turn, so that I should heal them'" (Matthew 13:15).

FORCE OF WRATH
Wrath means "hot anger, passion, or fierceness. It is an abiding and settled habit of the mind with the purpose of revenge" (*Unger's*). "As the churning of milk produces butter, and wringing the nose produces blood, so the forcing of wrath produces strife" (Proverbs 30:33).

Based on those Scriptures in the chart, journal about which piece of advice you needed to hear the most right now in your life, and why.

. . . .

. . . .

. . . .

. . . .

10. James exhorts believers to be "swift to hear" the word of truth. Check off the things that dull your ability to hear God's Word clearly.

— Advice from friends   — Self-help books
— Hollywood hype   — Talk show tips
— Political pundits   — Latest gossip
— Your own ideas   — Other_____

11. We know that people's wrath does not produce righteousness. Use the word *ANGRY* as an acronym to describe some things that provoke you to anger.

A (Example: Arrogant people who think they know it all.)

. . . .

N . . . .

. . . .

G . . . .

. . . .

R . . . .

. . . .

Y . . . .

. . . .

Now journal a prayer asking God to help you become slow to wrath.

. . . .

. . . .

. . . .

. . . .

. . . .

A story is told of Franklin Roosevelt, who often endured long receiving lines at the White House. He complained that people paid no attention to what was said as they went through these lines. One day he tried an experiment. To each person who passed by, he murmured, "I murdered my grandmother this morning." The guests responded with, "Marvelous!" "Keep up the good work." "God bless you, sir." Finally, Roosevelt greeted the ambassador from Bolivia, who actually heard the president's words. Nonplussed, the ambassador leaned over and whispered, "I'm sure she had it coming."

Sometimes we, too, are "hard of hearing." There are times when our eyes glaze over and people's words just float through our ears and past the brain. Haven't we all responded with a vague "Uh huh" to a story we're not really listening to? Or maybe at dinner we say a cursory "That's nice, dear" in response to our husband's stories about work?

When it comes to hearing God, many times we are also spiritually hard of hearing. Like the people in the receiving line, we want to be in a position to hobnob with God, but we don't *really* listen to what He says. Often we are so busy thinking of what we want to say to God that we don't pay attention to what He's saying to us. The next time you spend time with God, spend more time listening than talking.

contemplation

Half an hour's listening is essential except when you are very busy. Then a full hour is needed.
St. Francis de Sales

DAY 2 DO YOU DO?

preparation

Lord, I don't want to deceive myself. Help me to hear Your Word clearly and then do what You say. Amen.

WORD

How can a young [wo]man cleanse [her] way? By taking heed according to Your word. Psalm 119:9

Only time will tell whether a person is an authentic fruit-bearing Christian or a showy imposter. By outward appearances it is impossible to determine whether those who attend church are saints or ain'ts. In Matthew 13 Jesus told a parable of the tares and the wheat to illustrate the problem of mistaken identity—those who seem to be Christians in word but never in deed. Tares are a kind of darnel weed that grow in grain fields. Tares appear identical to wheat and barley, with a similar beard and stature. Ancient Jews considered tares degenerate wheat because the seeds are poisonous to man and animals, producing sleepiness, nausea, convulsions, and even death. The plants can be separated only at the time of harvest—to divide them earlier would destroy the good wheat.

God wants spiritual fruit, not religious nuts. He can tell the difference between the frauds and the fruitful: "Do not be deceived, God is not mocked; for whatever a man sows, that he will also reap" (Galatians 6:7).

James teaches that a person of Living Faith is one who produces fruit by incorporating four key elements into her Christian walk:
1) Repenting of all filthiness; 2) Receiving the Word of Truth;
3) Reproducing righteousness through doing what God says;
and 4) Realistically examining one's life in light of God's Word.

exploration

We have learned to be swift to hear and slow to speak because we've received the word of truth. "Therefore" we must *do* something with what we've received.

Read James 1, then focus on verses 21-22.

> ***Therefore lay aside all filthiness and overflow of wickedness, and receive with meekness the implanted word, which is able to save your souls.*** James 1:21

1. James began this verse with a "therefore." Whenever you see a "therefore," it's good to find out what it's there for. Look back to verse 20 and write the scriptural principles James connected with verses 21-22.

. . . .

2. Describe what James wants us to lay aside. . . . .

. . . .

3. Once we've weeded out, what should we receive, and how?

. . . .

4. What is the spiritual benefit of meekly receiving God's Word?

. . . .

> **But be doers of the word, and not hearers only, deceiving yourselves.** James 1:22

5. What are we to be, and not to be? . . . .

. . . .

6. What is the danger of being only hearers? . . . .

. . . .

transformation

7. Laying aside sinful behavior is like weeding a garden. Fill in the following chart to discover what weeds must be pulled from the garden of your heart.

SCRIPTURE	LAY ASIDE
Eph. 4:22-24	
Col. 3:8-10	
Heb. 12:1	
1 Pet. 2:1-2	

explanation

2

LAY ASIDE
To *lay aside* means to put away, cease, or depart from. James tells us to prepare the soil of our hearts by pulling out the weeds. Before God can produce righteousness in us, we must weed out the sin that stands between us and the fruits of righteousness.

3

IMPLANTED
James compares God's Word to seed and the human heart to soil. Metaphorically, God's Word is implanted in our hearts at salvation. In the parable of the sower, Jesus describes four types of soil: 1) hard heart; 2) shallow heart; 3) crowded heart; 4) fruitful heart (Matthew 13).

5

DO YOU DO?
Some people mistakenly believe that attending church or hearing a good sermon makes them grow as Christians. However, it is not the hearing but the doing that brings about spiritual fruit. We must *do the Word.* Don't just mark your Bible; let the Bible mark your life.

MEEKNESS
We are to receive the implanted word with meekness. *Meekness* is an attitude of humility toward God and gentleness toward others, springing from a recognition that God is in control. God promises blessings for those who exhibit this characteristic. "The meek shall inherit the earth" (Psalm 37:11).

DECEIT
In Lesson 3 we learned that Satan deceives us, tempting us to sin. Self-deception is every bit as dangerous as Satan's deception. It's important not to *fool ourselves* and, as a result, act *foolishly*. "If we say that we have no sin, we deceive ourselves" (1 John 1:8).

8. God desires to implant His Word deep in our hearts, bringing forth fruit. In the parable of the sower (Matthew 13:3-9, 18-23), Jesus described the kinds of soil (hearts) God's Word encounters.

Journal about some of the people you know who have hearts similar to those described below. Write a prayer asking God to make their hearts fruitful.

Hard Heart: Does not understand or receive the Word of God, so it does not bring forth fruit.

. . . .

. . . .

Shallow Heart: Receives the Word with great emotion but has no depth, so it withers over time and bears no fruit.

. . . .

. . . .

Crowded Heart: Lacks repentance and permits sinful attitudes and behaviors to crowd out the Word, so it bears no fruit.

. . . .

. . . .

Fruitful Heart: Receives the Word, allows it to take root, and produces a bountiful harvest.

. . . .

. . . .

9. James warned against self-deception. Paul gave the Corinthians a list of those who would not inherit the kingdom of God because they had been deceived.

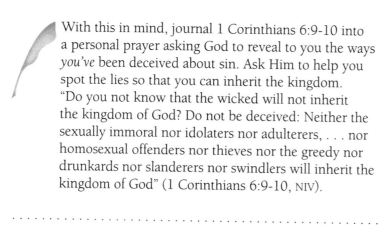

With this in mind, journal 1 Corinthians 6:9-10 into a personal prayer asking God to reveal to you the ways *you've* been deceived about sin. Ask Him to help you spot the lies so that you can inherit the kingdom. "Do you not know that the wicked will not inherit the kingdom of God? Do not be deceived: Neither the sexually immoral nor idolaters nor adulterers, . . . nor homosexual offenders nor thieves nor the greedy nor drunkards nor slanderers nor swindlers will inherit the kingdom of God" (1 Corinthians 6:9-10, NIV).

. . . .

. . . .

. . . .

. . . .

. . . .

Along with discovering electricity, Benjamin Franklin discovered a way to make his harvest more fruitful. He learned that plaster sown in the fields would make things grow better. He told his neighbors, but they didn't believe him and turned a deaf ear to his advice. He said no more about it, but he went into the field early the next spring and sowed some grain. Near the path where his neighbors walked, he traced some letters with his finger, sowed seed, and fertilized it with plaster. After a couple of weeks, the seed sprang up. As his neighbors passed that way, they were surprised to discover a message in bright green letters growing from the soil, "This has been plastered." Benjamin Franklin never needed to argue with his neighbors again about the benefit of plaster for the fields— the fruit of his labor said it all.

God has sown something amazing in the soil of our hearts—the implanted Word. For the Word to grow, not only do we need to weed out "all filthiness," but we must also make our hearts more fertile by doing what the Word instructs us to do. God's Word is much more than water to a parched soul; it is Miracle-Gro that will produce a bountiful harvest in the lives of Christians who have Living Faith.

contemplation

There are two things to do about the Gospel— believe it and behave it.
Susanna Wesley

DO YOU SEE?

preparation

Lord, thank You for offering a mirror that truly reflects what I look like, inside and out. Help me to see myself the way You see me. Amen.

OBSERVE

Whoever is wise will observe these things, and they will understand the lovingkindness of the Lord. Psalm 107:43

A cameraman working on the Merv Griffin show kept circling the waif-like model Twiggy during the pre-show lighting check. Merv became distracted then irritated with the constant movement of the man and his camera. Finally, Merv asked why the man kept rotating around Twiggy. The cameraman answered, "I always check our guests for their bad side, but Twiggy looks great from every angle."

Photographers say there are very few naturally beautiful people in the world. Careful lighting, posing, and airbrushing help people appear more attractive. Many are shocked to discover they have a crooked smile, one small eye, an off-centered nose, or some other flaw. Often when we look into a mirror, some type of activity like putting on makeup, plucking eyebrows, or combing hair distracts us. This is deceiving. When we're in motion, physical defects are not as noticeable. But when we're caught standing still, as in a photograph, our less-than-perfect features become obvious.

James reveals that in the spiritual realm, motion is also a great deceiver. When we read God's Word hastily, as we would read the daily news, we fail to see our spiritual flaws and stop long enough to do something about them. Today as you hold the mirror of God's Word up to your life, don't rush away before you have the chance to ask yourself, "Do I really see myself?"

exploration

We have read James's exhortation to "be doers of the word, and not hearers only." Now James challenges us to remember what we look like when we gaze into the mirror of God's Word.

Read James 1, then focus on verses 23-25.

For if anyone is a hearer of the word and not a doer, he is like a man observing his natural face in a mirror; for he observes himself, goes away, and immediately forgets what kind of man he was. James 1:23-24

1. Describe the "anyone" James refers to here. . . . .

. . . .

2. To whom is this person compared? . . . .

. . . .

3. What shows that this person's observation has little impact?

. . . .

. . . .

But he who looks into the perfect law of liberty and continues in it, and is not a forgetful hearer but a doer of the work, this one will be blessed in what he does. James 1:25

4. What does James encourage us to look into? . . . .

. . . .

5. How do you know that this action is more than just a glance?

. . . .

. . . .

6. Describe the person who continues in "the perfect law of liberty."

. . . .

. . . .

7. What does God promise this kind of person? . . . .

. . . .

explanation

2

MIRROR
Ancient mirrors were polished brass or bronze. Only the rich could afford mirrors of gold or silver. These metal mirrors, more primitive than the glass mirrors developed in the fourteenth century, gave distorted reflections. "For now we see in a mirror, dimly" (1 Corinthians 13:12).

3

GLANCE
The word *observes* implies that people often merely glance at their reflection. The problem with glancing is that we're likely to forget what we've seen. So, too, when we only give God's Word a cursory glance, we're less likely to remember what we've read.

4

PERFECT LAW
God's Word is *perfect* because it is inerrant, flawless and complete. The *law* emphasizes God's commands requiring obedience. *Liberty* focuses on redemption from sin and bondage. "The law of the Lord is perfect, reviving the soul" (Psalm 19:7, NLT).

DO YOU SEE?
The purpose of a mirror is to see yourself as you are and do something about what you see. The mirror of God's Word reflects the true nature of our hearts. "The Word of God . . . exposes us for what we really are" (Hebrews 4:12, NLT).

LOOK INTENTLY
The *looking* that James encourages comes from a word meaning "to bend beside; lean over; peer within; look intently; or stoop down" (adapted, *Strong's*). In contrast to casually observing an image in a mirror, to gaze carefully and with serious intent at God's Word requires time, attention, and sincere devotion.

GOD'S WORD
The Bible is such an indescribable book that one name alone can't convey all it contains. "*Scripture*"; "*our daily bread*"; "*the perfect law of liberty*"; "*the sword of the spirit*"; "*pure milk*"; and "*water*" are just a few names given for God's Word.

transformation

8. Looking into God's Word helps us to really see our spiritual appearance. Answer the questions by circling your response.

   a. How often do you look into a mirror to check your physical appearance?

   Never Once/month Once/week Once/day Twice/day or more

   b. Do you like what you see?

   Never Sometimes Frequently Usually Always

   c. How often do you look into the mirror of God's Word?

   Never Once/month Once/week Once/day Twice/day or more

   d. Do you like what you see?

   Never Sometimes Frequently Usually Always

9. Today we learned that we must continually look into God's Word, putting into practice what we read.

   Journal a prayer to God committing to live out what you have learned from God's Word by rewriting the following Scripture: "This Book of the Law shall not depart from your mouth, but you shall meditate in it day and night, that you may observe to do according to all that is written in it. For then you will make your way prosperous, and then you will have good success" (Joshua 1:8).

   . . . .

   . . . .

   . . . .

   . . . .

10. James called the Bible "the perfect law of liberty." Read Psalm 19:7-9, then fill in the chart to record what this psalm teaches you about God's Word.

WHAT IT'S CALLED	WHAT IT IS	WHAT IT DOES
Law of the Lord	Perfect	Converts the soul

. . . .

. . . .

. . . .

. . . .

. . . .

When you get what you want in your struggle for self
And the world makes you king for a day,
Just go to God's mirror and look at yourself,
And see what The Man has to say.
For it isn't your father or mother or wife
Who judgment upon you will pass;
The fellow whose verdict counts most in your life
Is the One whose Word is the glass.
Some people may think you're a straight-shootin' chum
And call you a wonderful guy,
But the "Man of the Glass" says you're only a bum
If His Word you've neglected to try.
God's the One you must please, never mind all the rest,
For it's Him that you'll meet in the end,
And you've passed your most dangerous, difficult test
If the "Man of the Glass" is your friend.
You may fool the whole world down the pathway of years
And get pats on the back as you pass,
But your final reward will be heartaches and tears
If you forsake the "Man of the Glass."

(adapted, *PC Study Bible*)

DO YOU SPEAK?

A man sat down to dinner with his family and solemnly said, "Let us pray." Everyone bowed their heads and the father intoned, "Thank You, Lord, for this food and for the hands that prepared it." During the meal, however, he began to complain: "This bread is stale!" "I don't like broccoli!" "This coffee's too weak!" And on it went throughout the meal.

As dessert was served, his young daughter asked, "Dad, do you think God heard you when you said grace today?" He answered confidently, "Of course." Then she asked, "Do you think God heard what you said about the bread, the broccoli, and the coffee?" Less confidently he answered, "Yes, I believe so." The little girl then asked, "Well, which of your words do you think God believed?"

To all appearances, this fault-finding father was very religious: he made sure he prayed with his family. But his words told a different story. The same is true with us. What we say speaks volumes about our character. Our words expose whether we are compassionate or critical; loving or hateful; generous or greedy.

We've all heard the saying that actions speak louder than words. But the Bible teaches that our words loudly proclaim the condition of our hearts. It has been estimated that we spend one-fifth of our lives talking, speaking at least eighteen thousand words per day. Today James reminds us to ask ourselves, "*What do I speak?*" because what we say reveals whether we are righteous or merely religious.

exploration

This week we have learned the importance of receiving God's Word, looking intently into it, and responding in obedience. Now we discover that true religion, based upon God's Word, will result in righteous speech.

Read James 1, then focus on verse 26.

> **If anyone among you thinks he is religious, and does not bridle his tongue but deceives his own heart, this one's religion is useless.** James 1:26

1. What phrase lets you know that James is addressing everyone who professes faith?

. . . .

2. What specific type of person is James addressing here?

. . . .

3. Describe the action this person fails to take. . . . .

. . . .

4. What impact does this failure have on the heart?. . . . .

. . . .

5. Jesus revealed that the tongue and the heart are intimately linked. Explain the connection, according to Matthew 12:34.

. . . .

. . . .

6. Looking back at James 1:26, what does an unbridled tongue reveal about a person's religion?

. . . .

7. Read Mark 7:6-7. How do Jesus' words about hypocrisy expand on James's point here?

. . . .

. . . .

2

RELIGIOUS
To *be religious* means to be pious concerning ceremonial observance—to carefully participate in the outward rituals of religious service such as liturgies and other ceremonies. The apostle Paul used the same root word to describe his former life as a Pharisee.

3

BRIDLE
A *bridle* is "anything that restrains, like the head harness of a horse" (*Webster's*). While it is impractical to put a physical bridle on our mouths, it is smart to put on a mental bridle. "Keep your tongue from evil, and your lips from speaking deceit" (Psalm 34:13).

5

DO YOU SPEAK?
What is in our heart will spill out of our mouth. If we hide God's Word in our heart, goodness will overflow. If we harbor sin, corrupt words will spill out. "A good [wo]man out of the good treasure of [her] heart brings forth good things" (Matthew 12:35).

GODLINESS

Godliness speaks of piety or reverence toward God. More than religious profession, it is the power of a vital union with God that results in godly speech and conduct. "But you . . . pursue righteousness, godliness, faith, love, patience, gentleness" (1 Timothy 6:11).

HOLY SPEECH

The words that we believers speak are a reflection of the One we serve. If we speak carelessly or thoughtlessly, we misrepresent God. Before speaking we should pray, "Let the words of my mouth and the meditation of my heart be acceptable in Your sight, O Lord" (Psalm 19:14).

EDIFICATION

As believers, we should exalt God and uplift one another with our speech. To *edify* literally means to build up. Christians are edified not only by godly speech but also by understanding spiritual truth through the work of evangelists, pastors, and teachers.

transformation

8. Rather than engaging in outward religious rituals for the sake of appearances, the Bible instructs us to pursue inner godliness for the sake of disappearances—"He must increase, but I must decrease" (John 3:30).

> With this in mind, journal the following passage into a personal prayer, asking God to help you grow in godliness: "Giving all diligence, add to your faith virtue, to virtue knowledge, to knowledge self-control, to self-control perseverance, to perseverance godliness, to godliness brotherly kindness, and to brotherly kindness love" (2 Peter 1:5-7).

. . . .

. . . .

. . . .

. . . .

. . . .

9. James encourages us to bridle our tongues. Check the areas in which you struggle to determine if you need a muzzle for your mouth.

— I chatter mindlessly

— I gossip brutally

— I boast about accomplishments

— I speak about God

— I never talk

— I remind people I'm religious

— I talk if it's quiet

— I interrupt conversations

10. What we say reflects what is in our heart and our relationship with God. Fill in the chart to discover how to engage in godly speech.

Ps. 35:28 . . . .

Ps. 119:171-172 . . . .

Eph. 4:15 . . . .

Eph. 4:29 . . . .

"You're grounded, Penny," my mom exclaimed when I used a swear word at home. "You've got an awful potty mouth!" When I was a teenager, all the cool kids cussed. And it was important to me to be cool. Though I had been raised in the church and knew better, I became proficient at profanity. Sadly, what came out of my mouth was a picture of what I had allowed into my heart. I had turned my back on my faith, thinking it was much more important to be a popular party girl than a prim and proper church girl. My friends swore, the movies I watched were drenched in bad language, and the music I listened to should have been rated R.

After I rededicated my life to Christ, one of the first sins God brought to my attention was my bad language. I repented and made a conscious effort to delete all expletives from my vocabulary. I didn't want my children to learn swear words from me. But old habits die hard. Recently I was teaching my oldest daughter to drive and she made a scary move. Without thinking I yelled, "%@X!#, Erin, watch where you're going!" She looked at me and said, "Mom, you've got a potty mouth." I realized that my words made me look like a total hypocrite in front of my daughter. I asked her to forgive me, and I asked God to cleanse my heart and tongue.

contemplation

Never let an indecent word slip from your mouth. Even if you don't mean it in an evil way, others may be offended. An evil word dropping into a weak person grows and spreads like a drop of oil on linen.
Frances de Sales

5 DO
YOU GO?

preparation

Father, I want to go
where You say, to love
whom You love, to keep
myself unsullied by the
world. Please empower
me to exhibit pure and
undefiled religion.
Amen.

UNDEFILED
Blessed are the
undefiled in the way,
who walk in the law of
the Lord! Psalm 119:1

Having grown up an atheist, in college I decided that if there truly
was a God, I would do a little investigating. I started this pursuit
of God by taking a class on eastern religions. It gave an overview
of Hinduism, Buddhism, Taoism, and Islam. From this smorgas-
bord of religious options, I admired Hinduism the most because
of the Hindu belief that all paths lead to God. It was so nice of this
religion to accommodate hundreds of millions of gods; perhaps I
could sample the "flavor of the month" god.

Simultaneously I began to take random surveys of my friends'
religious belief systems. When I asked, "Do you believe in God?"
they would respond, "I'm a Catholic," or "I go to the Lutheran
church." While attending the same party, drinking from the same
keg, and smoking the same joint, my pseudo-religious friends
would condemn me to hell for disbelief in "a God," as they sat
smugly secure in their church membership, without practicing
their faith. They had been inoculated by a religious system that
prevented them from catching the real thing—a relationship with
God rather than with a denomination.

James had encountered some people who were similar to my
friends. They said they were religious, but they had never repented.
They had all the right rituals, but they weren't living righteously.
So James decided to give some clear instruction on what makes
Christians relevant.

exploration

James has taught us that true inward conversion is manifested
outwardly with righteous speech. Now we examine some other
marks of true religion.

Read James 1, then focus on verse 27.

Pure and undefiled religion before God and the Father is this: to visit orphans and widows in their trouble, and to keep oneself unspotted from the world. James 1:27

1. What two words relating to cleanliness did James use?

. . . .

2. What should remain uncontaminated? . . . .

. . . .

3. What phrase used by James indicates that God notices your religion?

. . . .

4. How will those with pure religion help the helpless? . . . .

. . . .

5. According to Psalm 68:5, what will our holy God be for widows and orphans?

. . . .

6. Read Matthew 25:35-40. Explain whom Jesus encourages us to help, and whom we're *really* helping when we do this.

. . . .

7. According to James 1:27, if we have pure religion, how will we look after ourselves?

. . . .

. . . .

8. What has the potential for blemishing a believer's life?

. . . .

. . . .

explanation

2
RELIGION
The word *religion* comes from *religare*, which means reading over or paying careful attention to divine things. It refers to a system of worship with specific patterns of behavior. Religious rituals are not bad so long as they reflect true reverence and obedience to God.

4
HELPLESS
To God, neglecting helpless widows and orphans is as bad as witchcraft, lying, or adultery. "'I will be a swift witness against sorcerers, against adulterers, against perjurers, against those who exploit . . . widows and orphans . . . because they do not fear Me,' says the Lord" (Malachi 3:5).

7
STAIN FREE
Unspotted means unstained. The spiritual stains of sin can only be washed clean by Christ's blood. Once cleansed we can stay clean through obedience and confession. "If we confess our sins to him, he is faithful and just to forgive us and to cleanse us from every wrong" (1 John 1:9, NLT).

transformation

PURE

Pure means clean; *unde-filed* means free from contamination. Spiritually, religion becomes defiled when mixed with sinful motives. "The commandments and doctrines of men . . . have an appearance of wisdom in self-imposed religion, . . . but are of no value" (Colossians 2:22-23).

9. James has encouraged us to be pure concerning our religion. Fill in the table to discover in what areas of your life God expects purity.

SCRIPTURE	BE PURE IN . . .
Prov. 21:8	
Matt. 5:8	
1 Tim. 3:9	
2 Pet. 3:1	

DO YOU GO?

To *visit* means more than casually dropping by. It means to look out for, care for, and offer relief. In the early church, the neediest people were orphans and widows who, without the benefit of life insurance or welfare programs, were often in desperate straits.

10. Today we learned that God's desire is for His people to help the helpless.

> Think about a widow or orphan you know personally. Journal about when you will visit this person, and how you will help her or him.
>
> . . . .
>
> . . . .
>
> . . . .
>
> . . . .

WORLD

The *world* refers not to planet earth but to fallen humanity alienated from God. The world's systems of ungodly philosophies and values oppose God's holy precepts. Paul said, "We have received, not the spirit of the world, but the Spirit who is from God" (1 Corinthians 2:12).

11. James strongly urges us to remain unspotted from the world. Fill in the table to discover some characteristics of the world.

SCRIPTURE	WORLD
John 7:7	
Gal. 4:3	
Col. 2:8	
1 John 5:19	

Hundreds of women became widows and thousands of children orphans on September 11, 2001. As I watched the September 11 attacks, my thoughts became a prayer, *What can I do, Lord?* Thinking about the thousands killed proved too difficult to wrap my brain around. Instead I needed to pray for one widow. I remembered the POW bracelet I once wore and thought, *Perhaps a similar bracelet could be made to remember the victims and offer their families mercy.*

With the Lord's leading, I founded an organization called Mercy B.A.N.D. (Bearing Another's Name Daily), manufacturing bracelets to serve as a reminder to pray for the survivors and a living memorial to those who died so tragically. Within a week a jeweler, a silver provider, and a manufacturer were on board. Compassionate Christians donated computers, telephones, graphic design, and printing. Within four months, over forty thousand people had donned the bracelets. After a *New York Daily News* story, calls began coming from New York City. A mother who lost a son wanted bracelets engraved with his name. Four widows in a support group passed the phone around, spelling their husbands' names for me. To date, over 150 victims' family members have received the bracelets.

It's my hope that these simple silver bands will make a difference to the widows and orphans. I want the families to know that although there are a few people with evil in their hearts, there are infinitely more people who have mercy in their hearts—and now on their wrists. (See www.mercyband.org)

contemplation

Please give me those daily graces necessary to be fruitful in virtue and in good works.
Marie of the Incarnation

Class Warfare

Class warfare has many different faces: the haves versus the have-nots; Democrats versus Republicans; and educated versus uneducated. In India, Hindus organized society into groups called *castes,* which determined one's social class within the community. The caste system included the Brahmans (priests and scholars), Kshatriyas (rulers and warriors), Vaisyas (merchants and professionals), Shudras (artisans, laborers, and servants), and Dalits (menials known as the untouchables). The caste system was strictly enforced: no one could intermarry or find employment above his or her station in life.

Medieval Europeans had their own caste system known as *feudalism,* based on the social system of large manor estates. The social classes within this system were the lords (the rulers of the land), the vassals (aristocrats and warriors), and the peasants (farmers and servants). Socially, the peasants were at the bottom of the heap.

Ancient Israel was guilty of class warfare, ranking the rich above the poor and the Jews above the Gentiles. Obviously, it's human nature to put people into categories and rank them by their looks, clothing, social status, intelligence, ethnicity, or bank accounts. James urges believers to abolish class warfare because in God's eyes we are all equal. God does not show favoritism toward anyone, and neither should we. "For the Lord your God is God of gods and Lord of lords, the great God, mighty and awesome, who shows no partiality" (Deuteronomy 10:17).

DAY 1
A Class of His Own

DAY 2
Classy Clothes

DAY 3
Low Class

DAY 4
Class Act

DAY 5
Class Rules

A CLASS OF HIS OWN

preparation

Lord Jesus, I praise You that we are all precious in Your sight. I pray You will open my eyes to see others around me with Your love, dignity, and compassion. Amen.

THE KING SAYS
The King will answer and say to them, "Assuredly, I say to you, inasmuch as you did it to one of the least of these My brethren, you did it to Me."
Matthew 25:40

explanation

1

LORD OF GLORY
Glory is part of God's character emphasizing His greatness and authority. While God's glory is not a substance, at times God reveals His perfection and presence visibly. Such a display is often seen as fire or dazzling light, but sometimes it's seen as an act of power.

exploration

Last week we learned that believers with Living Faith will obey the Word of God. Today we will see that those with Living Faith realize that believers should treat one another equally.

Read James 2, then focus on verse 1.

> **My brethren, do not hold the faith of our Lord Jesus Christ, the Lord of glory, with partiality.**
> James 2:1

1. What title did James give to Jesus?. . . . .

. . . .

2. Read 2 Corinthians 4:6. In whose face did the glory of God shine?

. . . .

3. Read 1 Corinthians 6:19-20. Where does the Lord of glory reside today?

. . . .

4. What did James warn his brethren not to do? . . . .

. . . .

5. Read Job 34:19. What does this Scripture say about why God is not partial?

. . . .

. . . .

6. Look up the following Scripture references. Record in the space provided some of the people to whom Jesus ministered while on earth.

SCRIPTURE   JESUS' MINISTRY

Matt. 8:5-7 . . . .

Luke 18:35 . . . .

Luke 19:1-2 . . . .

Luke 23:32 . . . .

John 8:3 . . . .

7. Based on the definition of partiality and what you discovered from the chart, do you think Jesus was partial or impartial toward people? Why?

. . . .

. . . .

8. Jesus' genealogy included notable and godly believers such as Abraham, David, and Solomon. Skim Matthew 1:1-16. What other people with socially unacceptable pasts did God choose to include, with impartiality, in the bloodline of the Savior?

. . . .

. . . .

transformation

9. Jesus is the Lord of glory. His glory is revealed in His character, His miraculous deeds, and His transforming work within His people.

3

OUR GLORY
After Old Testament times, God's glory is shown mainly in Christ and His church. Christ shares His glory with us, transforming us into the glorious image of God. "We can be mirrors that brightly reflect the glory of the Lord" (2 Corinthians 3:18, NLT).

4

PARTIALITY
Partiality can be translated "favoritism" or "with respect of person." Originally, the word referred to raising someone's face or elevating the person. It came to refer to exalting someone strictly on a superficial, external basis, such as appearance, race, wealth, rank, or social status (adapted, *MacArthur*).

8

BLACK SHEEP
Tamar committed incest by seducing her father-in-law, Judah, to bear a child. Rahab was a prostitute in Jericho who hid the Israelite spies. Ruth was a Gentile from the despised Moabites, a race the Jews were strictly forbidden to marry. Bathsheba, Uriah's wife, committed adultery with King David.

REFLECTION
We reflect Jesus' glory through developing godly character; doing good deeds; operating in His miraculous gifts; and separating ourselves from sin. "When Christ, who is your real life, is revealed to the whole world, you will share in all his glory" (Colossians 3:4, NLT).

10
FAVORITISM
Playing favorites with friends or family may cause others to stumble through jealousy and strife. When Jacob favored Joseph over his brothers, they were jealous and lashed out. When James and John requested places of honor in heaven, it caused strife among the other disciples.

11
CRITICAL SPIRIT
We usually dislike in others what we dislike about ourselves. Instead of taking care of our own sin, it's easier to point the finger at someone else's. Jesus spoke against this hypocrisy. "You also outwardly appear righteous to men, but inside you are full of hypocrisy and lawlessness" (Matthew 23:28).

Using the word *GLORY*, journal about some of the ways you have beheld the Lord of glory.

G (Example: God's miraculous deliverance of my life from sin.)

. . . .

L . . . .

. . . .

O . . . .

. . . .

R . . . .

. . . .

Y . . . .

. . . .

10. James exhorts us to be impartial toward others. By what criteria do you show partiality or judge people?

___ Past experiences   ___ Color of skin
___ Initial impressions   ___ Social standing
___ Level of education   ___ God's view of them
___ Way they dress   ___ Other_____

11. Jesus said the way you treat others will determine how others will treat you. Place the phrases from the following verse that contain YOU or OTHERS in the appropriate column.

"Stop judging others, and you will not be judged. For others will treat you as you treat them. Whatever measure you use in judging others, it will be used to measure how you are judged. And why worry about a speck in . . . [another's] eye when you have a log in your own?" (Matthew 7:1-3, NLT).

YOU	OTHERS
. . . .	
. . . .	

. . . .

. . . .

. . . .

With just a tad of self-righteousness, my father would say, "I don't smoke, I don't chew, and I don't go with girls who do." It was his funny way of saying there were plenty of people worse than him in this world. Have you ever overheard other believers talk about things that made you feel spiritually inferior? "I don't go to the movies!" "I'm a home-schooler—I'd never send my kids to public school." "If he'd cut his hair and take those earrings off, he'd look more like a Christian."

Jesus told a parable about people who compare themselves with others. "One was a Pharisee, and the other was a dishonest tax collector. The proud Pharisee stood by himself and prayed this prayer: 'I thank you, God, that I am not a sinner like everyone else, especially like that tax collector over there! For I never cheat, I don't sin, I don't commit adultery, I fast twice a week, and I give you a tenth of my income.' But the tax collector stood at a distance and dared not even lift his eyes to heaven as he prayed. Instead, he beat his chest in sorrow, saying, 'O God, be merciful to me, for I am a sinner.' I tell you, this sinner, not the Pharisee, returned home justified before God" (Luke 18:9-14, NLT).

Comparing ourselves with others is futile: there's always someone better or someone worse. Instead, we should judge ourselves by the Lord of glory. Everyone else pales in comparison.

contemplation

The greatest, in the judgment of God, are the least in their own opinion; the more worthy they are, the more humility will be seen in them.

Thomas à Kempis

DAY 2 CLASSY CLOTHES

In a simple experiment, two friends of equal education, background, and economic status—one Caucasian, the other African-American—visited a Midwestern city to see if they would be treated alike. When they went into a shoe store, the white man was welcomed with a handshake; the black man waited for more than four minutes and never got waited on. At the car dealership, the white man got a better deal. At the apartment for rent, he was encouraged to look it over, but his African-American friend was told that the unit had already been taken. When interviewed, the people in this experiment who had shown prejudice said they weren't biased at all. But their actions betrayed their words.

Prejudice is a preconceived judgment or opinion. It is an irrational attitude of hostility directed against an individual or groups of people. Humans are susceptible to prejudice and partiality, but God has never had a prejudiced thought. Jill Briscoe offers some practical suggestions to overcome prejudice and partiality: 1) Become friends with someone you don't like because of their religious or political views, race, or economic standing; 2) Join a club whose members come from different socioeconomic levels; 3) Invite people you feel prejudice against into your home for a meal.

exploration

James has told us that personal prejudice and the gospel of Jesus Christ cannot coexist. Today he introduces us to two imaginary visitors—one in classy clothes and one in dirty duds—to illustrate the evils of partiality.

Review James 2, then focus on verses 2-4.

For if there should come into your assembly a man with gold rings, in fine apparel, and there should also come in a poor man in filthy clothes, . . . James 2:2

1. Who was the first visitor, and what was he wearing?

. . . .

2. Who was the second visitor, and what was he wearing?

. . . .

3. What phrase lets you know this scenario took place in the church?

. . . .

. . . and you pay attention to the one wearing the fine clothes and say to him, "You sit here in a good place," and say to the poor man, "You stand there," or, "Sit here at my footstool" . . . James 2:3

4. Describe how the man wearing fine clothes was treated.

. . . .

. . . .

5. Explain how the poor man's treatment was different.

. . . .

. . . .

. . . have you not shown partiality among yourselves, and become judges with evil thoughts? James 2:4

6. What question did James ask the brethren? What was the result of their partiality?

. . . .

. . . .

1

CLASSY CLOTHES
In ancient Israel, well-to-do people wore numerous rings on their fingers to parade their wealth. These people were referred to as "gold-fingered." Fine clothing was also a status symbol. The word *fine* literally means "bright or brilliant." These people tried to dazzle others with glitter and glamour.

2

DIRTY DUDS
The poor could afford only cheap clothing—probably castoffs. Water was such a precious commodity that they had less opportunity to wash. The sin was not that the first man wore finery or that the second man wore dirty duds. The sin was that the people treated them differently based on appearances.

5

DISRESPECT
Failing to offer a visitor a footstool was extremely disrespectful. Telling a visitor to sit down beside one's footstool was a double show of contempt, essentially saying, "Sit by my stool like a dog."

transformation

7

CLASS WARFARE
Class warfare works both ways. Oftentimes it's the rich judging the poor. But the poor can be guilty of judging the rich, thinking they don't deserve their money or have obtained it easily. Lydia, the seller of purple, worked hard for her money and used it to further the gospel.

FILTHY RAGS
Humans obsess about what they wear on their bodies, but the Bible teaches we should be more concerned about how our hearts are adorned. "We are all infected and impure with sin. When we proudly display our righteous deeds, we find they are but filthy rags" (Isaiah 64:6, NLT).

RESPECT
Respect means to look back or to give particular attention and consideration. We don't just ignore the poor; oftentimes we don't even see them or their plight. Train yourself to notice, then considerately meet their needs. More than giving them a handout, offer them a hand up.

7. James gave a scenario of two different types of people—now it's your turn. Picture yourself standing in the checkout line at the grocery store. A woman wearing diamonds and designer clothes is waiting in front of you. What judgments do you make about her because of her apparel?

— "I bet she's a snob."
— "Her children probably go to a private school."
— "Her money can't buy her happiness."
— "I wonder if she is rich in the Lord?"
— Other_____.

Now imagine yourself sitting in your car at a stoplight. A man in filthy clothes is sitting on the corner with a "Will Work For Food—Jesus Loves You" sign. What judgments do you make about him?

— "He needs to get a job."
— "If I give him money, he'll go buy liquor."
— "He doesn't know Jesus—he's just using His name."
— "I wonder if he would let the Lord change his life?"
— Other_____.

8. Can you recall a time when you tried to impress others by wearing classy clothes? How did it make you feel? Did others respond like you expected?

. . . .

. . . .

. . . .

9. James told about the poor who were treated with disrespect in the early church. Name some people or groups today that modern society marginalizes or treats with disdain.

. . . .

. . . .

Choose one of the people you named and journal about how you will treat him or her respectfully this week.

. . . .

. . . .

. . . .

. . . .

Children are naturally greedy and selfish. Their favorite words are *I, me,* and *mine.* Our son was no different than other pre-schoolers, so my husband, Skip, found a way to train him to be generous and not show prejudice. One night while reading the Bible together, they read: "Do not be hard-hearted or tightfisted toward [the poor]. Instead, be generous and lend them whatever they need" (Deuteronomy 15:7-8, NLT). Skip tightly clenched his hands into fists and said, "Don't be tightfisted." Then he opened his fists, holding out his hands and said, "Be open-handed." With childlike exuberance, Nathan imitated his father, walking around the house clenching and releasing his fists, chanting, "Don't be tightfisted, be open-handed!"

One day this lesson was put to the test. Nathan and I drove by a homeless person holding a sign, "Will Work For Food." Nathan said, "Mama, let's be open-handed and give him some money." I didn't want to quench Nathan's generosity, but I didn't want our money to be squandered. Then I got an inspired idea. "Let's go to the grocery store and buy him some food." After that, we prepared a dozen lunch bags filled with nonperishable food and a note about God to carry wherever we traveled. Keep your eyes open this week to your hidden prejudices, and ask God for new ways to share His love without favoritism.

contemplation

Very few people take the trouble to use their brains as long as their prejudices are in working condition.
Roy L. Smith

3 LOW CLASS

preparation

Lord, I praise You that no matter what my social status is, You have blessed me abundantly with faith to believe the gospel, be saved, and persevere to eternal life. Amen.

THE LORD IS RICH
There is no distinction between Jew and Greek, for the same Lord over all is rich to all who call upon Him. Romans 10:12

Everybody knows some of the basic rules of etiquette: "Don't talk with your mouth full." "Respond to an R.S.V.P. within five days of receiving an invitation." "Offer your seat to a lady or your elders." Etiquette is a code of behavior that helps people get along with one another. Many people think it applies to high-class members of society who have a rigid set of rules concerning appropriate party attire and proper table manners. But true etiquette doesn't exist to make you look good; its goal is to make others feel good. Like my grandma used to say, "A person with good manners will always make others feel comfortable."

Emily Post, who made a career out of good manners, wrote, "Best Society is not a fellowship of the wealthy, nor does it seek to exclude those who are not of exalted birth; but it *is* an association of gentle-folk, of which good form in speech, charm of manner, knowledge of the social amenities, and instinctive consideration for the feelings of others, are the credentials by which society the world over recognizes its chosen members." In other words, you can posses the impeccable manners of high society, but if you make other people feel bad about themselves, you behave like a member of the lower class, not the upper crust.

Our instructor James wants to make sure we have proper etiquette when it comes to our dealings with others, especially the poor.

exploration

Yesterday we learned that being rich or poor is not a sin, but playing favorites is. Today we discover that God's grace produces people rich in faith, and that those who treat the poor badly exhibit low-class behavior.

Review James 2, then focus on verses 5-7.

> *Listen, my beloved brethren: Has God not chosen the poor of this world to be rich in faith and heirs of the kingdom which He promised to those who love Him?*
> James 2:5

1. What phrase did James use to gain his readers' attention?

. . . .

2. Describe whom God has chosen, and why. . . . .

. . . .

3. Read Psalm 41:1-3. List the blessings for those who consider the poor and weak.

. . . .

. . . .

4. What promise did God make in James 2:5 to those who love Him?

. . . .

> *But you have dishonored the poor man. Do not the rich oppress you and drag you into the courts? Do they not blaspheme that noble name by which you are called?*
> James 2:6-7

5. How had the poor man been treated? Reflect on yesterday's lesson, then describe how this had happened within the church.

. . . .

. . . .

6. What question did James use to remind his readers how the rich had treated them?

. . . .

. . . .

2
RICH FAITH
When God speaks of riches, He doesn't necessarily mean money. He wants us to be rich in faith, mercy, and good works, and then He will take care of the rest. "Seek first the kingdom of God and His righteousness, and all these things shall be added to you" (Matthew 6:33).

4
KINGDOM
The kingdom of heaven, the kingdom of God, and eternal life are one and the same. People who have placed their faith in Jesus Christ have the kingdom of God reigning in their hearts *now*, and *later* they will enter the kingdom of heaven and experience eternal life.

7. When the rich oppress poor believers, what are they really doing (v. 7)?

. . . .

. . . .

transformation

8. Often the financially poor are rich in faith. But there is another type of poverty the Bible teaches about: "Blessed are the poor in spirit, for theirs is the kingdom of heaven" (Matthew 5:3). Think about how you were "poor in spirit"—spiritually bankrupt—before you experienced the kingdom of heaven.

Journal about how, in God's grace, you've become spiritually rich in faith, mercy, or good deeds.

. . . .

. . . .

. . . .

. . . .

. . . .

9. God has promised that those who believe will be heirs to His kingdom. Fill in the chart to discover some of the riches we will inherit.

SCRIPTURE	INHERITANCE
Ps. 37:11	
Prov. 3:35	
Matt. 19:29	
Rev. 21:7	

BLASPHEMY
Blasphemy is cursing, slandering, showing contempt or lack of reverence for God. In the Old Testament, blaspheming God was a serious crime punishable by death. "Anyone who blasphemes the Lord's name must be stoned to death by the whole community of Israel" (Leviticus 24:16, NLT).

POOR IN SPIRIT
In order for you to be rich in faith, Jesus became poor in spirit. "You know how full of love and kindness our Lord Jesus Christ was. Though he was very rich, yet for your sakes he became poor, so that by his poverty he could make you rich" (2 Corinthians 8:9, NLT).

HEIRS
In heaven we will all be rich in the things that really matter. Every child of God equally inherits eternal life, a heavenly home, crowns for the faithful, and a place at the Lord's table. "Since we are his children, we will share his treasures" (Romans 8:17, NLT).

10. We have seen that in the early church the rich often oppressed the poor.

Read the definition of oppression in the sidebar, then journal about some ways people are oppressed today.

. . . .

. . . .

. . . .

. . . .

OPPRESSION
To *oppress* someone is to crush or burden them by an unjust exercise of power or authority; to weigh down mentally; a sense of heaviness or obstruction in the body or mind. Besides the poor, the Bible exhorts, "Do not oppress widows, orphans, [or] foreigners" (Zechariah 7:10, NLT).

Shrink the earth's population to a village of one hundred people and it looks something like this:

- 57 Asians, 21 Europeans, 14 from the Western Hemisphere, and 8 Africans
- 52 female, 48 male
- 70 non-Christian, 30 Christian

Six people would possess 59 percent of the entire world's wealth, and all six would be from the United States. Eighty people would live in substandard housing, seventy would be unable to read, fifty would suffer from malnutrition, one would be near death, one would be near birth, one (yes, only one) would have a college education, and only one would own a computer.

When you consider our world from such a compressed perspective, the following is something to ponder:

- If you have food in the refrigerator, clothes on your back, a roof overhead, and a place to sleep, you are richer than 75 percent of this world.
- If you have never experienced war, imprisonment, torture, or the pangs of starvation, you are ahead of 500 million other people.
- If you have money in the bank, in your wallet, and spare change in a dish someplace, you are among the top 8 percent of the world's wealthy.

For those of us who have much, James's teaching reminds us to honor the poor, not insult them or play favorites. This is the way to a Living Faith that is truly rich.

contemplation

Half the world is starving; the other half is on a diet. We are not privileged because we deserve to be. Privilege accepted should mean responsibility accepted.
Madeleine L'Engle

DAY 4 CLASS ACT

preparation

Thank You, Lord, for liberating me from the bondage of sin and for clothing me with Your perfect righteousness. Thank You that I'm a brand new person in Christ Jesus, free to obey, serve, and live a faithful, righteous life. Amen.

LOVE ONE ANOTHER
A new commandment I give to you, that you love one another; as I have loved you, that you also love one another. John 13:34

Catherine Booth, wife of William Booth and "Mother" of the Salvation Army, was truly a class act. "Wherever Catherine Booth went," said G. Campbell Morgan, pastor of Westminster Chapel, "humanity went to hear her. Princes and princesses merged with paupers and prostitutes."

One night Morgan shared in an evangelistic meeting with Mrs. Booth, and a great crowd of lower-class people attended. Her message of compassion to the downtrodden brought many to Christ. After the meeting, Morgan and Mrs. Booth went to a fine home for dinner. The elegant lady of the manor, dressed in the latest fashions, said, "My dear Mrs. Booth, that meeting was dreadful!" In her down-to-earth way, Mrs. Booth asked, "What do you mean, dearie?" "Well, when you were speaking, I was looking at those people and their faces were so terrible! I don't think I shall sleep tonight!" "Madame, you mean to say you don't know them?" Mrs. Booth asked. The hostess replied in a huff, "Certainly not!" "That is very interesting," Mrs. Booth said. "I did not bring them with me from London; they are *your* neighbors!"

It's easy to love the lovely, but it's godly to love the unlovely. Mrs. Booth demonstrated true class by extending her hand to those less fortunate than herself, treating them with the same dignity she would offer to those who were well-to-do. James reminds us that believers should obey Christ's royal command to love our neighbors as ourselves.

exploration

Our lesson yesterday taught us that rich or poor, those who love Jesus and have placed their faith in Him will inherit God's kingdom. Now we will learn that if we obey the royal law of love, in God's eyes we'll be a class act.

Review James 2, then focus on verses 8-11.

> **If you really fulfill the royal law according to the Scripture, "You shall love your neighbor as yourself," you do well.** James 2:8

1. What did James encourage his readers (and us) to fulfill?

. . . .

2. Explain the royal law and the commendation for keeping it.

. . . .

> **. . . but if you show partiality, you commit sin, and are convicted by the law as transgressors.** James 2:9

3. What behavior did James consider sinful? . . . .

. . . .

4. How do you know this behavior is sinful? . . . .

. . . .

> **For whoever shall keep the whole law, and yet stumble in one point, he is guilty of all. For He who said, "Do not commit adultery," also said, "Do not murder." Now if you do not commit adultery, but you do murder, you have become a transgressor of the law.** James 2:10-11

5. If a person breaks even one of God's laws, what is that person guilty of?

. . . .

6. What two commandments did James mention? . . . .

. . . .

. . . .

1

ROYAL LAW
James quotes Leviticus 19:18 here, reminiscent of the Golden Rule: *Do unto others as you would have them do unto you.* "Whatever you want men to do to you, do also to them, for this is the Law and the Prophets" (Matthew 7:12). By doing this we fulfill the royal law.

4

LAW BREAKERS
To *sin* means to miss the mark of God's holy purity. *Transgress* means to go over or beyond; to willfully violate God's laws. Transgression implies rebellion. If God drew a line in the sand, then sinners would inadvertently stumble over the line while transgressors would willfully step over it.

5

LAW MAKER
The Law—the Ten Commandments—comes from God, reflecting His nature of holiness, righteousness, and goodness. As the great King, God gave laws that were binding on His people. Furthermore, His laws are universal and are an expression of His love for His people.

7. By comparing the sin of partiality to the sins of adultery and murder, what was James saying about partiality?

. . . .

transformation

8. We've been told to love our neighbor, but "who is my neighbor?" Read Luke 10:29-37 to see how Jesus answered that question.

   a. Describe what happened to the traveler (v. 30).

. . . .

   b. How did the priest and Levite treat the traveler (vv. 31-32)?

. . . .

   c. Explain how the Samaritan responded (vv. 33-35).

. . . .

   d. Describe what a good neighbor is (v. 37).

. . . .

9. To love our neighbors as ourselves is to fulfill the Golden Rule.

> Journal about a specific way you can "do unto others as you would have them do to you" this week. Then do it!

. . . .

. . . .

. . . .

. . . .

10. The Ten Commandments (see Exodus 20) were given to govern our relationships with God and with others. Place each commandment in the appropriate column: Have no other gods besides God / Do not take God's name in vain / Do not make idols / Keep the Sabbath / Honor your father and mother

---

8

GOOD NEIGHBOR
Samaritans were a mixed race (Jewish and Gentile), contaminated by foreign blood and false worship, and had built a rival temple on Mt. Gerizim. The Samaritans were hated by the Jews. The "Good Samaritan," a despised foreigner, was a better neighbor than a pious priest.

9

GOLDEN RULE
Sin of *commission* means doing something you know is wrong. Sin of *omission* is not doing what you know is right. The Golden Rule is of no value until you practice it. "To him who knows to do good and does not do it, to him it is sin" (James 4:17).

10

COMMANDMENTS
The ten laws given by God are guidelines for daily living. They are part of a covenant between God and His people. Although given more than three thousand years ago, they're still relevant today. Jesus upheld them and summed them up into two commandments: 1) Loving God and 2) Loving others.

/ Do not murder / Do not commit adultery / Do not steal /
Do not bear false witness / Do not covet

GOD	OTHERS

. . . .

. . . .

. . . .

. . . .

. . . .

. . . .

. . . .

Following World War II, soldiers were released from a prison
camp in Siberia. Although the officers tried to repatriate as many
men as possible, it looked like many would have to remain in
the bitter cold region when winter threatened to close up the
port. As the last boat prepared to sail, it was apparent that only
a few would be welcomed aboard. Among those waiting to be
transported were two buddies who had developed a deep friendship throughout the war. Only one man was selected; the other
seemed doomed to remain behind.

Those who were leaving were limited to one piece of luggage.
The lucky soldier who was chosen to board the ship emptied his
duffle bag of his prized souvenirs and personal belongings, then
told his best friend to get into the canvas sack. Carefully lifting the
bag on his shoulders, he boarded the ship with his friend as his
single possession. This man truly loved his neighbor as himself.

Loving your neighbors requires sacrifices of time, energy, and
resources. Jesus showed his love by sacrificing everything for us.
He fulfilled the royal law by giving His life for everyone. "Greater
love has no one than this, than to lay down one's life for his
friends" (John 15:13). He was completely impartial. He died for
the whole world—from Ted Bundy to Mother Teresa—including
you and me, and He challenges you to follow in His footsteps.
Show how much you love Him by loving your neighbor, no
matter who it is.

contemplation

*Though we do not
have our Lord with us
in bodily presence,
we have our neighbor,
who, for the ends of
love and loving service,
is as good as our Lord
himself.*
Teresa of Avila

preparation

Lord, I long to do what is pleasing and good in Your sight. Help me to love and extend mercy to everyone who needs it, just as You extend mercy to me. Amen.

MERCY
The Lord has already told you what is good, and this is what he requires: to do what is right, to love mercy, and to walk humbly with your God.
Micah 6:8, NLT

Many years ago, a well-to-do Christian who abhorred slavery paid a high price for a slave at auction. When the two met for the first time, the wealthy man said, "I have bought you, but I did it only to free you from the terrible bondage you have known." Then he handed the other man some papers that guaranteed his freedom.

The slave looked at him in sheer amazement. "Am I truly free? May I go where I wish?" "Yes," said the Christian, "that's why I bought you, so you could be loosed from those chains forever." Overwhelmed by these words, the slave fell at the feet of his liberator and said with heartfelt devotion, "Then my greatest joy and freedom will be to stay with you and serve you gladly for the rest of my life."

The Bible is the story of God's quest to liberate humanity. His Son, Jesus, paid a very high price—His life. Through His sacrifice, those who call on His name are set free from the bondage of sin. The only reasonable response for those of us who have been liberated by His mercy is to serve Christ gladly in all that we say and do for the rest of our lives. Like the former slave we will be able to say, "Serving Christ has been my greatest joy and freedom." James teaches us that showing love and mercy are part of the class rules in the school of faith.

exploration

We have found that Living Faith obeys the royal law of God by extending love to our neighbors. Today we discover that we must follow the class rules and uphold God's merciful law of liberty.

Review James 2, then focus on verses 12-13.

So speak and so do as those who will be judged by the law of liberty. James 2:12

1. Based on yesterday's lesson, explain the "law" that should affect our speech and actions.

. . . .

. . . .

2. According to James, how should we speak and act?. . . . .

. . . .

3. By what standard will we be judged?. . . . .

. . . .

4. The law of liberty was designed to set us free from sin. Read Galatians 5:13-14. What should we *do* and *not* do with the liberty we've been given?

. . . .

. . . .

For judgment is without mercy to the one who has shown no mercy. Mercy triumphs over judgment. James 2:13

5. What type of judgment did James focus on at the beginning of verse 13?

. . . .

. . . .

6. When do you think this type of judgment will be delivered?

. . . .

7. Describe the power of mercy. . . . .

. . . .

explanation

2
JUDGED?
Believers are judged differently than unbelievers. The judgment seat of Christ does not judge a believer's sins; those have been atoned for by Christ's death. Rather, the works of every child of God will be evaluated, resulting in reward or loss of reward (adapted, *Unger's*). See 2 Corinthians 5:10.

3
LAW OF LIBERTY
The Ten Commandments were the law of Moses; the gospel of Christ represents the law of liberty because it sets transgressors free from the bondage, judgment, and penalty of sin. "If the Son sets you free, you will indeed be free" (John 8:36, NLT).

7
MERCY
Mercy moves God to help the miserable just as grace moves Him to forgive the guilty. *Mercy* implies compassion that withholds punishment even when it is deserved. "Our God is merciful and forgiving, even though we have rebelled against him" (Daniel 9:9, NLT).

transformation

YOUR GOSPEL
"You are writing a gospel, a chapter each day, by the things that you do and the words that you say. People hear what you say and they see what you do. Say, what is the gospel according to you?" (Anonymous)

9

BONDAGE
People think they can handle a little sin. "Just one drink, then I'll quit." When we obey sin, it becomes our master. "You can choose sin, which leads to death, or you can choose to obey God and receive His approval" (Romans 6:16, NLT).

10

TRIUMPH
Triumph refers to the celebratory parade hailing a Roman general's victory over an enemy. Jesus was triumphant over the power of sin, ensuring that mercy could prevail. "Having disarmed principalities and powers, [Jesus] made a public spectacle of them, triumphing over them" (Colossians 2:15).

8. We've been urged to speak and do as those obeying the royal law. Fill in the chart to discover some things believers are to speak or do.

SCRIPTURE	SPEAK/DO
John 13:15 . . . .
1 Cor. 11:25 . . . .
Eph. 4:25 . . . .
Titus 2:1 . . . .

9. Many people think that God's laws are restrictive. James says it is a law of liberty setting us free from the bondage of sin. Check off the things that have held you captive.

— Food   — Drugs
— Relationships   __ Bitterness
— Legalism   __ Materialism
— Tobacco   __ Swearing
— Lust

10. James taught that mercy triumphs over judgment. With this in mind, complete the following steps:

Step One: Write the name of someone you know in bondage to sin who needs God's mercy.

. . . .

Step Two: Describe the circumstances this person is in and the consequences that may occur because of his or her actions. (Example: My friend has been gambling at the casino and could squander the rent.)

. . . .

. . . .

. . . .

Step Three: Journal a prayer of mercy for your friend by rewriting the following verse: "So let us come boldly to the throne of our gracious God. There we will receive his mercy, and we will find grace to help us when we need it" (Hebrews 4:16, NLT).

. . . .

. . . .

. . . .

. . . .

What if things were reversed? Think about what would happen if God's judgment triumphed over His mercy. Break one, just *one,* of the Ten Commandments and you're toast. No second chances; immediate death sentence. That moment of loving your child more than God? Death! That little white lie you told your husband? Death! That instant of longing for your neighbor's new car? Death!

Now think about society. If judgment triumphed over mercy, then the moment you broke the speed limit, your license would be rescinded. The first class you missed would be your last—you'd be expelled from school. No calling in sick to work—judgment doesn't allow for sick days. At home, every time your child acted naughty—immediate punishment. Your husband broke his promise and came home late—no smiles of understanding, only the cold shoulder. You mention a handsome movie star and end up in divorce court. No mercy, only judgment.

Living under judgment would make the world a desperate and despairing place. Perhaps the birds would not sing nor the grass turn green. People wouldn't smile or laugh—why should they? There'd be no need for prayer because we couldn't be forgiven.

Aren't you grateful that God is a God of mercy? His very name is mercy; His character is mercy; He delights in mercy; His mercy is new every morning; His mercy is never ending. And, hallelujah, His mercy triumphs over judgment!

contemplation

There's a wideness in God's mercy.
Frederick William Faber

Flatline Faith

The eerie scream of sirens shatters the lazy afternoon. Paramedics rush into the ER calling out, "Code Blue! We've got a flatline!" Quickly doctors assess the patient then pull out the defibrillation paddles, sending bursts of electricity into the body to shock the heart into activity. While the patient is being hooked up to an EKG to measure the heart rate, a doctor pulls out her stethoscope and listens intently to the patient's breathing to make sure the lungs are working properly. The crisis is averted—the patient will survive.

Human beings need two vital organs to survive: a heart and lungs. Without both functioning properly, life will cease. You can't stay alive if you stop breathing. You can't stay alive if your heart stops beating. These two functions are inseparable: The heart pumps the blood and the lungs oxygenate the blood. If either system fails, you're dead.

Just as physical bodies need the heart and lungs to work together, the spirit needs two vital components to function together: faith and works. Faith and works are to our souls what the heart and lungs are to our bodies. We must have both to be spiritually alive. Faith allows us to be born again—it gives us spiritual breath. Works help us grow to maturity, pumping spiritual vitality into our lives. This week James reminds us that people without the two functioning elements of faith and works are in a spiritual crisis, resulting in flatline faith—faith that is dead.

DAY 1
Doubting Faith

DAY 2
Dead Faith

DAY 3
Demonic Faith?

DAY 4
Divine Faith

DAY 5
Dynamic Faith

1

DOUBTING
FAITH

preparation

*Father, I want my faith
to be genuine, beyond
any doubt. Help me
examine myself closely
and determine whether
I merely say I believe,
or whether I show what
I believe in both word
and deed. Amen.*

FAITH
*Examine yourselves as
to whether you are in the
faith. Test yourselves.
2 Corinthians 13:5*

explanation

PROFIT
*Profit means "a return
above an expenditure;
a gain or advantage."
In God's eyes, when
we expend godliness,
we gain contentment.
"Now godliness with
contentment is great
gain" (1 Timothy 6:6).
Following God provides
many advantages that
money can't buy.*

exploration

Lesson 5 taught us that people with Living Faith will not show partiality based on worldly wealth. Now James goes on to say that there is good reason to doubt the sincerity of those who profess faith in Christ if they fail to put their words into action. People with Living Faith will not just say they believe; they will show it.

Read James 2, then focus on verse 14.

> **What does it profit, my brethren, if someone says he has faith but does not have works? Can faith save him?**
> James 2:14

1. How do you know James was addressing professing Christians here?

   . . . .

2. What question did James begin with? . . . .

   . . . .

3. Put in your own words what the hypothetical person in verse 14 was saying.

   . . . .

4. According to Romans 10:9, in order for us to be saved, what must accompany our words?

   . . . .

5. Returning to James 2:14, what does this hypothetical person who says he has faith fail to do?

. . . .

6. What is the bottom-line question, according to James 2:14?

. . . .

7. Based on the tone of this question, what answer do you think James expects us to give?

. . . .

8. Read Ephesians 2:8-10 and answer the following questions:

a. According to Paul, how have we been saved (v. 8)?

. . . .

b. Explain what has *not* purchased our salvation and why (vv. 8-9).

. . . .

c. Why did God create us in Christ Jesus (v. 10)? . . . .

. . . .

transformation

9. We've seen that God desires for us to profit spiritually. However, to benefit God's kingdom, we must invest something.

Using the acrostic *PROFIT*, journal about how *you* will invest in kingdom work.

Pray for _____.

Remind _____ that Jesus loves them.

Offer my time to _____.

Forgive _____.

Invest in _____ ministry.

Tell _____ about Christ.

3
F.A.I.T.H.
Faith is firm belief in God involving commitment to His will; a personal surrender to Christ. Faith could be an acrostic: Forsaking All I Trust Him (adapted, Lockyer, *All the Doctrines of the Bible*). "Faith is the substance of things hoped for, the evidence of things not seen" (Hebrews 11:1).

5
WORKS
Our works can be either good or bad. Works are bad when they are works of darkness, works of the flesh, idolatry, hypocrisy, or works of the law. "Have no fellowship with the unfruitful works of dark-ness, but rather expose them" (Ephesians 5:11).

9
PROFITABLE
God isn't concerned whether we make a financial profit; He is concerned that we prosper spiritually. By investing in good works, we will reap eternal treasures. Jesus said, "What profit is it to a man if he gains the whole world, and loses his own soul?" (Matthew 16:26).

SAYING

Saying something doesn't make it true. You can say you're twenty-nine, but that doesn't make it so. You can say you have faith, but your actions might betray you. "We are lying if we say we have fellowship with God but go on living in spiritual darkness" (1 John 1:6, NLT).

DOING

Christians will do what the Bible instructs, revealing a genuine faith. Jesus rebuked the scribes and Pharisees for saying the right words without doing the right deeds. "They say, and do not do" (Matthew 23:3). Doing good works will not save us, but it does prove we are saved.

10. Not all who *say* they have faith truly do have saving faith. Read Matthew 7:21 and answer the following questions.

a. What will people *say* to Jesus? . . . .

. . . .

b. What does Jesus reveal about some of these people's eternal fate?

. . . .

c. Explain who will enter the kingdom of heaven. . . . .

. . . .

11. James revealed that those with Living Faith will not only say they believe but also will do good works. Fill in the table to discover some good works we are instructed to do.

SCRIPTURE	GOOD WORKS
1 Tim. 5:10 . . . .
1 Tim. 6:18 . . . .
Titus 2:6-9 . . . .
Heb. 6:10 . . . .

Journal about which of the above good works you exhibit in your life, then write a prayer asking God to help you incorporate the good works you do not yet exhibit into your life.

. . . .

. . . .

. . . .

. . . .

. . . .

. . . .

A Christian man worked transporting tourists across a lake in his rowboat. Sometimes he presented the gospel in a most unusual way. He painted the word FAITH on one oar of his rowboat and the word WORKS on the other. Stopping in the middle of the lake, he would row with just the oar marked "faith," causing the boat to go in circles to the left. Reversing the process, he'd row with just "works" and circle in the opposite direction. The bewildered passengers would ask what he was doing. Explaining the truth of salvation, he would add, "You see, neither faith nor works can go it alone. They are twins that cannot be separated."

This story is reminiscent of Lazarus' two sisters: Mary, the faithful devotee and Martha, the hardworking servant. When Jesus came to their home for dinner, Mary was found worshipping at the Lord's feet while Martha was spinning her wheels in a flurry of activity. Disgruntled, Martha said, "Lord, doesn't it seem unfair to you that my sister just sits here while I do all the work?" Jesus defended Mary's choice saying, "My dear Martha, you are so upset over all these details! There is really only one thing worth being concerned about. Mary has discovered it—and I won't take it away from her" (Luke 10:40-42, NLT).

As Christians, there are seasons when we become more involved in the work and less concerned about the worship, and that's when we go in fruitless circles. Pray for a balance of believing and doing in your faith walk.

contemplation

Only the Word of God makes us wholesome and blessed. The divine Word brings faith. Faith brings love. Love results in good deeds.
Martin Bucer

2 DEAD FAITH

Mother Teresa said, "The poor come to all of us in many forms. Let us be sure that we never turn our backs on them, wherever we may find them. For when we turn our backs on the poor, we turn them on Jesus Christ." Is this true? Did Mother Teresa really mean that neglecting the poor is neglecting Christ?

Jesus explained this phenomenon during the Olivet Discourse. He warned that upon His return He will separate the sheep from the goats. The sheep represent those followers who express Living Faith through generous works. The goats are those who display dead faith by not practicing what they preach. This litmus test of dead or living faith was based on the treatment of the poor and needy.

Jesus takes it personally when the poor are neglected. He chastised the goats, "Depart from Me, . . . for I was hungry and you gave Me no food; I was thirsty and you gave Me no drink; I was a stranger and you did not take Me in, naked and you did not clothe Me, sick and in prison and you did not visit Me" (Matthew 25:41-43). The dismayed goats couldn't understand how they had neglected Jesus. He said, "Inasmuch as you did not do it to one of the least of these, you did not do it to Me" (Matthew 25:45).

James's litmus test for true faith is the same as our Lord's. Will we assist the poor or avoid them? Your answer reveals whether you are more like a sheep or a goat.

exploration

James has asked us to contemplate whether merely *saying* we have faith proves we truly believe. Now we learn that true Living Faith expresses itself not only in good words but in generous works as well.

Review James 2, then focus on verses 15-17.

> *If a brother or sister is naked and destitute of daily food, and one of you says to them, "Depart in peace, be warmed and filled," but you do not give them the things which are needed for the body, what does it profit?*
> James 2:15-16

1. James used another hypothetical situation to reflect the lifelessness of faith without works. Describe the condition of the needy people in this situation.

. . . .

2. What platitude did the church offer the needy brother or sister?

. . . .

3. Describe what the church failed to do. . . . .

. . . .

4. What question did James repeat from verse 14? . . . .

. . . .

5. John also addressed people who say the right words but fail in acts of mercy. Read 1 John 3:17-18 and answer the following questions.

   a. Describe the kind of people John is addressing here.

   . . . .

   b. Explain the true nature of their relationship with God.

   . . . .

   c. Contrast the way John expects true believers to behave.

   Not:

   . . . .

   But:

   . . . .

explanation

1

DESTITUTE
Destitute means "to be forsaken or abandoned; suffering extreme poverty." The world thinks the rich get ahead while the poor are left behind, but Jesus said, "The last will be first, and the first last" (Matthew 20:16), and "I will never leave you nor forsake you" (Hebrews 13:5).

3

FAMILY OF GOD
We are to help anyone in need. But if the needy are members of God's own family, we should treat them especially well. "Whenever we have the opportunity, we should do good to everyone, especially to our Christian brothers and sisters" (Galatians 6:10, NLT).

Thus also faith by itself, if it does not have works, is dead. James 2:17

LONELY FAITH
The New Century Version translates this verse, "Faith that is alone—that does noth-ing—is dead." It is faith alone that saves us, but faith that saves us can never be alone. Just as Jesus sent the disciples out two by two, faith and works must keep each other company.

NATIONAL SIN
If individuals neglect the poor, so will the nation. "This was the sin of your sister Sodom: . . . her daughters were arro-gant, overfed and unconcerned; they did not help the poor and needy. . . . Therefore I did away with them as you have seen" (Ezekiel 16:49-50, NIV).

EMPTY WORDS
Words of caring without acts of sharing are a sham. Jesus saw through people who say one thing but do another: "You hypocrites! Isaiah was prophesying about you when he said, 'These people honor me with their lips, but their hearts are far away'" (Mark 7:6-7, NLT).

6. What was the conclusion James reached about faith?

. . . .

7. What does faith need to be alive?. . . . .

. . . .

transformation

8. In the Old Testament book of Jeremiah, the Lord rebuked His people for neglecting the poor. Read Jeremiah 5:28-29, then answer the following questions:

a. How are these people described?. . . . .

. . . .

b. What two things had they failed to do? . . . .

. . . .

c. What indictment did God make against them and what are the consequences?

. . . .

. . . .

9. The people in today's lesson offered pious platitudes instead of necessary nourishment. Check off some modern platitudes you've heard offered to those in need.

— "God bless you."
— "Have you called the homeless shelter?"
— "I'll pray for you."
— "I feel your pain."
— "Will Medicaid cover that?"
— "What about food stamps?"
— "I gave at the office."
— "God helps those who help themselves."

10. Actions really do speak louder than words.

> Journal about a time when you showed your faith by your actions rather than your words.

. . . .

. . . .

. . . .

. . . .

10

DEAD FAITH
People with dead faith know the proper prayers and can quote memory verses, but fail to live what they've learned. Any proclamation of faith that does not result in the performance of good deeds is in danger of dying. Does your faith need to be resuscitated?

During the Great Depression, a group of Christians gathered to pray for a family that had lost everything when the stock market crashed. While one of the men was praying fervently on their behalf, the young son of a local farmer knocked loudly at the door. "What do you want?" they inquired. "Pa says he can't join you at this prayer meetin', but he asked me to bring his prayers in the wagon!" They went outside to see what the young boy meant. When they reached the wagon, they saw that Pa's "prayers" consisted of potatoes, flour, beef, oatmeal, turnips, apples, jars of jelly, fruit, and a bundle of clothing. Convicted for failing to take action, the group decided to become the answer to their own prayers. That same day, they each loaded up a wagonload of "prayers" to help their needy neighbors.

Like James, Jesus taught that we can become the answer to our own prayers. At the conclusion of Matthew 9, He told the disciples, "The harvest truly is plentiful, but the laborers are few. Therefore pray the Lord of the harvest to send out laborers into His harvest" (Matthew 9:37-38). Matthew 10 begins with Jesus sending the disciples themselves out to become the answer to their own prayers: "These twelve Jesus sent out and commanded them, saying, . . . 'As you go, preach, saying, "The kingdom of heaven is at hand"'" (Matthew 10:5, 7).

contemplation

You do right when you offer faith to God; you do right when you offer works. But if you separate the two, then you do wrong. For faith without works is dead; and lack of charity in action murders faith.
Bernard of Clairvaux

DAY **3** DEMONIC
FAITH?

BELIEF
*Without faith it is impos-
sible to please Him, for
he who comes to God
must believe that He
is, and that He is a
rewarder of those who
diligently seek Him.
Hebrews 11:6*

All I really need to know about demons I learned from deviled ham! The Gospels of Matthew, Mark, and Luke all provide an in-depth course in Demonology 101 when they record how Jesus exorcised demons from a possessed man, sending them into the herd of swine. The demons knew more about Jesus Christ's position of authority, His power, and the judgment to come than the twelve disciples did. Let's look at the unclean spirits' response to Jesus more closely.

That the demon-possessed man "ran and worshiped him" (Mark 5:6) showed the demons' profound respect for Jesus. Bible teacher John MacArthur says, "Demons hate and loathe everything about God, yet they are powerless to do anything but bow down before Him when in His presence."

They called Jesus the "Son of the Most High God" (Luke 8:28), revealing that the demons understood His incarnation—the Son, fully man, and Most High God, fully deity.

Their statement, "If you cast us out" (Matthew 8:31), proves that the evil spirits knew that Jesus had compassion for this man and that He had the power to destroy them.

The question "Have You come here to torment us before the time?" (Matthew 8:29) shows the demons knew there would be a divinely appointed time for judgment and eternal damnation. Their eschatological theology was impeccable.

James knew about Jesus' power, too, and about what real faith in Christ was. As he continues his discussion of faith and works, he uses the demons' faith to make a point.

 *exploration*

We have found that faith without works is dead faith. Today we learn that mere intellectual faith, the type even the demons have, is not Living Faith either.

Review James 2, then focus on verses 18-20.

> *But someone will say, "You have faith, and I have works." Show me your faith without your works, and I will show you my faith by my works.* James 2:18

1. What might a person say to separate faith from works?

   . . . .

2. In response, what did James ask to see?. . . . .

   . . . .

3. How was James willing to prove that belief and behavior are inseparable?

   . . . .

> *You believe that there is one God. You do well. Even the demons believe—and tremble! But do you want to know, O foolish man, that faith without works is dead?* James 2:19-20

4. What did James acknowledge that the reader believed?

   . . . .

5. What sarcastic commendation did he give those who say they believe?

   . . . .

6. Describe the others who believed in one God and their response to Him.

   . . . .

   . . . .

3

SHOW ME
James was from the "Show Me" state. He knew that seeing is believing. How can you tell an apple tree from a peach tree? By the fruit! Jesus said, "You can detect them by the way they act, just as you can identify a tree by its fruit" (Matthew 7:16, NLT).

4

ORTHODOX
Jewish orthodoxy believes the *Shema*: "Hear, O Israel: The Lord our God, the Lord is one! You shall love the Lord your God with all your heart" (Deuteronomy 6:4-5). Christian orthodoxy says, "There is one God and one Mediator between God and men, the Man Christ Jesus" (1 Timothy 2:5).

6

UNORTHODOX
Demons are monotheistic; their orthodoxy *believes* in one true God, but they don't love Him. This intellectual belief cannot save them. They accept Deuteronomy 6:4 without obeying Deuteronomy 6:5, and that kind of faith is worthless. As a result, they tremble at their certain judgment to come.

SHOW AND TELL
"Do you love me?"
a young wife asks her
husband. "Of course
I do. I married you,
didn't I?" he replies.
"If you *really* love me,
then why don't you
show me?" she
responds. True love
will both show and
tell sincere devotion.
Jesus said, "If you
love me, obey my
commandments"
(John 14:15, NLT).

FOOLISH
Only a fool would fail to
act upon what he or she
knows. If you know an
earthquake is coming,
you fortify your house.
If you know a flood is
flowing, you head for
higher ground. Don't be
foolish. If you know that
Jesus saves, make sure
He's your Savior.

7. Summarize James's main point and explain why you think
   James repeats this message.

. . . .

. . . .

transformation

8. James challenged people to show him their faith without works,
   while he would show them his faith by his works.

   Journal about a time when someone told you how much
   they loved you but failed to show you that they really
   cared. How did it make you feel?

. . . .

. . . .

. . . .

. . . .

9. James commended his readers for believing in the one true
   God. But what we believe should impact how we behave.
   Make a list of the things you believe about God.

. . . .

. . . .

. . . .

   Now journal about what you will do in response to what
   you believe.

. . . .

. . . .

. . . .

. . . .

10. The demons, as well as their leader Satan, believe in God and are afraid. Fill in the chart to learn what they know.

SCRIPTURE	WHAT EVIL POWERS KNOW
Matt. 4:5-6	
Matt. 25:41	
Luke 4:33-35	

The demons are one example of spiritual beings who believe but are doomed anyway. Even Satan believes. Let's imagine a conversation between God and Satan.

Satan smoothly approaches the pearly gates and beseeches, "Let me into heaven. I *believe* in You." God replies, "Let me give you the test of faith and we'll see. First, do you believe that I created the heavens and the earth?" Satan smugly says, "Of course I believe that. I was there!" Next God says, "Do you believe that Jesus is God made man?" "Of course I do. I was stalking—I mean watching Him in Bethlehem." "But do you believe that My Son died for humanity's sins?" Satan quickly answers, "I believe that. I saw the crucifixion," then mutters to himself, "I thought I had Him there." "Do you believe," God asks, "that Jesus rose from the dead and now sits beside me in glory?" "Unfortunately, I wasn't able to stop the stone from being rolled away. I saw Him walking and talking after His resurrection—yes, I believe." "Well, then," said God, "what good works have you done to further my kingdom?" Lucifer thinks for a long time but can't come up with one single good work. Firmly God says, "Though you believe in my Son, you oppose Him. You have done only evil works. You would never call Him Lord. Depart, you worker of iniquity; you have no place here."

But to those who believe and obey, our loving Father says, "Well done, good and faithful servant" (Matthew 25:21).

contemplation

The devil is perfectly willing for a person to profess Christianity, so long as he doesn't practice it.
Anonymous

DAY 4 — DIVINE FAITH

FAITHFUL FATHERS

These all died in faith, not having received the promises, but having seen them afar off were assured of them, embraced them and confessed that they were strangers and pilgrims on the earth.
Hebrews 11:13

Faith has made people do some pretty peculiar things. John the Baptist wore camel's hair, ate locusts, and lived out in the wilderness. The prophet Ezekiel ate an entire book, locked himself in the house bound in ropes, lay on his right side for forty days, then alternated to his left side for forty more days. Hosea married a prostitute knowing she would be unfaithful and gave her lovers food and clothing to provide for her. Why did they do these things? Because, by faith, they heard God speak and they obeyed.

What would you do if you "heard" a strange inner voice telling you: "Say good-bye to everyone you know, pack up, and move to a place you have never seen"? Perhaps your well-intentioned mother would call Dr. Phil on the Oprah Show, or some misguided zealot would try to cast out the demon of deception. Or maybe, as a last resort, you'd swallow a small white lithium pill to make the voices stop.

Abraham had no Bible, no TV or radio evangelist, no pastor, no church, and no prayer partner when he heard God say, "Leave your country, your relatives, and your father's house, and go to the land that I will show you" (Genesis 12:1, NLT). But amazingly he responded to God's unfamiliar voice with absolute obedience. God considered this a response of faith, "and it was accounted to him for righteousness" (James 2:23). Today James presents Abraham as an example of a man who possessed divine faith.

exploration

James has shown that a belief in God is useless if it is only intellectual in nature. Now we learn that a faith that acts is what God seeks.

Review James 2, then focus on verses 21-23.

> **Was not Abraham our father justified by works when he offered Isaac his son on the altar? Do you see that faith was working together with his works, and by works faith was made perfect?** James 2:21-22

1. What was Abraham called? . . . .

. . . .

2. How was he justified? . . . .

. . . .

3. What was working together in Abraham's life? . . . .

. . . .

4. Explain the result of these working together. . . . .

. . . .

> **And the Scripture was fulfilled which says, "Abraham believed God, and it was accounted to him for righteousness." And he was called the friend of God.** James 2:23

5. What was fulfilled through Abraham's actions? . . . .

. . . .

6. Because Abraham believed God, what was put into his spiritual account?

. . . .

. . . .

7. Describe the honor Abraham received. . . . .

. . . .

2

JUST FAITH
Justified means
1) Acquittal: to declare and treat a person as righteous, and 2) Vindication: evidence of righteousness. To *be justified* means we are *excused* from judgment and give *evidence* of our faith through obedience to God. "The doers of the law will be justified" (Romans 2:13).

4

PERFECT FAITH
The Greek translation for *perfect* means "completeness, fully grown, or mature." Absolute perfection is an attribute of God alone. In the highest sense, He alone is complete, wanting nothing. His perfection is eternal and without defect and is the standard of all other perfection (adapted, *Unger's*).

6

RIGHT FAITH
Righteousness is conforming to God's will, obeying God's commands, or fulfilling God's requirements. Abraham accepted God's Word through faith and submitted himself to its control. Therefore God accepted him as one who fulfilled the whole of His righteous requirements (adapted, *Vine's*).

transformation

8

FORESHADOWING
Abraham's good works were a mere foreshadowing of God's best work. Abraham willingly offered his only son on an altar on Mount Moriah, pointing to the time when God would willingly sacrifice His only begotten Son on a cross on a hill called Calvary.

9

IMPERFECT
Abraham was faithful, not sinless. Twice he lied about his wife, saying Sarah was his sister. However, the majority of Abraham's life he faithfully obeyed God. Christians aren't perfect either, just forgiven. "If we confess our sins, He is faithful and just to forgive us our sins" (1 John 1:9).

10

GOD'S FRIEND
You might think God chooses friends based on their stellar qualities. But Jesus came to be "a friend of tax collectors and sinners!" (Matthew 11:19). When Jesus becomes your friend, He's "a friend who sticks closer than a brother" (Proverbs 18:24).

8. Read Hebrews 11:8-10 and 17-19 to learn more about Abraham and his acts of faith.

   a. In what way did Abraham first display his faith in God (vv. 8-9)?

   . . . .

   b. How did Abraham's faith affect his future (v. 10)?

   . . . .

   c. What test of faith did he endure (vv. 17-18)?

   . . . .

   d. What knowledge of God prompted this faithful response (v. 19)?

   . . . .

   . . . .

9. Fill in the table to learn more about Abraham, the father of faith.

SCRIPTURE	ABRAHAM
Gen. 20:2-7	
Neh. 9:7-8	
Isa. 41:8	
John 8:56	
Rom. 4:2-3	

10. Today we learned that Abraham believed God and so was considered a friend of God. Jesus also called Christians His friends.

   Journal a prayer thanking God for calling you His friend by rewriting the following verse: "You are my friends if you obey me. I no longer call you servants, because a master doesn't confide in his servants. Now you are my friends, since I have told you everything the Father told me" (John 15:14-15, NLT).

. . . .

. . . .

. . . .

. . . .

What is faith anyway? Is it an overwhelming feeling or a serene inner state of consciousness? Since faith is at the core of practical Christian living, it's very important to understand what it is and what it is not.

In the classic book *The Fight,* John White writes, "Faith is man's response to God's initiative. . . . To realize that faith is your response to something God does or says will take pressure off you and enable you to adopt a more constructive attitude to it. Do not look inside yourself and ask, 'How much faith do I have?' Look to God and ask, 'What is He saying to me? What would He have me do?' When Jesus praised the great faith of different men and women in the Gospels, He was not praising a mystical inner state. He was usually commenting on a concrete action by which someone responded to Him. It might have been the action of the Roman centurion who sent his servants to Christ asking only that Christ speak the word of power, or the pathetic struggle of a feeble woman to touch His robe. . . . [Faith] was the person's response, usually in overt action, to God's call."

Abraham is called the "father of faith" because of his obedient response to God's voice. By leaving his home, journeying to the Promised Land, circumcising his flesh, and offering up Isaac, Abraham made step-by-step decisions to obey God. Do *you* follow in Father Abraham's footsteps?

contemplation

Faith is not only a means of obeying, but a principal act of obedience; not only an altar on which to sacrifice, but a sacrifice itself.
Edward Young

preparation

I know, Lord, that I am a sinner. Thank you for allowing Your Son, Jesus Christ, to justify me before You. Thank You for viewing me just as if I'd never sinned. Amen.

JUSTIFIED

All have sinned and fall short of the glory of God, being justified freely by His grace through the redemption that is in Christ Jesus.
Romans 3:23-24

James might logically follow his teaching on Abraham, the "father of faith," with other examples of godly, faithful men—maybe David, the man after God's own heart, or Elijah, the miracle-working prophet. Instead, James tells us about Rahab. In James's day, Rahab had three strikes against her: she was a Gentile pagan, a prostitute, and a woman! But James chose an unlikely Old Testament character to make his point that faith is available to all who will hear and obey God's call on their lives.

Jesus chose unlikely people too. He called lowly fishermen, despised tax collectors, and radical zealots to follow Him. He also called women. One woman was like Rahab—a desperate woman with a past. Remember the story? A Pharisee invited Jesus to his house for dinner and didn't even offer the common courtesy of washing Jesus' feet. Then a woman, who was a known sinner, came to the house and stood at Jesus' feet, weeping. "She began to wash His feet with her tears, and wiped them with the hair of her head; and she kissed His feet and anointed them with the fragrant oil" (Luke 7:38). The Pharisee rebuked Jesus for allowing this prostitute near Him. But Jesus commended her, saying, "Her sins, which are many, are forgiven, for she loved much" (Luke 7:47). From these unlikely women, we learn that dynamic faith is love put in action.

exploration

James continues his discussion on faith and works showing that we exhibit a dynamic faith when we believe in and obey God despite all obstacles.

Review James 2, then focus on verses 24-26.

You see then that a man is justified by works, and not by faith only. Likewise, was not Rahab the harlot also justified by works when she received the messengers and sent them out another way? James 2:24-25

1. Based on Abraham's example, what, then, are we supposed to see?

....

2. What key phrase reveals that faith is but one phase in justification?

....

3. What Old Testament figure did James next mention?

....

4. Why did he mention her here? ....

....

5. Describe the good works she performed....................

....

6. Skim Matthew 1:5-16, then describe the honor Rahab received for her allegiance to God.

....

....

For as the body without the spirit is dead, so faith without works is dead also. James 2:26

7. Summarize James's comparison here by filling in the blanks.

Just as the body needs the spirit to be _____,

faith must have works to prove it is _____.

2

PROCESS
Justification—being acceptable to a holy God—is a process. The order of events in justification is 1) Grace: "By grace you have been saved" (Ephesians 2:8); 2) Faith: ". . . through faith" (Ephesians 2:8); 3) Good works: ". . . created in Christ Jesus for good works" (Ephesians 2:10).

3

RAHAB
Rahab was a pagan Gentile who lived in Jericho, the first city conquered by the Israelites (Joshua 2:1). Rahab is described as a harlot, but she also manufactured and dyed linen. According to rabbinic tradition, Rahab was one of the four most beautiful women in the world.

5

TREASON?
Rahab risked her life for the Jews, her people's enemies. Harboring spies was a treasonable offense that would bring the death penalty not only to her but to her family as well. By choosing to ally herself with God's friends, Rahab found new life.

8.

ROLE MODELS
Those in the Hall of
Faith are role models of
faith for believers. But
these people were not
sinless. Jacob stole his
brother's inheritance,
Moses murdered a man,
and David was an adul-
terer. Their lives teach
that God is not looking
for perfect people, only
faithful ones.

9.

HEARING
Rahab heard about
God's mighty power,
and it brought her to
a dynamic Living Faith.
She became one of
God's own despite
her despised race, occu-
pation, and gender.
"There is no longer Jew
or Gentile, slave or free,
male or female. . . . You
are one in Christ Jesus"
(Galatians 3:28, NLT).

transformation

8. This week we have learned that Living Faith is a process—the
   grace of God leads to faith in God resulting in good works for
   God. The "Hall of Faith" found in Hebrews 11 is a monument
   to those who exhibited this kind of faith.

   a. Skim Hebrews 11. Write down the members of the Hall of
      Faith who stand out to you, then describe the good works
      that accompanied their faith.

   HALL OF FAITH   ACT(S) OF FAITH

   . . . .

   . . . .

   . . . .

   b. Which of these people would *you* most want to be like?
      Why?

   . . . .

   . . . .

9. Rahab is the only Gentile mentioned by name in the Hall of
   Faith. Read part of her story in Joshua 2:8-14, then answer the
   following questions.

   a. Explain what she realized and how she came to this realiza-
      tion (v. 9).

   . . . .

   . . . .

   b. Describe what the inhabitants of Jericho had heard about the
      Lord and their response (vv. 10-11).

   . . . .

   . . . .

   c. What declaration of faith did Rahab make to the spies
      (v. 11)?

   . . . .

d. Explain what she asked of the spies, and what they promised in return for her help (vv. 12-14).

. . . .

. . . .

10. Rahab received mercy for herself as well as the members of her household because of her faith.

> Journal the following Scripture into a personal prayer asking God to show mercy to the members of your household: "Believe on the Lord Jesus Christ, and you will be saved, you and your household" (Acts 16:31).

. . . .

. . . .

. . . .

10
FAMILY FAITH
Faith is not passed on genetically; birth into a family of faith does not ensure salvation. However, being born into a family who believes has advantages. Families can pass on a faith heritage by teaching Scripture, living godly lives, and praying for those who are not yet saved.

A king once organized a great race ending in the courtyard of his palace. Every young man in the kingdom participated, hoping to win the bag of gold offered to the winner. The runners lined up and the starting bell rang out. They set off quickly but were dismayed to find a great pile of rocks and stones in the middle of the course. The runners frantically scrambled over and around the obstacle to complete the race.

Every runner but one crossed the finish line in record time. But the king did not declare a winner. Finally, a solitary runner came through the gate. Lifting a bleeding hand, he said, "O King, forgive my tardiness! I found a pile of rocks and stones in the road, and I wounded myself removing the obstacles from the path." Then he lifted his other hand, saying, "But I found this bag of gold beneath the pile." The king proclaimed, "My son, *you* have won the race, for he runs best who makes the way safe for others to follow."

Like the runner, Rahab's course was not easy. She faced the obstacles of being a woman and a pagan Gentile. She risked everything she had—including her life—to pave the way for others to enter God's kingdom. Yet her victory was assured. Because of her faith working together with faithfulness, she holds a place in Messiah's genealogy, stands proudly in the Hall of Faith, and wears a victor's crown in heaven.

contemplation

We can prove our faith by our committal to it, and in no other way. . . . And it might shock some of us profoundly if we were brought suddenly face-to-face with our beliefs and forced to test them in the fires of practical living.
A. W. Tozer

Loose Lips Sink Ships

On December 7, 1941, Japanese aircraft attacked Pearl Harbor in Hawaii. This sneak attack disabled much of the U.S. Pacific naval fleet and destroyed many aircraft, propelling enraged Americans to arms. World War II took place on both land and sea, but it was clear that, for the war being waged in the Pacific, aircraft carriers were the most important weapon.

The fear of enemy spies finding out key locations of U.S. naval vessels prompted the government to wage a publicity campaign. They sent advice to GIs about what to say and not say when writing letters home, when carrying on conversations, or if captured by the enemy. Posters carried the message to the home front: *Loose Lips Might Sink Ships.*

The epistle of James also warns those in the Lord's army that the lips can do devastating damage: our lips can make our ships sink or float! Last week James emphasized what we do—our works—not what we say. Just in case his readers got the wrong idea, James gave clear instructions to counterbalance the works-only idea: *Saying* and *doing* go hand in hand.

Modern Christians have the same problem with works, thinking, *If I don't drink, smoke, or swear, I'm okay.* Yet they engage in gossip, slander, and backbiting. They may build up the body of Christ with their actions while their loose lips spring leaks in the body of Christ.

preparation

Heavenly Father, I know whatever is in my heart eventually will come out of my mouth. Please help my words and my actions honor You. Amen.

ACCEPTABLE WORDS
Let the words of my mouth and the meditation of my heart be acceptable in Your sight, O Lord, my strength and my Redeemer. Psalm 19:14

explanation

1
NAVIGATOR
Teacher means "master or instructor," carrying the idea of ruling over another. A teacher, like a navigator, charts the course for others to follow. Since there's a danger in leading others astray, not everyone in the church should teach. Too many navigators could take a ship off course.

exploration

It is interesting to note that every chapter in the book of James includes an admonition about our speech. As James begins his teaching on loose lips, he reminds us that those who teach God's Word are held to a higher standard as they help navigate their students through troubled waters.

Read James 3; then focus on verses 1-2.

> **My brethren, let not many of you become teachers, knowing that we shall receive a stricter judgment.**
> James 3:1

1. What phrase lets you know that teaching is not for everyone?

. . . .

2. How do you know that James included himself as a teacher?

. . . .

3. What phrase reveals that God holds teachers to a higher standard?

. . . .

4. To learn more about the gift of teaching read Ephesians 4:11-12.

   a. Who decides what gift an individual receives?

. . . .

b. How do you know that not everyone has the same gift?

. . . .

c. Why are these gifts given? . . . .

. . . .

5. Teachers offer spiritual instruction. Yet, teachers themselves must be taught. Fill in the table to learn who teaches the teacher.

SCRIPTURE	THE TEACHER
Job 36:22.	
John 13:13.	
John 14:26.	

> *For we all stumble in many things. If anyone does not stumble in word, he is a perfect man, able also to bridle the whole body.* James 3:2

6. Explain what all human beings do. . . . .

. . . .

7. Describe the three outstanding characteristics of someone who does not have loose lips.

. . . .

. . . .

transformation

8. In the school of life, some are pupils and some are teachers. God calls and gifts people to be teachers of spiritual truth. Name some of the people appointed by God to be your spiritual teachers.

. . . .

. . . .

3

INSPECTOR
Some desire to be spiritual leaders for power or prestige, forgetting that how and what they teach will affect their eternal reward. Jesus said, "Much is required from those to whom much is given, and much more is required from those to whom much more is given" (Luke 12:48, NLT).

6

PERFECTER
Stumble means "to fall, trip, sin, or offend." Stumble in word and you'll stumble in deed. Controlling your tongue helps you become *perfect*—mature or complete. Christ is our perfecter, so "Let us fix our eyes on Jesus, the author and perfecter of our faith" (Hebrews 12:2, NIV).

8

GIFTED TEACHER
The "gift of teaching" is the ability to understand and communicate Christian truths clearly. The result is the maturing of believers into more effective Christian disciples. "Preach the word of God. . . . Patiently correct, rebuke, and encourage your people with good teaching" (2 Timothy 4:2, NLT).

MILLSTONE
A *millstone* was part of a mortar used to grind wheat or olives. About two feet thick, a millstone weighed hundreds of pounds. Just like cement shoes, a millstone would make you sink like a rock! "A woman on the roof threw down a millstone that . . . crushed his skull" (Judges 9:53, NLT).

LIGHT OR DARK?
Jesus said, "If anyone walks in the day, he does not stumble. . . . But if one walks in the night, he stumbles, because the light is not in him" (John 11:9-10). Advance into the light and you'll be sure-footed. March into darkness and you're headed for a fall.

Journal about some of the spiritual truths you have learned from them.

. . . .

. . . .

. . . .

. . . .

. . . .

. . . .

9. If a teacher stumbles, he or she often causes the pupils to stumble as well. The Gospel of Matthew teaches about the consequence of causing others to trip up spiritually. Read Matthew 18:6-7 and describe the offense and resulting punishment.

. . . .

. . . .

. . . .

10. The apostle Peter said if you add some key elements to your Christian faith, "you will be neither barren nor unfruitful in the knowledge of our Lord Jesus Christ. . . . If you do these things *you will never stumble!*" (2 Peter 1:8, 10, emphasis added). Read 2 Peter 1:5-10. Place a + by the elements you have added, and a – by those things you lack.

___ faith in the Lord
___ "add to your faith virtue"
___ "to virtue [add] knowledge"
___ "to knowledge [add] self-control"
___ "to self-control [add] perseverance"
___ "to perseverance [add] godliness"
___ "to godliness [add] brotherly kindness"
___ "to brotherly kindness [add] love"

11. Those who do not stumble are considered perfect, mature
    in the faith.

> Journal a prayer by rewriting the following verse and
> asking God to help you to stand tall in the faith: "All
> glory to God, who is able to keep you from stumbling,
> and who will bring you into his glorious presence
> innocent of sin and with great joy." (Jude 24)

. . . .

. . . .

. . . .

. . . .

An article in the *U.S. Naval Proceedings* told of two battleships that
had been at sea in heavy weather for several days. The visibility
was poor with patchy fog, so the watchful captain of one of the
ships remained on the bridge. Shortly after dark, the lookout
reported, "Steady light, bearing on the starboard bow!" A steady
light meant their ships were on a dangerous collision course.

The captain then called out, "Signal that ship: 'We are on a
collision course; advise you change course twenty degrees.'"

Back came the signal, "Advisable for you to change course
twenty degrees."

The captain said, "Send: 'I'm a captain; change course twenty
degrees.'"

"I'm a seaman second-class," came the reply. "You had better
change your course twenty degrees."

By that time the captain was furious, "Send: 'I'm a battleship;
change course twenty degrees.'"

Back came the flashing light, "I'm a lighthouse."

They immediately changed course. Smart move. A lighthouse
has a few good characteristics: 1) warns of potential danger;
2) signals safe harbor; 3) is stronger than a storm; 4) shines
brightest in the fog.

God's Word is like a lighthouse. Some "teachers" challenge the
veracity of God's lighthouse, taking their shipload of parishioners
into dangerous waters. But wise teachers will chart a sure course,
using the light of God's Word to guide their ships to safe harbor.

contemplation

A teacher affects
eternity; he can never
tell where his influence
stops.
Henry Gardiner Adams

2 STEERING THE SHIP

preparation

Lord, I realize that many small things hold sway over me: Small words of kindness make my day; sometimes my small thinking holds me back. Help me to remember that small things can make a big impact. Amen.

SMALL THINGS
Who has despised the day of small things? Zechariah 4:10

On April 14, 1912, the unthinkable happened to the unsinkable *Titanic* on her maiden voyage. Near midnight the luxury liner struck an iceberg that ripped a 300-foot hole through the hull, sinking her in just two and a half hours. *Titanic* had encountered no rough seas or bad weather; however, she had received urgent warnings of dangerous ice floes.

April 13: *Rappahannock* warns by signal lamp of heavy pack ice ahead and ice denting her bow and twisting her rudder.

April 14, 9:00 A.M.: *Coronia* reports "bergs, growlers, and field ice."

April 14, 11:40 A.M.: *Noordam* reports "much ice."

April 14, 1:42 P.M.: *Baltic* warns of "icebergs and large quantity of field ice" 250 miles ahead of *Titanic's* position.

April 14, 1:45 P.M.: *Titanic* intercepts message from *Amerika* reporting two passing icebergs and relays it to the U.S. Hydrographic Office.

April 14, 7:30 P.M.: *Californian* warns of "three large bergs" only 50 miles ahead of *Titanic*.

Finally, April 14, 9:40 P.M.: *Mesaba* reports "great number large icebergs." While talking to Cape Race about menus for the passengers' arrival, *Titanic* tells *Mesaba,* "Shut up. . . . You are jamming my signals." The captain should have altered *Titanic's* course. But he failed to make the slight adjustment of turning the ship's relatively small rudder in order to avert a huge disaster.

Today James warns that unless we get our "small rudders"— our tongues—under control, our "ships" are headed for destruction.

James has reminded us that not many should be teachers, warning that our words can make others stumble. Now he uses some comparisons to show the tongue's power.

Review James 3; then focus on verses 3-4.

> ***Indeed, we put bits in horses' mouths that they may obey us, and we turn their whole body.*** James 3:3

1. James used natural illustrations to help us see the impact small things have on large things. In the first illustration, what small instrument is put into the mouth of a large horse?

. . . .

2. What two things result from the small bit? . . . .

. . . .

> ***Look also at ships: although they are so large and are driven by fierce winds, they are turned by a very small rudder wherever the pilot desires.*** James 3:4

3. Name the two things that make a ship difficult to maneuver.

. . . .

4. What small thing turns the ship and keeps it on course?

. . . .

5. Who is at the controls? . . . .

. . . .

transformation

6. In Psalm 32:8-9, David speaks of God bringing him to repentance after he had fallen into sin. Read these verses, then answer the following questions.

    a. What does God promise to do for David (v. 8)?

    . . . .

4

RUDDER

A *rudder* is a broad, flat device used to direct a ship's course. A ship controlled by a rudder carries precious cargo to wonderful places. A tongue controlled by God will spread the good news wherever it goes. "Go therefore and make disciples of all the nations" (Matthew 28:19).

5

PILOT

Bits control the wild nature of horses; the rudder overcomes winds that drive ships astray. Therefore, a strong hand must control both. The tongue controlled by God's hand can be tamed. "Take control of what I say, O Lord, and keep my lips sealed" (Psalm 141:3, NLT).

6

MULISH

David's refusal to repent resulted in his "groaning all the day long" (Psalm 32:3). God used this discomfort to rein in his mulish behavior: "Your hand was heavy upon me" (v. 4). Repentance restored his health and relationship to God: "I acknowledged my sin" (v. 5).

James gave sound
advice about reining in
your tongue. The differ-
ence between a wise
person and a foolish
one is their speech.
"Babbling fools fall flat
on their faces" (Prov-
erbs 10:8, NLT), while
"the words of the
wise keep them out
of trouble" (Proverbs
14:3, NLT). Which one
are you?

8

CONSECRATION
To *consecrate* means
"to dedicate or set
apart for worship or
service." Job dedicated
his tongue to God:
"As long as I live, . . .
my lips will speak no
evil, and my tongue
will speak no lies"
(Job 27:3-4, NLT).
Starting today, will
you consecrate your
tongue to God?

b. What does God warn David (and us) against (v. 9)?

. . . .

c. What are the characteristics of these beasts (v. 9)?

. . . .

7. The Psalms are full of exhortations about our tongues turning toward right or wrong. Look up the verses, indicate which direction they went (**R**ight or **W**rong), and describe how they were used.

SCRIPTURE	R/W	DESCRIPTION
Ps. 10:7 . . . .
Ps. 12:2-4 . . . .
Ps. 15:2-3 . . . .
Ps. 52:2-5 . . . .
Ps. 66:16-17 . . . .
Ps. 119:172-173 . . . .

8. Think of your life as a ship. Do you allow God's Word to be your "rudder"? Are you consecrating your words to His glory and honor?

Journal about a time when God helped you steer your tongue toward speech that is edifying. What did you say, and how did it make others feel?

. . . .

. . . .

. . . .

. . . .

. . . .

Now journal of a time when you steered your tongue toward trouble. What did you say, and what were the consequences?

. . . .

. . . .

. . . .

. . . .

After nearly completing his first overseas cruise, a young ensign was given an opportunity to prepare for and take the ship out to sea. With a stream of commands, the decks were buzzing with men, and soon the ship was sailing out of the channel.

His efficiency established a new record for getting a destroyer under way, and he was not surprised when a seaman approached him with a message from the captain. He was surprised, though, to find that it was a radio message that read: "My personal congratulations upon completing your underway preparation exercise according to the book and with amazing speed. However, you overlooked one of the unwritten rules—make sure the captain is aboard before getting under way."

We may pilot our own ships, but we've discovered that we must follow the directions of our divine Captain. Our tongues are like rudders. When controlled by strong hands and good hearts, the tongue guides us to desired destinations. However, if held loosely and with wrong intentions, our tongues can do devastating damage, leaving us shipwrecked. If your tongue has taken you into uncharted waters and your hand is not strong enough to navigate the storm, don't forget the Captain. If you let Him, He'll steady your hand, curb your tongue, and quiet your heart. With God at the helm, you're headed for smooth sailing.

preparation

Lord, this week I have become so aware of the power my tongue has to hurt others. Please purify my heart so that my words will be pure. Amen.

PURE WORDS
The words of the Lord are pure words, like silver tried in a furnace of earth, purified seven times. Psalm 12:6

To plan a honeymoon, you do some research on Carnival Cruise Lines and discover the "fun ship" *Ecstasy* offering exotic vacations from Miami to the Bahamas. This floating paradise offers a health club featuring state-of-the-art equipment and body and facial treatments; the Blue Sapphire Lounge showcasing Las-Vegas-style venues; the Crystal Palace Casino with over two hundred slot machines and sixteen blackjack tables; three luxurious pools, one boasting a heart-pounding waterslide; a library lined with mahogany bookshelves stocked with classics and best-sellers; and elegant meals in two dining rooms.

You immediately call your travel agent and book passage for the vacation of a lifetime beginning July 19, 1998. But two days into the cruise, there's trouble in paradise. You realize there's one place you should have checked before setting sail—the engine room! When a disastrous fire disables the engines, the ship is left crippled. You begin to swelter in your cabin: no air conditioning. The kitchens serve leftovers: no oven. The casino lights go dim and discotheques go silent: no electricity. The fire is extinguished as a tugboat pulls the ship back to Miami. Your dream vacation has become a nightmare.

Ships have powerful engines. But if even a small fire gets out of control, the power source can be damaged, and the whole ship can be crippled. James likens our tongue to fire. When our words rage out of control, others get burned and our lives go up in smoke.

exploration

We've seen that our tongues can either bring smooth sailing or cause shipwrecks. Now we find that our words can cause great destruction below deck as well.

Review James 3; then focus on verses 5-6.

> **Even so the tongue is a little member and boasts great things. See how great a forest a little fire kindles!**
> James 3:5

1. James draws our attention to the tongue. Contrast what the tongue does in comparison to its size.

. . . .

2. What did James liken it to? . . . .

. . . .

> **And the tongue is a fire, a world of iniquity. The tongue is so set among our members that it defiles the whole body, and sets on fire the course of nature; and it is set on fire by hell.** James 3:6

3. James builds on the analogy of the forest fire to explain how dangerous a tongue out of control can be. What phrase describes how sinful the tongue can be?

. . . .

4. What negative impact does the tongue have on the body?

. . . .

5. How can the fire extend beyond the body? . . . .

. . . .

6. Who did James imply was the originator of sins of the tongue?

. . . .

. . . .

transformation

7. The tongue can ignite a huge fire of trouble. In 2 Corinthians 12:20-21, Paul describes some tongue trouble. Reflecting upon

4

DEFILE
Defiled means "stained, contaminated." "The whole body" implies the entire vessel is permeated. Plutonium is good fuel on a nuclear submarine. But if it leaks, the whole ship is defiled with radiation. "Evil words come from an evil heart and defile the person who says them" (Matthew 15:18, NLT).

5

COURSE
Course of nature is also translated "your whole life" (NLT), and "the whole course of his life" (NIV). The destructive impact of ruinous speech burns and spreads to everyone we encounter throughout our life. Our past, present, and future can be destroyed by a slip of the tongue.

7

FIRE AND WATER
Fire out of control brings destruction, especially to dry places. If your spiritual life is dry, perhaps you have neglected your water source. Jesus said, "He who believes in Me, . . . out of his heart will flow rivers of living water" (John 7:38).

8

INIQUITY
The Bible often uses
iniquity to describe evil,
wickedness, unrigh-
teousness, or lawless-
ness. Iniquity suggests
different types of evil:
transgressions of spiri-
tual law; crimes against
God; moral or legal
wrongs; depravity; and
sin in general. "Under
his tongue is trouble
and iniquity" (Psalm
10:7).

9

HEAVENLY FIRE
Jesus came to "baptize
you with the Holy Spirit
and fire" (Matthew
3:11). "The Spirit, like
fire, melts the heart,
separates and burns up
the dross, and kindles
pious and devout affec-
tions in the soul. . . .
This is that fire which
Christ came to send
upon the earth"
(*Matthew Henry*).

your life, place a check in the space where you have the most
trouble taming your tongue.

— Quarreling

— Slander

— Factions

— Outbursts of anger

— Jealousy

— Gossip

— Disorder

— Arrogance

> Journal a prayer to God asking Him to extinguish the
> verbal flames you have ignited. If you have harmed
> others, ask Him to heal their wounds and restore their
> hearts.

. . . .

. . . .

. . . .

. . . .

. . . .

8. James reminds us the tongue is a "world of iniquity"—full of
sin. Read Proverbs 6:16-19 and list the sins of the tongue.

. . . .

. . . .

9. Though sins of the tongue are "set on fire by hell," there is
a kind of speech set on fire by heaven. Acts 2 tells how, on
the day of Pentecost, tongues of fire came upon the believers
(see Acts 2:1-4). Read Acts 2:38-39, then answer the following
questions to discover what Peter spoke as a result of this
heavenly fire.

a. What message did he speak (v. 38)? . . . .

. . . .

b. What promise did he make (v. 38)? . . . .

. . . .

c. Who did this promise include (v. 39)?. . . . .

. . . .

d. Who will you take this message to? . . . .

. . . .

The summer of 1947 was an unseasonable scorcher in Brantford, Ontario. So when Roddie, his big brother, Dennis, and Mac went for a weenie roast in the forest, they had no problem finding scrub brush for kindling. With the wrappers from the buns placed on top of the pile, a mere strike of Roddie's match quickly ignited the pile. Sparks flew upward as the wind snatched up fragments of the burning plastic, then hurtled them back down like meteors all around the campsite. Dennis began huffing and puffing like the big bad wolf in an attempt to extinguish the fire. Instead, it fanned the flames. All three boys began stomping wildly on the burning embers, waving their arms in the air and screaming like Indians on the warpath. This billowed the flames even higher. Then the boys did what any twelve-year-old would have done— they ran for their lives! Looking back in horror, they saw the entire ten-acre woods going up in smoke.

My dad—fondly nicknamed "Hot Rod"—learned that it literally only takes a spark to get a forest fire burning. James warns that our fiery tongues can wreak havoc too. Angry accusations, contentious comments, or godless gossip can burn others, leaving lives in ruin. Remember that those who heat things up verbally are playing with hellfire. "As charcoal is to burning coals, and wood to fire, so is a contentious man to kindle strife" (Proverbs 26: 21).

DAY 4 FIRE TORPEDOES!

Most of us would agree that wielding weapons in public is not good for anyone's health. Yet most of us are carrying a potentially deadly weapon around with us all the time—a weapon that is not good for our spiritual or emotional health. The psalmist said that some people "sharpen their tongues like swords and aim their words like deadly arrows. They shoot from ambush at the innocent man" (Psalm 64:3-4, NIV). Spiteful words spewed from vengeful hearts can blow others away, critically wounding their spirits. But, the truth is, hateful words can backfire on us, hurting ourselves as much as those we've attacked.

During World War II, the U.S. submarine *Tang* surfaced under cover of darkness to fire on a large Japanese convoy off the coast of China. Since previous raids had left the American vessel with only eight torpedoes, the accuracy of every shot was absolutely essential. The first seven missiles were right on target; but when the eighth was launched, it suddenly deviated and headed right back at their own ship. The emergency alarm to submerge rang out, but it was too late. Within a matter of seconds, the U.S. sub received a direct hit and sank almost instantly.

Instead of doing battle with the enemy, Christians often use God's Word like a torpedo to attack one another. With precisely aimed missiles of criticism, contempt, or callousness, we can cripple the body of Christ, of which we are all members. You cannot sink someone else's end of the boat and still keep your own afloat.

exploration

Yesterday we found that the tongue was described as a fire that is ignited by hell. Today we discover that the tongue can be full of deadly poison.

Review James 3; then focus on verses 7-8.

> **For every kind of beast and bird, of reptile and creature of the sea, is tamed and has been tamed by mankind. But no man can tame the tongue. It is an unruly evil, full of deadly poison.** James 3:7-8

1. Name the four categories of animals James mentioned.

. . . .

2. What phrase makes you think the animal kingdom has been subdued?

. . . .

3. How is the tongue different from wild animals? Why?

. . . .

4. What is the tongue full of? . . . .

5. Think back to yesterday's lesson concerning the force behind the sinful tongue. Relate this to the tongue full of poison— why is this an appropriate illustration?

. . . .

transformation

6. James exhorts us to tame, or humble and tone down, our tongues.

Using the word *TAME* as an acrostic, journal about some ways you can tone down your tongue.

T (Example: Talk without using sarcastic wit.)

. . . .

A . . . .

M. . . . .

E . . . .

explanation

2

TAME

Tame means "to domesticate from a state of wildness to usefulness; to be made submissive; to humble or tone down." No animal— or tongue—willingly consents to being tamed; it goes against their nature. "Will the wild ox consent to being tamed?" (Job 39:9, NLT).

3

UNRULY

Unruly means "undisci-plined." The term describes someone not easily ruled and implies stubborn resistance to control. Believers have a responsibility to help control those whose words are out of control. "We exhort you, brethren, warn those who are unruly" (1 Thessalonians 5:14).

6

CAGE IT!

We've caged the mighty lion, encased poisonous reptiles in terrariums, and placed the killer whale Shamu in a tank. God in His infinite wisdom placed our tongues in a cage of their own: behind two lips and surrounded by sharp teeth. If your tongue raises its ugly head—bite it.

7

GOOD WORDS
Tongues produce a world of good when we pray, praise, or preach the gospel. "Love your enemies, bless those who curse you, . . . and pray for those who spitefully use you and persecute you" (Matthew 5:44).

8

ANTIDOTE
People say, "My lips are sealed," pretending to lock the door and throw away the key, only to blab anyway. We can't control our tongues, but God can if we give Him the keys. "Take control of what I say, O Lord, and keep my lips sealed" (Psalm 141:3, NLT).

7. Our unruly tongues need to be disciplined. Discipline includes both stopping bad habits and starting good ones. In other words, don't just bite your tongue; bless others with it instead. In the columns record some biting words you've said in the past, then edit those words into a blessing.

BITING WORDS	BLESSING WORDS
(Example: You're too old to wear that.)	(Example: You're so young at heart.) . . . .
. . . .	. . . .
. . . .	. . . .
. . . .	. . . .

8. The tongue was described as "full of deadly poison." Below are some words that describe the symptoms of poisoning.

☠ sweating
☠ weakness
☠ paralysis
☠ increased pulse rate
☠ pain
☠ restricted breathing

Briefly journal about a time when poisonous words affected you in one of these ways.

. . . .

. . . .

. . . .

. . . .

Gossip can be one of the most potent poisons, infecting everyone who comes in contact with it. Here are some symptoms of gossip poisoning followed by the antidote guaranteed to neutralize this deadly venom.

Symptoms of Gossip Poisoning:

1. **Dislike:** Developing bitterness even though the person involved did not directly offend you.
2. **Disapproval:** Criticizing those involved. Acting as the judge in the matter while recruiting others to "your side."
3. **Distortion:** Searching out more gossip and using it to give the worst possible impression of others or to make yourself look spiritual.
4. **Deception:** Believing that such actions are actually accomplishing God's will and using prayer to spread the rumors further.

Antidotes to Gossip Poisoning:

1. **Repentance:** Ask God to cleanse your mind and to forgive you for poisoning others with gossip. *"If we confess our sins, He is faithful and just to forgive us our sins and to cleanse us from all unrighteousness"* (1 John 1:9).
2. **Restoration:** Pray for a genuine love for everyone involved. If you've sinned against someone, make it right. *"If you bring your gift to the altar, . . . first be reconciled to your brother, and then come and offer your gift"* (Matthew 5:23-24).
3. **Renewal:** Be transformed by renewing your mind with truth instead of lies. God's Word is the antidote of the soul. *"You are already clean because of the word which I have spoken to you"* (John 15:3).

When you lose the urge to spread bad reports about others, have more compassion, and begin to genuinely care about the people involved, then God is working to cure the poison of gossip in your life and to build up a Living Faith.

contemplation

Never believe anything bad about anybody unless you positively know it to be true; never tell even that unless you feel that it is absolutely necessary— and remember that God is listening while you tell it.

Henry Van Dyke

DAY 5 — GOURMET GALLEY

Have you noticed how people inevitably gather in the kitchen? It doesn't matter that the living room is decorated beautifully or the den has a big-screen TV. These rooms simply don't have the magnetic pull of the kitchen. The kitchen just feels like home. It's the place where you can pour a cup of coffee as you pour your heart out and where homespun wisdom is offered with a pinch of love.

The same is true of a ship's galley. At all hours passengers can find a warm fire burning, savory soups simmering, and fresh bread baking. Daphne White, director of the Lion and Lamb Foundation, took a journey on a schooner and discovered the galley was the most enticing place of all. "It didn't take me long to realize that while I love the idea of cooking, it is even more fun to sit back in a cozy galley and watch someone else do the work—all the while knowing you will be entitled to A Little Something as soon as it came out of the oven."

However, the galley can be a dangerous place when high seas cause hot broth to slosh from cauldrons or pitch the novice sailor against a hot grill. Sometimes, in the galley, people get burned. James reminds us that our words can be as inviting as a gourmet galley when they offer "A Little Something" known as a blessing, or they can be as scalding as a sea-tossed pot of stew when they spew curses.

exploration

This week's lesson has exposed the power of the tongue. Today we find that our tongues can quickly switch from gourmet to garbage.
Review James 3; then focus on verses 9-12.

*With it [the tongue] we bless our God and Father,
and with it we curse men, who have been made in the
similitude of God.* James 3:9

1. What good do we do with our tongue? . . . .

. . . .

2. What evil do we do with our tongue? . . . .

. . . .

3. Explain why cursing people is evil in God's sight.

. . . .

*Out of the same mouth proceed blessing and cursing.
My brethren, these things ought not to be so.*
James 3:10

4. Explain the hypocrisy some professing Christians exhibit with
their mouths.

. . . .

5. What strong warning does James give concerning this type
of hypocrisy?

. . . .

*Does a spring send forth fresh water and bitter from the
same opening? Can a fig tree, my brethren, bear olives,
or a grapevine bear figs? Thus no spring yields both salt
water and fresh.* James 3:11-12

6. James used the natural imagery of water and fruit to demonstrate his point.

   a. What is a fresh spring unable to produce? . . . .

. . . .

   b. What is a fig tree or grapevine unable to produce?

. . . .

1

BLESS GOD
Bless means "to speak
well of or celebrate
with praises." We bless
God by praising His
divine characteristics
and expressing grati-
tude for His mercies
(adapted, *Vine's* and
Unger's). "I will bless
the Lord at all times;
His praise shall continu-
ally be in my mouth"
(Psalm 34:1).

3

CURSE OTHERS
A *curse* is a prayer for
evil or misfortune on
another. God made
everyone in His image.
"When God created
people, he made them
in the likeness of God.
. . . and he blessed
them" (Genesis 5:1-2,
NLT). Those God has
blessed, we have no
right to curse.

6

THE SOURCE
Water often speaks of
the refreshing power
of the Holy Spirit, and
fruit often represents
the love, joy, and
peace the Spirit
produces in our lives.
This divine source of
love will spill out of
our hearts and lips to
refresh others.

7. What does this analogy teach you about the words you speak?

. . . .

. . . .

transformation

8. Today we learned that one of our primary functions as believers is to bless God. Read Psalm 103:2-5, and list all the reasons we have to praise God.

. . . .

. . . .

Now journal a personal psalm of praise to God, thanking Him for one or more of these blessings in your life.

. . . .

. . . .

. . . .

. . . .

9. In the Old Testament, God warned his people against cursing others. Fill in the chart to learn about these warnings.

SCRIPTURE	DO NOT CURSE
Exod. 21:17 . . . .
Exod. 22:28 . . . .
Lev. 19:14 . . . .
Eccles. 10:20 . . . .

10. As believers, we are called to speak refreshing words, not words that are bitter or stinging. Think of a friend who might need to hear good words. In the space provided, draw a cup and fill it to overflowing with words that will

8
SING PSALMS
Psalms are prayers, poems, and hymns that focus the worshiper's thoughts on God in praise and adoration. You don't have to be a songwriter to write a psalm; you simply need a heart of praise. "Sing psalms to Him; talk of all His wondrous works!" (Psalm 105:2).

9
CAN'T CURSE
Balak, the king of Moab, hired Balaam to curse the Israelites. But God wouldn't allow him to speak curses; instead, He caused Balaam to bless them. "What have you done to me? I took you to curse my enemies, and look, you have blessed them bountifully!" (Numbers 23:11).

10
FRESH WATER
Without fresh water, there can be no life. 97 percent of the earth's water is salty, making it unusable for drinking or farming. Only 3 percent is fresh water. How does your speech compare with these statistics—mostly bitter and only a little bit refreshing?

bless that person. (Example: Thank you; I love you; I appreciate your kindness.)

Journal about how words of blessing have helped you, and then write when you will speak refreshing words to the person you named above.

. . . .

. . . .

. . . .

. . . .

Xanthus, the philosopher, once told his servant to prepare for dinner guests and get the best thing he could find in the market. The philosopher and his guests sat down the next day at the table. They had nothing but tongue—four or five courses of tongue— tongue cooked in this way and tongue cooked in that way. The philosopher finally lost his patience and said to his servant, "Didn't I tell you to get the best thing in the market?" The servant said, "I did get the best thing in the market. Isn't the tongue the organ of sociability, the organ of eloquence, the organ of kindness, the organ of worship?"

Then Xanthus the philosopher said, "Tomorrow I want you to get the worst thing in the market." And on the morrow the philosopher sat at the table, and there was nothing but tongue—four or five courses of tongue—tongue in this shape and tongue in that shape. The philosopher lost his patience again and said, "Didn't I tell you to get the worst thing in the market?" The servant replied, "I did; for isn't the tongue the organ of blasphemy, the organ of defamation, the organ of lying?"

The tongue can be used for evil or for good, for blessing or for cursing. If the people in your life were asked what type of words you've served them, what would they say?

The Moral of the Story Is...

*E*veryone loves fables. The characters are usually animals that act like people, and the moral of each story is told at the end of the fable in the form of a wise proverb. Aesop, a Greek slave, was the father of fables. His tales illustrated the failings and virtues of human nature in a simple, humorous way.

James also wanted to impart wisdom to his readers, teaching them the difference between earthly and heavenly wisdom. This week join us in rediscovering some of Aesop's fables that help illustrate the wisdom James wants us to develop.

The Ant and the Grasshopper

One summer day a Grasshopper was chirping to its heart's content. An Ant passed by bearing a heavy ear of corn to his nest. "Come chat with me," said the Grasshopper, "instead of toiling in that way."

"I am helping lay up food for the winter," said the Ant, "and so should you."

"Why bother about winter?" said the Grasshopper. "We've got plenty of food now." The Ant continued its toil anyway. When winter came the Grasshopper had no food and was starving to death, while the ants distributed grain from the stores they'd collected in the summer. The Grasshopper learned the hard way; it's best to prepare for days of necessity during days of plenty.

The Moral of the Story Is . . . Wisdom is revealed by what you do with what you know.

DAY 1
What You Do with What You Know

DAY 2
Pride Comes before the Fall

DAY 3
Every Man for Himself

DAY 4
Virtues Worth Cultivating

DAY 5
Only God Can Change Our Nature

1

WHAT YOU DO WITH
WHAT YOU KNOW

exploration

Last week we learned that what we say indicates the condition of
our heart. This week we will learn that the kind of life people live
reveals the kind of wisdom they possess.

Read James 3, then focus on verse 13.

> **Who is wise and understanding among you? Let him
> show by good conduct that his works are done in the
> meekness of wisdom.** James 3:13

1. Who was James looking for? . . . .

. . . .

. . . .

2. Fill in the following chart with the lessons you learn about
understanding.

SCRIPTURE	LESSONS ON UNDERSTANDING
Deut. 1:13	
1 Sam. 25:3	
1 Kings 3:9	
Ps. 111:10	
Prov. 1:5	

3. According to verse 13, what should a believer show?

. . . .

4. What does this conduct produce? . . . .

. . . .

5. Describe how these works should be done. . . . .

. . . .

6. In Proverbs 2:2-7, Solomon gave advice concerning how to gain wisdom. Read the passage then answer the questions.

a. What actions should we take to seek wisdom (vv. 2-4)?

. . . .

b. To what are wisdom and understanding likened (v. 4)?

. . . .

c. What does God promise if we take these actions (vv. 5-7)?

. . . .

transformation

7. James sought people with wise understanding. Ephesians 1:18-19 speaks of people with enlightened understanding, while Ephesians 4:18-19 describes those with darkened understanding. List the characteristics of each.

ENLIGHTENED MIND	DARKENED UNDERSTANDING
. . . .	. . . .
. . . .	. . . .
. . . .	. . . .
. . . .	. . . .

3

GOOD CONDUCT
Good conduct means "manner of life," and isn't a one-time action but a consistent life-style. NKJV says, "Only let your conduct be worthy of the gospel of Christ" (Philippians 1:27). NLT translates, "You must live in a manner worthy of the Good News about Christ."

5

GET WISDOM!
Wisdom is the ability to judge correctly—taking the best course of action based on knowledge. The first principle of biblical wisdom is to humble ourselves before God in reverence and obedience to His commands. "Fear of the Lord is the beginning of wisdom" (Proverbs 9:10, NLT).

7

ENLIGHTENMENT
The Age of Enlightenment began in the 1600s when philosophers contrasted superstitious religion with scientific reason. True enlightenment begins with Jesus. "I am the light of the world. He who follows Me shall not walk in darkness, but have the light of life" (John 8:12).

Imitation is the sincerest form of flattery. Christians are encouraged to follow their leaders' lifestyles. "Remember your leaders, who spoke the word of God to you. Consider the outcome of their way of life and imitate their faith" (Hebrews 13:7, NIV). Whom do you model your life after?

ACT WISELY
Wisdom not demonstrated in righteous acts is as useless as faith without works. To know something doesn't make you wise. You can be book smart but common-sense foolish if you never alter your actions based on your knowledge. When you act upon what you know, you are truly wise.

8. Today we learned that good conduct is a lifestyle. Rather than the *Lifestyles of the Rich and Famous,* James commends the *Lifestyles of the Righteous and Faithful.*

> Using two words from the following list (or think of your own), name your lifestyle program. Then journal about how you've developed this manner of life:

Righteous, meek, kind, faithful, humble, trustworthy, loving, stable, strong, quiet, gentle, funny, unpredictable, proud, shy, helpful, flamboyant, artistic, perfectionist, creative, athletic, scholarly, busy, lazy, loud, bossy, organized, chaotic.

Lifestyles of the _____ and _____.

. . . .

. . . .

. . . .

. . . .

. . . .

9. Wisdom is the practical application of what we know. The following is a list of things a wise person must know and do. Place an ✗ beside the items you know but do not practice, and a ✔ beside those things you know and act upon.

___ Increases learning (Prov. 1:5)

___ Departs from evil (Prov. 14:19)

___ Increases in strength (Prov. 24:5)

___ Controls her feelings (Prov. 29:9)

___ Doesn't glory in his wisdom (Jer. 9:23)

___ Hears and obeys Jesus (Matt. 7:24)

___ Settles disputes among Christians (1 Cor. 6:5)

When a young man applied for a job as a farmhand, he listed one qualification: "I can sleep when the wind blows." The farmer was puzzled, but he'd taken a liking to the young man, so he hired him. A few days later, a violent storm awakened the farmer and his wife from a deep sleep. They jumped out of bed and, to their surprise, they found the shutters securely fastened and a supply of logs neatly stacked beside the fireplace. The tools were placed in the shed so they wouldn't rust, the tractor was parked in the garage, and the barn was locked with the animals safely inside. All was well.

At that moment the farmer realized the meaning of the young man's claim, "I can sleep when the wind blows." Because the farmhand had conducted good works when the skies were clear, he was prepared for the storm when it broke. When the wind blew, he had no fear and could sleep peacefully.

This young man could have given the farmer a long list of skills when applying for the job. Instead he gave the farmer a humble statement backed by diligent actions. He showed he was truly wise by preparing for a rainy day when the sun was shining. In the same way, believers will display their wisdom by "good conduct . . . done in the meekness of wisdom" (James 3:13).

DAY 2 PRIDE COMES BEFORE THE FALL

Godly wisdom is identifiable by an important attitude—meekness. James warns us that there is another type of wisdom in opposition to this godly wisdom, which should be avoided at all costs. This pseudo-wisdom manifests itself with the attitudes of envy, egotism, and exaggeration.

The Jay and the Peacock
A Jay venturing into a yard where Peacocks used to walk found a number of feathers, which had fallen from the Peacocks. He tied them all to his tail and strutted toward the Peacocks. When he came near them, they discovered the cheat and pecked at him until they plucked away his borrowed plumes. The Jay was forced to go back to the other Jays, who had watched his behavior. They were annoyed with him and said: "It is not only fine feathers that make fine birds."

Wisdom that is demonic envies, covets, and cunningly attempts to elevate itself to a place of prominence. This describes Satan's flaw that led to his ultimate fall. Ezekiel 28 says that before Satan landed in Eden, he was "the anointed cherub" who had access to the "holy mountain of God." He was "perfect" until one proud day "iniquity was found" in him. His "heart was lifted up because of [his] beauty." Therefore God condemned him, saying, "You corrupted your wisdom for the sake of your splendor." And then God cast him to the ground.

The Moral of the Story Is . . . Pride comes before the fall.

We've seen that Living Faith possesses the meekness of wisdom manifested in good works. Now James describes a wisdom that parades itself as heavenly but is, in fact, demonic.

Review James 3, then focus on verse 14-15.

> *But if you have bitter envy and self-seeking in your hearts, do not boast and lie against the truth.* James 3:14

1. What are the first two sinful attitudes mentioned here?

. . . .

2. Where do these attitudes originate? . . . .

. . . .

3. What prideful behavior are we warned against? . . . .

. . . .

4. When we boast because of envy and self-seeking, what are we really doing?

. . . .

> *This wisdom does not descend from above, but is earthly, sensual, demonic.* James 3:15

5. How do you know this wisdom is not heavenly? . . . .

. . . .

6. What three titles does James give it? . . . .

. . . .

7. Match the following Scriptures with the corresponding characteristics of worldly wisdom.

Philippians 3:18-19   Sensual

2 Corinthians 11:13-14   Earthly

Jude 16-19   Demonic

BITTER ENVY

Bitter means "pointed, sharp, prickly, or pungent." *Envy,* like jealousy, is a painful awareness of an advantage enjoyed by another coupled with a desire to possess that advantage. Bitter envy describes the worst type of envy, one that completely disregards the feelings and well-being of others.

BRAGGART

Here James describes an arrogant person. In modern society boasting and self-seeking are viewed as acceptable qualities. Boasting is rampant among politicians, sports figures, and celebrities. But a Christian who exhibits arrogance reveals a lack of divine wisdom.

UNHOLY TRINITY

The three types of worldly wisdom correspond with our three enemies. *Earthly* symbolizes the world, *sensual* the flesh, and *demonic* the devil. "All that is in the world—the lust of the flesh, the lust of the eyes, and the pride of life—is not of the Father" (1 John 2:16).

transformation

7
DEMONIC
Demonic means demon-like. Demons disseminate errors to seduce believers. One deception is the belief that through mediums people can converse with deceased humans, which is forbidden. "Do not rely on . . . psychics, for you will be defiled by them" (Leviticus 19:31, NLT).

8
JEALOUSY
Bitter envy manifests itself in a striving jealousy that competes with others for attention. Jealousy originates with pride, displays itself in covetousness and evil desires, and ends in destruction. "A heart at peace gives life to the body, but envy rots the bones" (Proverbs 14:30, NIV).

9
BOAST
While the Bible teaches that we are not to boast in ourselves, we are encouraged to use our lips to boast about others. "Do not boast . . . Let another man praise you, and not your own mouth; a stranger, and not your own lips" (Proverbs 27:1-2).

8. James warned against bitter envy. This type of envy can wear three different faces. Below is a description of each.

> Journal about a time when your face was marked by these devilish displays of jealousy.
>
> Saddened when others got ahead.

. . . .

☺ Gladdened when others fell behind.

. . . .

☹ Maddened when you didn't get all the credit.

. . . .

9. Boasting in ourselves is lying against the truth because we are taking credit for something God has created. If you are beautiful, thank God for creating you that way. If you have a brilliant mind, honor God with your thoughts.

> With this in mind, journal a prayer boasting in God alone by rewriting the following verse: "I will boast only in the Lord; . . . Come, let us tell of the Lord's greatness; let us exalt his name together" (Psalm 34:2-3, NLT).

. . . .

. . . .

. . . .

. . . .

10. Circle the three words in these verses that describe how God views worldly wisdom.

"For the wisdom of this world is foolishness with God. For it is written, 'He catches the wise in their own craftiness'; and again, 'The Lord knows the thoughts of the wise, that they are futile'"(1 Corinthians 3:19-20).

Corrie Ten Boom told the story of a proud woodpecker who was tapping away at a dead tree when the sky unexpectedly turned black and the thunder began to roll. Undaunted, he went right on working. Suddenly a bolt of lightning struck the old tree, splintering it into hundreds of pieces. Startled but unhurt, the haughty bird flew off, screeching to his feathered friends, "Hey, everyone, look at me! Look what I did!"

That old woodpecker is a lot like people who think more highly of themselves than they ought. You know the ones—the ones who are so busy bragging about their achievements that they fail to recognize God as the source of their abilities. They suffer from spiritual delusions of grandeur.

James reminds us that godly wisdom will be humble—giving God the credit—while demonic wisdom will take all the credit. The next time you're tempted to brag or say, "Look at me!" remember: "This is what the Lord says: 'Let not the wise man gloat in his wisdom, or the mighty man in his might, or the rich man in his riches. Let them boast in this alone: that they truly know me and understand that I am the Lord who is just and righteous, whose love is unfailing, and that I delight in these things'" (Jeremiah 9:23-24, NLT).

WORLDLY

Worldliness is devotion to this world rather than spiritual affairs. Worldly people are so earthly minded they are no heavenly good. Worldliness can be seen in those who elevate ecology over theology and recycling over religion. "Set your mind on things above, not on things on the earth" (Colossians 3:2).

contemplation

To have a low opinion of our own merits and to think highly of others is an evidence of wisdom.
Thomas à Kempis

DAY 3 EVERY MAN
FOR HIMSELF

We have been strongly warned against the attitudes of envy
and self-seeking based on worldly wisdom. Envy and self-seeking
promote a lifestyle of "every man for himself." This lifestyle is
completely contrary to Christ's command that we live with an
attitude of sacrificial love. Jesus said, "A new commandment
I give to you, that you love one another; as I have loved you"
(John 13:34).

The Three Tradesmen

A great city was besieged. The frightened inhabitants came
together and consulted about the best way to protect their town
from the enemy. A Bricklayer recommended bricks as the best
material for resistance. A Carpenter proposed timber as a better
method of defense. A Hunter said, "Sirs, I beg to differ. There
is nothing so good as leather for protection." Because they were
confused about which to choose, each man began setting up
defenses as he saw fit. On one side of the city, a wall of brick
was erected, on another side a wall of wood, and on a third side
a wall of leather. But one side was left defenseless, and that's
where the enemy came in and conquered the city.

The Moral of the Story Is . . . Every man for himself brings
destruction.

exploration

James has shown how worldly wisdom is demonic and devoid
of spiritual truth. Now he shows the consequences of living by
self-gratification.

Review James 3, then focus on verse 16.

For where envy and self-seeking exist, confusion and every evil thing are there. James 3:16

1. List the two types of worldly wisdom repeated here.

. . . .

2. What happens to the mind of the envious, self-seeking individual?

. . . .

3. What things surround this type of person? . . . .

. . . .

4. How many evil things accompany envy and self-seeking?

. . . .

5. Early in biblical history, self-seeking people took an action that resulted in great confusion for the world. Read Genesis 11:4-9 to learn about this time, then answer the following questions.

a. Explain what these people wanted to build and the self-seeking motive behind it (v. 4).

. . . .

b. Who came to inspect this endeavor, and what problem did He foresee (vv. 5-6)?

. . . .

c. Describe the action taken by the Lord and the result (vv. 7-9).

. . . .

6. Another story in Genesis tells about a time when envy brought about great evil. Read Genesis 4:1-8. Explain the role you think envy played in this evil event and why.

. . . .

. . . .

explanation

1

SELF-SEEKING
Self-seeking can be translated "selfish ambition." The self-seeking person is selfish and loves to stirs up strife in order to get ahead. But God has harsh words for the selfish: "To those who are self-seeking . . . [God will render] indignation and wrath, tribulation and anguish" (Romans 2:8-9).

2

CONFUSION
Confusion literally means "disorder" and speaks of instability, perplexity, and tumult. Since God is a God of order, His people are noted for their stability and confidence rather than chaotic disorder: "God is not the author of confusion but of peace" (1 Corinthians 14:33).

4

EVERY EVIL
"Every evil thing" speaks broadly of the results of worldly wisdom. In one sense, *evil* means "worthless or futile." In another sense, it means "vile and contemptible." In other words, nothing good and everything bad are the results of envy and self-seeking.

7

ESTEEM
The world promotes
tearing others down.
The Bible promotes
building others up.
When you esteem
others, you will be
esteemed. "Let not
mercy and truth forsake
you . . . and so find
favor and high esteem
in the sight of God and
man" (Proverbs 3:3-4).

8

IN THE FLESH
The *flesh* refers to our
carnal, earthly nature
apart from God's divine
influence. The flesh
represents our evil lusts
and desires. The flesh
is prone to sin and
opposed to God. "So
then, those who are in
the flesh cannot please
God" (Romans 8:8).

7. James strongly warned against self-seeking or selfish ambition.
In Philippians 2:2 Paul gives the antidote to these evil attitudes:
"Let nothing be done through selfish ambition or conceit, but
in lowliness of mind let each esteem others better than himself."
With this in mind, honestly examine your heart, then journal
the following steps.

Step One: Name a position or attribute you are jealous
of someone else possessing. (Example: I'd be a better
president of the P.T.A. than Jane Doe.)

. . . .

Step Two: Journal a prayer asking God to give you
a humble spirit, "lowliness of mind."

. . . .

. . . .

Step Three: In order to esteem others better than
yourself, list the good qualities and qualifications of the
person you are envious of.

. . . .

. . . .

8. One consequence of envy and self-seeking is confusion. People
are confused because they think the things of the world—"the
works of the flesh"—will satisfy them.

Read about the specific works of the flesh found in
Galatians 5:19-21, then describe how one of these fleshly
works has brought confusion into your life. (Example:
I thought it was fine to watch a psychic on TV, but what
she said did not match God's Word.)

. . . .

. . . .

. . . .

9. James has warned against allowing evil things to impact us. The prophet Isaiah taught that doing good is a personal choice. Read Isaiah 1:16-17 and explain how we can cease to do evil.

. . . .

. . . .

. . . .

. . . .

9
PARDON
Evil is the failure of free beings to conform in character and conduct to the will of God, bringing about sin. However, God offers pardon to all who turn from their evil ways to Him. "You are God, ready to pardon, gracious and merciful" (Nehemiah 9:17).

Imagine a few scenarios that depict the potential evil caused by jealous, self-seeking individuals.

Think of the confusion on a football team if jealous guards tried to play quarterback instead of blocking. Serious harm could come to the unprotected quarterback. What if selfish ambition occurred on a commercial airliner? The passengers would be in extreme jeopardy if an ambitious but unqualified stewardess decided to pilot the plane. In politics, confusion and evil would abound if the legislative, executive, and judicial branches failed to carry out their constitutional tasks and seized one another's jobs in a power grab.

In the same way, serious evil can come to our relationships at home, work, or church if we allow envy and self-seeking to rule our life. A wife who doesn't think her husband is "keeping up with the Joneses" might willingly destroy her marriage. A coworker envious of another's promotion could easily obliterate a reputation through slanderous comments. A church member who feels over-looked might split a congregation by spreading seeds of discontent and criticism.

Not surprisingly, self-seeking and envy were the emotions that led to the crucifixion of Jesus Christ. Judas selfishly betrayed Jesus for thirty pieces of silver, and "it was out of envy that the chief priests had handed Jesus over" (Mark 15:10, NIV). But Christ showed a different way: "being in the form of God, . . . [He took] the form of a bondservant, . . . humbled Himself and became obedient to the point of death" (Philippians 2:6-8). Let's follow the wisdom of Christ.

contemplation

One year of
Self-surrender
Will bring
Larger blessings
Than fourscore
Years of
Selfishness.
Henry van Dyke

After warning against cultivating worldly values that lead to lives of vice, James turns our attention back to heavenly wisdom—godly actions and attitudes that result in godly virtues.

The Lion and the Little Mouse

A big Lion was awakened when a little Mouse began scurrying up and down his back. The Lion trapped the mouse in his huge paw and opened his jaws to swallow him. "Pardon, O King!" cried the little Mouse. "If you forgive me, I'll never forget it! Perhaps I can do you a good turn someday!" The Lion was so amused at the idea of the little Mouse helping him that he let the Mouse go in peace. Soon after, the Lion was caught in a trap. The hunters tied him to a tree while they searched for a wagon to carry him off. Just then the little Mouse happened to pass by. Seeing the sad plight of the Lion, the Mouse gnawed away the ropes that bound the King of the Beasts. "Was I not right?" said the little Mouse, "I *was* able to help you!" The moral? Little friends may prove great friends.

The Lion went against his nature by listening to the little Mouse and granting him mercy, and that is what saved him in the long run. The same is true for believers: We must stand against our sin nature and against worldly wisdom. When we do, we find heavenly rewards.

The Moral of the Story Is . . . Godly virtues are worth cultivating.

exploration

This week's lesson is a study in contrasts: the wisdom of the world as opposed to the wisdom from above. We have learned the dark truth that the world's wisdom results in confusion and every evil thing. Now we step into the light and discover that those who possess the wisdom from above demonstrate Living Faith through godly attributes.

Review James 3, then focus on verse 17.

> **But the wisdom that is from above is first pure, then peaceable, gentle, willing to yield, full of mercy and good fruits, without partiality and without hypocrisy.**
> James 3:17

1. James used the word "But" to change our focus from wisdom that does not descend from above to wisdom that does come from above. What did James say was the first virtue of godly wisdom?

. . . .

2. "Then" what is the second virtue of divine wisdom?

. . . .

3. Name the next two qualities that are evident in heavenly wisdom.

. . . .

4. Describe what wisdom from above is filled with. . . . .

. . . .

5. What two vices does this wisdom *not* exhibit? . . . .

. . . .

6. Remembering Lesson 5 (James 2:1-13), define again *partiality* and *hypocrisy*.

Partiality:. . . . .

Hypocrisy:. . . . .

transformation

7. The wisdom of God is peaceable, bringing harmony to relationships with both God and people. Name a relationship of yours, in the past or present, that has hit a sour note.

. . . .

explanation

PEACEABLE
In almost every book of the New Testament, *peaceable* describes a) harmony between people and nations; b) freedom from molestation; c) order in government or church; d) harmonious relationship with God; e) rest and contentment in Christ (adapted, *Vine's*).

YIELDING
Gentle means "to be moderate, meek, and mild." *Willing to yield* literally means "easily entreated or persuaded." One who is gentle will patiently listen and easily yield her will to follow God's will. But meek does *not* mean weak. A gentle believer will not yield to wrongdoing.

FRUITFUL
Fruit refers to deeds that show the power of the Holy Spirit working in believers who abide in Christ. This union generates "the fruit of the Spirit"—Christ's character reproduced in those who believe (adapted, *Vine's*). Jesus said, "You will know them by their fruits" (Matthew 7:16).

GOD'S WILL

The Spirit prays for us to do God's will: "The Spirit intercedes for the saints in accordance with God's will" (Romans 8:27, NIV). Jesus also prays: "He always lives to make intercession for them" (Hebrews 7:25). Won't you make it your prayer to do the will of the Father?

GOOD FRUIT

Root determines fruit. Jesus said, "I am the vine, you are the branches. He who abides in Me . . . bears much fruit" (John 15:5). Since Jesus, our root and vine, is pure and peaceable, as branches we should yield purity and peace.

Now journal a prayer to God by rewriting the following passage and asking Him to restore harmony: "May God, who gives this patience and encouragement, help you live in complete harmony with each other—each with the attitude of Christ Jesus toward the other. Then all of you can join together with one voice, giving praise and glory to God, the Father of our Lord Jesus Christ" (Romans 15:5-6, NLT).

. . . .

. . . .

. . . .

. . . .

8. Another virtue that demonstrates godly wisdom is a willingness to yield to God's will. When we fail to yield in traffic, we are likely to have a collision. So, too, when we fail to yield to God's will, we are likely to wreck our lives. With this in mind, fill in the chart to discover God's will for you. Draw a yield sign ∇ beside the areas in which you have yielded.

SCRIPTURE	GOD'S WILL	YIELDED?
Eph. 6:5-6		
1 Thess. 4:3		
1 Thess. 5:18		
1 Pet. 2:15		
2 Pet. 3:9		

9. Today James urged us to be fruitful by allowing the Holy Spirit to reproduce Christ's character in us. Circle the virtues of heavenly wisdom you need most in your life right now.

Pure	Peaceable
Gentle	Willing to yield
Full of mercy	Full of good fruits

Based on your knowledge of Scripture, journal about a situation when Christ exhibited these virtues in His life. What do you learn from this?

. . . .

. . . .

. . . .

. . . .

. . . .

We've all heard people say, "God loves you and has a wonderful plan for your life." Somehow we mistakenly conclude "God's will" brings only joy and allows no suffering. But that wasn't the case for Jesus, and it isn't the case for the rest of us.

God's plan included Jesus being born in a lowly stable; growing up in a blue-collar home; walking dusty roads with no place to lay His head; hearing the crowd shout, "Hosanna!" then yell, "Crucify!" God loved Jesus and had a wonderful plan for His life— His death. It wasn't always easy for Jesus to yield to the will of His Father. He struggled at Gethsemane, three times asking God to remove the cup of sorrow. But each time, He yielded to the Father's will: "Not as I will, but as You will" (Matthew 26:39). And so, Jesus was "first pure, then peaceable, gentle, willing to yield, full of mercy and good fruits, without partiality and without hypocrisy."

God loves *you*. He has a wonderful plan for your life—eternal life. But life on earth includes drinking from the cup of sorrow. A bad diagnosis, a rocky relationship, a prodigal child, financial struggles, or other difficulties make you plead as Jesus did, "Let this cup pass from me!" But God's will won't ever lead you where His grace will not keep you. Therefore, *you* can confidently pray, "Your will be done on earth as it is in heaven" (Matthew 6:10).

contemplation

God's will is not an itinerary but an attitude.
Andrew Dhuse

DAY 5 — ONLY GOD CAN CHANGE OUR NATURE

preparation

Jesus, I praise You that You are my peace. Thank You for the rich relationship I enjoy with You today. Teach me to plant the fruit of peace in the lives of those You place in my path. Amen.

PEACEFUL LIVING
The work of righteousness will be peace, and the effect of righteousness, quietness and assurance forever.
Isaiah 32:17

James has taught us to think and act with godly wisdom. While it is far more natural to act with worldly wisdom, we gain wisdom from above when God dwells in our hearts and plants His character in our lives.

The Scorpion and the Ladybug
A Scorpion befriended a Ladybug who became a loyal companion to him. A time came when the Ladybug struggled to cross a dangerous river, so the Scorpion offered to take her to the other side on his back. He had come to care for the Ladybug and had promised he would never harm her, so she accepted his offer of a ride. But, safely across the river, he stung her with his venomous tail. As she lay in greatest pain, she said, "But you promised you would never hurt me. Why did you?" He shrugged and said sadly, "Because it is my Nature." The moral of this story is: Regardless of our wishes or intent, it is to our Nature alone that we inevitably succumb.

James reminds us that God wants to change our nature from the inside out, allowing us to make true peace with Him that leads to peace with others.

The Moral of the Story Is . . . Only God can change our nature.

exploration

James now turns to an agricultural metaphor about righteous living. We discover that Christians who have God's wisdom planted in their hearts will sow a wonderful harvest.

Review James 3, then focus on verse 18.

Now the fruit of righteousness is sown in peace by those who make peace. James 3:18

1. What is the fruit or by-product of godly wisdom? . . . .

. . . .

2. Read Hebrews 12:11, and explain how God cultivates the fruit of righteousness in His children.

. . . .

3. According to James, how is this fruit sown? . . . .

4. Who sows (plants) the fruit of righteousness? . . . .

. . . .

5. According to Matthew 5:9, why are peacemakers blessed?

. . . .

6. Read 2 Corinthians 9:10 and answer the following questions.

   a. Who supplies the "seed" sown? . . . .

   . . . .

   b. In what two ways does He ensure that there is enough for everyone?

   . . . .

transformation

7. Today we discovered that Christians can bear "the fruit of righteousness." Fill in the chart to discover other fruits we can produce.

SCRIPTURE	SPIRITUAL FRUIT
John 4:35-36	
Rom. 6:22	
Gal. 5:22-23	

Col. 1:10 . . . .

Heb. 13:15 . . . .

8
PRUNING
Pruning away branches
is the method Jesus
used to increase fruitfulness. "He prunes the
branches that do bear
fruit so they will
produce even more"
(John 15:2, NLT). God
often uses His Word,
His Spirit, and providen-
tial circumstances to
"prune" or help His
children become more
productive.

8. Sometimes trees are pruned to produce more fruit. Christians, too, are chastened and disciplined to yield righteous fruit.

Using the word *PRUNE* as an acrostic, list some unfruitful behaviors God has cut away in your life, helping you reap a harvest of righteousness.

P (Example: Pride) . . . .

R . . . .

U . . . .

N . . . .

E . . . .

RECONCILIATION
Reconcile means to
"restore to friendship,
harmony, or commu-
nion." God desires us
to be reconciled to Him
and to other human
beings. "God . . . has
reconciled us to Himself
through Jesus Christ,
and has given us the
ministry of reconcilia-
tion" (2 Corinthians
5:18).

9. We have learned that peace is not a state of mind or the absence of war. Instead, peace carries the idea of reconciliation between conflicting parties.

With this in mind, journal through the steps found in Matthew 5.

Step One: Write about one of your relationships that has been severed through strife: "If you bring your gift to the altar, and there remember that your brother has some-thing against you" (v. 23).

. . . .

. . . .

Step Two: Write about what you'll do *today* to make things right with that person: "Leave your gift there before the altar, and go your way. First be reconciled to your brother" (v.24).

. . . .

. . . .

Step Three: Write a prayer thanking God for making you a peacemaker: "Then come and offer your gift" (v. 24).

. . . .

. . . .

. . . .

Charles Dickens, the great English novelist whose works include *A Christmas Carol, Oliver Twist,* and *A Tale of Two Cities,* and another great writer of the Victorian age William Makepeace Thackeray, the author of *Vanity Fair,* both loved to write about London and its often unequitable social structure. The two had been friendly rivals until they quarreled over an unknown matter.

Just before Christmas in 1863, they happened to meet in London but passed quickly by, refusing to speak to one another. Unhappy at their estrangement, Thackeray turned back to his old and dear friend, seized his hand, and told him he couldn't bear the coldness that existed between them. Dickens was so touched by the gesture that his anger and bitterness faded away. The two men were friends once again. On Christmas Eve, Thackeray died suddenly of an aneurysm. Dickens was one of the illustrious people to attend the funeral at Westminster Abbey. Sir Thomas Martin, who had been with the men that wintry day in London, said, "I saw Dickens . . . standing at the grave of his rival. He must have rejoiced, I thought, that he had shaken hands so warmly a few days before." Nearly seven years later, Dickens himself was buried at Westminster Abbey.

William Thackeray lived up to his middle name "Makepeace" and went to his grave at peace with his friend. And Charles Dickens could say along with his famous character Tiny Tim, "God bless us every one!"

contemplation

Sowing seeds of peace is like sowing beans. You don't know why it works; you just know it does. Seeds are planted, and topsoils of hurt are shoved away.
Max Lucado

War of the Worlds!

War is hell." I (Penny) know this adage is true because my father is a Korean War veteran. As a young girl, I would hear him scream in the middle of the night and anxiously listen as my mom soothed him back to sleep. In those days we hadn't heard of Posttraumatic Stress Disorder. However, there's no denying the long-term effects the war had on my dad.

PTSD is triggered by exposure to terrifying events. It often occurs among soldiers who have been in combat situations. Many people with PTSD experience flashbacks and nightmares. They also experience emotional numbness, sleep disturbances, depression, anxiety, irritability, or outbursts of anger. The effects of war are physical and emotional, long-lasting and far-reaching. War shapes the lives of those who have gone into battle and impacts their families and friends as well.

There are other kinds of wars that are just as traumatic as military conflict. They, too, cause adverse side effects. In the book of James, we have read about the war of the worlds—the kingdom of God against the kingdoms of men. This conflict had many battlefronts: war of words, class war, and spiritual warfare. The church was in the trenches and it was tough going!

But while war is hell, peace is heavenly. If you are suffering the trauma of kingdom warfare, look up! Jesus said, "In Me you may have peace. In the world you will have tribulation; but be of good cheer, I have overcome the world" (John 16:33).

DAY **1** DECLARATION OF WAR

preparation

Father, there is war without and war within. I am so thankful that You have sent the Prince of Peace to overcome my flesh and the world. Teach me to walk in peace with my brothers and sisters in Christ. Amen.

PEACE
The Lord will bless His people with peace. Psalm 29:11

explanation

1
WARS
Fights lead to war; wars are serious disputes resulting in combat. James used these words as metaphors for personal relationships in the church, which had become combative in nature. "His words are as smooth as cream, but in his heart is war" (Psalm 55:21, NLT).

exploration

Last week we learned that worldly wisdom causes conflict while godly wisdom promotes peace. Now we examine more closely the source of conflicts among people.

Read James 4, then focus on verses 1-2.

> *Where do wars and fights come from among you? Do they not come from your desires for pleasure that war in your members? James 4:1*

1. What is the first hypothetical question James asked?

. . . .

2. Why do you think James felt compelled to address the issue of wars and fights among the people?

. . . .

3. James answered his first question with another question. According to the second question, where do wars and fights come from?

. . . .

4. Where is the battle waged? . . . .

. . . .

> *You lust and do not have. You murder and covet and cannot obtain. You fight and war. Yet you do not have because you do not ask. James 4:2*

5. James now gives a list of "desires" that lead to conflict. Based on verse 2, fill in the chart to understand what you do and why you do it.

WHAT YOU DO	WHY YOU DO IT
. . . .
. . . .
. . . .

6. James says that wars begin with lust and covetousness. Read Genesis 26:12-22, then answer the following questions.

a. In what three ways did the Philistines respond to Isaac's prosperity?

(v. 14) _____

(v. 15) _____

(v. 16) _____

b. How did their quarrel continue to escalate, and finally end (vv. 17-22)?

. . . .

7. According to the last phrase in verse 2, what is one reason we don't have what we desire?

. . . .

transformation

8. Wars begin with "desires for pleasure." *Webster's Dictionary* gives three different definitions for pleasure. Beside each definition list some things that you find pleasurable.

1) Sensual gratification: . . . .

2) Frivolous amusement: . . . .

3) Source of delight or joy: . . . .

3
PLEASURE
The word *pleasure* stems from the word *hedonon,* from which we get the English words *hedonist* and *hedonism.* It conveys the idea of pursuing sensual desire and passion. God made us with a capacity for pleasure. Yet, uncontrolled desires for pleasure—hedonism—cause great conflict.

5
LUST
Lust is desire for the forbidden or an obsessive sexual craving. Although there are legitimate desires for which God makes provision, lust is desiring things that are contrary to God's will. "Make no provision for the flesh, to fulfill its lusts" (Romans 13:14).

6
COVETOUS
To *covet* is to wish for what one does not have; also translated "greed." Covetousness lies in discontentment with what one has. "Take heed and beware of covetousness, for one's life does not consist in the abundance of the things he possesses" (Luke 12:15).

9

SELFLESS
Human beings have
three favorite words: *I*,
Me, and *Mine*. Lust and
covetousness are
rooted in selfishness,
but godliness has its
roots in selflessness.
"Because He laid down
His life for us, . . . we
also ought to lay down
our lives for the breth-
ren" (1 John 3:16).

10

PROVIDER
Too often God's chil-
dren look for provision
in all the wrong places,
when God has a store-
house of supplies to
match every need.
"My God shall supply
all your need according
to His riches in glory
by Christ Jesus"
(Philippians 4:19).

Our pleasures can turn to poison when they become
excessive, obsessive, or aggressive. Journal about a situation when your desire for pleasure became poisonous.
(Example: My desire for amusement at the movies took
away my discernment to abstain from watching unscrip-
tural sex and unbridled obscenities.)

. . . .

. . . .

. . . .

. . . .

9. James warned that lust leads to conflict. Paul says, "Walk in the
Spirit, and you shall not fulfill the lust of the flesh" (Galatians
5:16). The following are Paul's lists of fleshly and spiritual
behaviors. Circle the ways you've indulged in the flesh, then
underline the fruit of the Spirit you've displayed.

> **Lust of the Flesh:** "Sexual immorality, impure thoughts,
> eagerness for lustful pleasure, idolatry, participation in
> demonic activities . . . quarreling, jealousy, outbursts of
> anger, selfish ambition, divisions . . . envy, drunkenness"
> (Galatians 5:19-21, NLT).

> **Fruit of the Spirit:** "Love, joy, peace, patience, kindness,
> goodness, faithfulness, gentleness, and self-control"
> (Galatians 5:22-23, NLT).

10. Today we discovered that conflicts escalate because of
prayerlessness—"you do not have because you do not ask."

With this in mind, make a brief list of the things you
don't have but wish you did. Beside each item, journal
a prayer asking God to be your provider.

. . . .

. . . .

. . . .

. . . .

Sibling rivalry is as old as Cain and Abel. So it's no surprise that the tug of war between my sister Suzanne and I began the day I was born. It started with a fight for our parents' attention. She thought Dad liked me best, and I felt that Mom favored her. Our conflict moved from relationships to possessions. One Christmas Grandma gave us matching baby dolls: hers was blue and mine was pink. But one day Suzanne discovered the blue doll's hair was missing and insisted that *hers* was the pink doll. I was left crying, clutching the bald blue doll. Thankfully we grew out of our animosity and now are *the* best of friends, unlike the sisters in the following story.

Two spinster sisters lived together. Because of an argument, they stopped speaking to one another. Unwilling to move out of their house, they used the same rooms, ate at the same table, and slept in the same bedroom. A chalk line divided their areas into two halves. Each could come and go, cook and eat, sew and read without ever crossing over into her sister's domain.

God's children can experience sibling rivalry too. Instead of dividing homes, they divide churches because of jealousy, envy and strife. Paul pleads with God's kids, "Brothers and sisters . . . stop arguing among yourselves. Let there be real harmony so there won't be divisions in the church. I plead with you to be of one mind." (1 Corinthians 1:10, NLT).

contemplation

The wars that rage within the world are a reflection of the wars that rage inside people.
Leighton Ford

DAY 2 ENEMIES OF GOD

preparation

Jesus, I am so grateful that You are my best friend. Please keep me from friendship with the world and draw me ever closer to You. Amen.

GOD'S FRIEND

But there is a friend who sticks closer than a brother. Proverbs 18:24

We entered the world just one week apart that cold wintry December in 1957. She was to be born breech but flipped during delivery and came out headfirst. I was headed in the right direction but at birth changed my mind and came out backwards. We are both left-handed, five foot seven inches tall, have ash-blonde hair and hazel eyes. That's why my cousin Valerie and I named ourselves "twin cousins." We were inseparable—until Gretchen McClure moved into the neighborhood.

Gretchen was a doctor's daughter and had all the cool toys, *Mystery Date* being the most coveted game of all. Everyone wanted to be her friend. But Gretchen liked to play favorites and develop exclusive friendships. If Valerie was "in," then I was "out," and vice versa. The one who was Gretchen 's friend was forced to treat the other cousin like a foe—no verbal exchanges allowed. We'd even walk on the opposite side of the street to avoid the enemy. But one bright day, Valerie and I realized that blood *is* thicker than water. Reunited we proclaimed, "Who needs Gretchen and her toys anyway?"

This week James declares that some friendships just don't mix. Like oil and water, God and this world are not compatible. We must make a choice: Will we be God's friend or foe? The death of Jesus has made us members of God's family, and His blood is thicker than any friendship this world has to offer.

exploration

Yesterday we discovered that conflicts and wars begin with selfish desires. Today we discover that lustful desires also result in a declaration of war against God.

Review James 4, then focus on verses 3-4.

> **You ask and do not receive, because you ask amiss, that you may spend it on your pleasures.** James 4:3

1. How does God respond to some of our requests? Why?

. . . .

. . . .

2. What impure motive hinders our prayers?. . . . .

. . . .

. . . .

> **Adulterers and adulteresses! Do you not know that friendship with the world is enmity with God? Whoever therefore wants to be a friend of the world makes himself an enemy of God.** James 4:4

3. What startling label did James give those consumed by the pursuit of pleasure?

. . . .

4. If you become the world's friend, how does that impact your relationship to God?

. . . .

5. What phrase reveals this was something they should already know?

. . . .

6. Therefore, what conclusion did James reach and to whom does it apply?

. . . .

. . . .

explanation

2

AMISS

Amiss means "off target" in a physical or moral sense. Prayers go amiss—off target— because of wrong motives. But our Father hits the bull's-eye every time. God doesn't always give us what we want; He gives us what we need. He'll say "No" to keep us on target.

3

ADULTERY

James is speaking metaphorically about spiritual, not sexual, infidelity. When people disobeyed God or practiced idolatry, the prophets accused them of spiritual adultery. The *Living Bible* interprets this verse, "You are like an unfaithful wife who loves her husband's enemies."

4

THE WORLD

The *world* does not refer to planet Earth, but to the spiritual reality of the humanistic, Satan-inspired value system opposed to God. The world system will entice us to be unfaithful to God. "He shall judge the world with righteousness, and the peoples with His truth" (Psalm 96:13).

transformation

7

ON TARGET

Prayer doesn't change God's mind, but it changes our hearts. When we pray for passing pleasure, our motives are wrong. When we pray for God's glory, our motives are on target.

8

IDOLATRY

In the Old Testament, idolatry was the worship of something created instead of the Creator Himself. In the New Testament, idolatry was the replacement of God in the mind of the worshiper. Therefore, anything that comes between God and us is an idol.

9

GOD'S FRIEND

Obey God, and you'll be His friend. Jesus said, "You are my friends if you obey me. I no longer call you servants, because a master doesn't confide in his servants. Now you are my friends, since I have told you everything the Father told me" (John 15:14-15, NLT).

7. Sometimes our prayers go amiss because we pray with impure motives. Draw a line connecting the Scriptures with the actions that will get our prayers back on target.

Mark 11:24	Keep commandments
Mark 11:25	Ask in Jesus' name
John 14:13	Forgive
John 15:7	Believe
1 John 3:22	Abide in Christ

8. James said that Christians who get too friendly with the world are committing spiritual adultery. Read Jeremiah 3:6-14, then answer the following questions.

a. How did Israel and Judah commit spiritual adultery (vv. 6-8)?

. . . .

b. What two options did these adulterous people face (vv. 8, 12, 14)?

. . . .

. . . .

c. Based on what you've learned today, are you being faithful or faithless toward God?

. . . .

9. *Idolatry* is putting anyone or anything before your devotion to God. Describe a potential area in your life that could turn into idolatry. (Example: I always put my children first. If their sporting events are on Sunday, we skip church. I'm so busy with their schedules that I don't have time to read my Bible and pray.)

. . . .

. . . .

Journal a prayer to God by rewriting the following verse; let Him know that you will choose Him first: "No one can serve two masters. For you will hate one and love the other, or be devoted to one and despise the other. You cannot serve both God and [anything else, including] money" (Matthew 6:24, NLT).

. . . .

. . . .

. . . .

. . . .

History is full of traitors, from Judas to Benedict Arnold. What makes traitors so grievous is that they are people we trusted. They are our friends, our neighbors, and our countrymen.

John Walker Lindh seemed like an all-American boy on a quest for truth. But when the U.S. Army found him consorting with the enemy in an Afghani prison camp, it was apparent that he had succumbed to wicked lies. He went from a teenage tourist to an alleged Taliban terrorist. His motto changed from, "In God we trust" to "In Osama we hope." CNN reports that Walker Lindh even received personal thanks from bin Laden for "taking part in jihad." Only time will tell whether he was a misguided youth or a malicious coconspirator. But many people think that any friend of Osama's is not a friend of ours.

Some things truly are black and white. You're either a patriot or a traitor. You're either God's friend or His enemy. Jesus said, "He who is not with Me is against Me, and he who does not gather with Me scatters abroad" (Matthew 12:30). God wants to know—are you His friend or foe?

contemplation

Man draws nearer to God as he withdraws from the the consolation of this world. How swiftly passes the glory of the world!
Thomas à Kempis

PSYCHOLOGICAL WARFARE

"Capture their minds and their hearts and souls will follow" is the PSYOP motto. Psychological Operations (PSYOP) are military tactics that convey selected information to enemy audiences to influence their emotions and reasoning. PSYOP employs two key tactics: 1) Diminish morale or the will to resist; 2) Give opponents a "carrot and stick" approach—cooperate and be rewarded; resist and face the consequences. Here are some examples.

During World War II, Toyko Rose's radio broadcasts became a major means of disseminating pro-Japanese propaganda to demoralize the Allied troops. During the Gulf War, the Allied coalition flew loudspeaker aerial missions around Faylaka Island broadcasting the message to surrender. The next day 1,405 Iraqis surrendered to the U.S. Marines. In the recent war on terrorism, U.S. planes dropped the leaflet, "Taliban Reign of Fear," over Afghanistan. On it Muslim leader Osama bin Laden's face was transformed into a fearful snarling Jinn. The *Koran* identifies the Jinn as creatures that practice deceit to do evil. Showing the Jinn with the Taliban was meant to capture the minds of the Afghans and show that these oppressive leaders had turned toward evil.

God knows that those who have rejected Him have made themselves His enemies, and He desires to capture their hearts, minds, and souls. Paul said, "Let God transform you into a new person by changing the way you think" (Romans 12:2, NLT). God even uses the "carrot and stick" approach—draw near to Him and be rewarded or reject Him and meet resistance.

exploration

This week we've learned that selfishness leads to wars with others and ultimately with God. Today we learn that God jealously desires for us to surrender to Him in a spirit of humility.

Review James 4, then focus on verses 5-6.

> *Or do you think that the Scripture says in vain, "The Spirit who dwells in us yearns jealously"?* James 4:5

1. What phrase in James's question reaffirms the truth of God's Word?

. . . .

2. Where does God's Spirit live? . . . .

. . . .

3. How does the He respond to spiritual infidelity? . . . .

. . . .

4. James said that God's Spirit lives in us. Read 1 Corinthians 6:15-20 and answer the following questions.

   a. What phrases reveal the believer's intimate relationship with God (vv. 15, 17, 19)?

   . . . .

   b. What does this passage add to our understanding of why God hates spiritual adultery?

   . . . .

> *But He gives more grace. Therefore He says: "God resists the proud, but gives grace to the humble."* James 4:6

5. Instead of condemnation, what is God willing to give and how much?

. . . .

6. How does your attitude impact God's response to you?

. . . .

---

explanation

3

GODLY JEALOUSY
Jealousy involves vigilance in guarding someone we love. A spouse who is jealous takes great care to guard the relationship from interlopers. In the same way, God guards His relationship with His bride—the church—to ensure that our affections are for Him alone.

5

AMAZING GRACE
Grace is undeserved favor. It is amazing that God would sign a peace treaty with wretched sinners like us. Yet, when you accept Jesus as your Lord and Savior, God pours out *more grace* than you could ever imagine. "Where sin abounded, grace abounded much more" (Romans 5:20).

6

ATTITUDE?
Pride says, "I don't need God." Humility says, "I can't live without God." Pride pushes God away; humility reaches *up* to God and *out* to others. Human pride in the Garden of Eden brought death; God's humility in the Garden of Gethsemane brought eternal life.

YEARNING
Yearn means "to experience longing or craving; feel tenderness and compassion." After a lengthy separation, Joseph "yearned for his brother; . . . and sought somewhere to weep" (Genesis 43:30). A woman facing the loss of her child "yearned with compassion for her son" (1 Kings 3:26).

7. Most people think jealousy is a negative trait. But in James we find that God yearns jealously for us in a positive way. The apostle Paul also yearned for the early church to stay pure and faithful: "I am jealous for you with godly jealousy. For I have betrothed you to one husband, that I may present you as a chaste virgin to Christ" (2 Corinthians 11:2). Name someone whom you long to see stay spiritually pure.

· ·

 Journal a prayer, based on 2 Corinthians 11:2, asking God to keep that person's faith unsullied by the world.

· ·

· ·

· ·

· ·

ABUNDANT GRACE
God has an "abundance of grace" (Romans 5:17). In other words, no matter what situation you may find yourself in, God has more than enough grace to help. "The Lord will give grace and glory; no good thing will He withhold from those who walk uprightly" (Psalm 84:11).

8. Many people associate grace with salvation alone. But we learned that God gives *more* grace. Now that you are saved, check the ways in which you need more grace.

— Grace for "different gifts" (Romans 12:6, NIV)
— Grace "for every good work" (2 Corinthians 9:8)
— Grace "sufficient for you . . . in weakness" (2 Corinthians 12:9)
— Grace for "eternal encouragement and good hope" (2 Thessalonians 2:16, NIV)
— Grace "to help us when we need it" (Hebrews 4:16, NLT)

HUMILITY
Greek philosophers despised humility for it implied weakness. But biblical humility grows out of the recognition that all we have and are comes from God. Jesus was the supreme example of humility. "Being found in appearance as a man, He humbled Himself" (Philippians 2:8).

9. The prideful meet resistance while the humble find grace. Read 2 Chronicles 7:14 to learn how to humble yourself before God, and what will result.

a. What three things must we do to humble ourselves?

· ·

· ·

b. What three things does God promise to those who humble themselves?

. . . .

. . . .

Journal about a situation where your stubborn pride has met God's resistance. Then write a prayer to God humbling yourself and asking for His blessings.

. . . .

. . . .

. . . .

. . . .

Giovanni Bernardone was born in Italy to a wealthy cloth merchant. He led a pampered and frivolous life, dreaming of heroic exploits. During adolescence he joined the militia and was captured during his first battle. He endured a year in prison. Upon his release, Giovanni encountered a poor leper and reconsidered his religious beliefs. Imitating Christ, Giovanni renounced all his belongings, including the clothes he was wearing, and accepted total poverty. He even renounced his family name. Now we know him as St. Francis of Assisi, the founder of the Franciscans, who devote themselves to preaching and caring for the poor and sick.

Someone once asked St. Francis how he was able to accomplish so much. He replied, "Maybe the Lord looked down from Heaven and said, 'Where can I find the weakest, littlest man on earth?' Then He saw me and said, 'I've found him. I will work through him, and he won't be proud of it. He'll see that I am only using him because of his insignificance.'"

James tells us that God resists the proud but gives grace to the humble. Because of his wealth and position, Giovanni was a proud young man seeking only adventure and acclaim. By humbling himself, he was given great grace to change and live a life that counted for eternity.

contemplation

Pride is spiritual cancer; it eats the very possibility of love or contentment, or even common sense.

C. S. Lewis

DAY 4 RESISTANCE MOVEMENT

Why do humans resist authority? The Pilgrims on the Mayflower resisted the oppressive demands of the church and government by fleeing Europe. The early American colonists resisted England's taxation without representation by dumping tea into Boston Harbor. Rather than submit to India's Salt Act, which forced impoverished citizens to buy salt at exorbitant prices from the government, Mahatma Gandhi protested by marching to the sea to make salt from seawater. In the 1960s, the hippies, whose resistance anthem was, "Make Love Not War," orchestrated "sit-ins" and picketed college campuses. In every household, on a daily basis, children resist their parents' authority.

The original resistance movement began long before the world was created. Satan attempted to stage a coup against God's authority in heaven. He said, "I will ascend above the heights of the clouds, I will be like the Most High" (Isaiah 14:14). It is believed that he enlisted one-third of the angels to join his ranks. But it didn't work, and "that serpent of old, called the Devil and Satan, who deceives the whole world; he was cast to the earth, and his angels were cast out with him" (Revelation 12:9).

Though he was cast out, his resistance movement of sin continues. Satan entices humanity to resist God using every trick in the book. Today James reminds us that God, our ultimate authority figure, wants us to learn how to resist the resistor.

exploration

Yesterday we learned that in order to make peace with God, we must wage war against ourselves—humble ourselves before God. Today we learn other steps toward peace with God.

Review James 4, then focus on verses 7-9a.

Therefore submit to God. Resist the devil and he will flee from you. James 4:7

1. Yesterday we learned that God gives more grace. "Therefore" James exhorted his readers to do what two things?

   . . . .

   . . . .

2. What does God promise those who resist the devil? . . . .

   . . . .

3. Skim Matthew 4:1-11. What "weapon" did Christ use to resist Satan?

   . . . .

   . . . .

Draw near to God and He will draw near to you. Cleanse your hands, you sinners; and purify your hearts, you double-minded. Lament and mourn and weep! James 4:8-9a

4. It is not enough to "resist the devil." What else must we do to make peace with God?

   . . . .

   . . . .

5. What does God promise if we do this? . . . .

   . . . .

6. Explain what sinners and double-minded people need to do.

   . . . .

   . . . .

7. With what attitude should we repent? . . . .

   . . . .

1

SUBMIT
Submission speaks of lowering, humbling, or being compliant. This military term means to yield oneself to the authority or will of another. A person with Living Faith willingly submits to God in the same way that a private willingly submits to a general.

2

RESIST
Another military term, *resist* means to battle against, set oneself against, exert opposition. People who have made themselves friends with God have become Satan's enemies. "Your enemy the devil prowls around like a roaring lion looking for someone to devour" (1 Peter 5:8, NIV).

7

LAMENT AND REPENT
Repentance is turning away from sin and turning back to God. It includes a change of mind and feelings of "godly sorrow" for sin. "Godly sorrow brings repentance that leads to salvation and leaves no regret" (2 Corinthians 7:10, NIV).

8

REBEL
To *rebel* means "to oppose or disobey authority." Rebellion can be open defiance or subversive resistance. God ranks spiritual rebellion among one of the worst sins. "Rebellion is as bad as the sin of witchcraft, and stubbornness is as bad as worshiping idols" (1 Samuel 15:23, NLT).

9

ARMOR
Christians battle against a great enemy. However, God is more powerful than our foe. He provides impenetrable armor to protect us. "Put on all of God's armor so that you will be able to stand firm against all strategies and tricks of the Devil" (Ephesians 6:11, NLT).

8. James encouraged believers to submit themselves to God. Submission is an attitude of yielding to one in authority. Using the word *SUBMIT* as an acrostic, list some of the areas in your life that need to be yielded to God.

S . . . .

U . . . .

B . . . .

M . . . .

I . . . .

T . . . .

9. We have been exhorted to resist Satan. Think of an area in your life where you have had difficulty resisting Satan. 1 Peter 5:8-9 (NLT) gives three practical steps to stand in opposition to the enemy.

Journal about how these steps can help you resist Satan more effectively in the future.

1) "Watch out for attacks from the Devil."

. . . .

. . . .

2) "Take a firm stand against him."

. . . .

. . . .

3) "Be strong in your faith."

. . . .

. . . .

10. We have learned that repentance is not just feeling sorry for yourself but being sorry that you've sinned against God. It is not regret for getting caught but remorse that brings change. Fill in the chart to discover more.

SCRIPTURE	REPENTANCE INCLUDES
Job 42:6	
Ezek. 18:30-32	
Mark 1:15	
Acts 26:20	

A teacher asked, "What does the word *repent* mean?" A little boy responded, "It's being sorry for your sins." Then a little girl raised her hand and added, "It's being sorry enough to quit." I experienced both of these aspects of repentance after a sad experience at the happiest place on earth.

During the summer of 1978, I was an "almost Christian," attending church and reading my Bible. But I had not yet repented of all my sins. Believe it or not, I was unsure whether smoking marijuana was sinful or not. A misguided churchgoer had advised me that God gave us all the herbs on earth for our enjoyment.

When my friends pulled out a joint on the gondola ride at Disneyland, I didn't participate, but I didn't disapprove of their behavior either. As our gondola reached the Matterhorn, the Disneyland police were waiting for us. They held me guilty by association. After calling our parents, they kicked us out of the park. I was not only sorry we were caught; I felt genuine repentance for not being a better witness. From this event I learned that submitting to God means not only changing our actions but also changing our mind about sin.

10
REPENTANCE
James spoke of both inward and outward repentance: "cleanse your hands" and "purify your hearts." Jesus told pretentious religious leaders that repentance begins in the heart. "You try to look like upright people outwardly, but inside your hearts are filled with hypocrisy and lawlessness" (Matthew 23:28, NLT).

contemplation

True repentance has a double aspect; it looks upon things past with a weeping eye, and upon the future with a watchful eye.
Robert Smith

DAY 5 UNCONDITIONAL SURRENDER

preparation

Holy Father, sometimes there are so many battles going on in my heart I don't know whether to laugh or cry. Let me know the joy of humbly repenting and surrendering all to You. Amen.

HONOR
Humility and the fear of the Lord bring wealth and honor and life.
Proverbs 22:4, NIV

I (Penny) was miserable. I thought I wanted out of my marriage, so I gave my husband Kerry an ultimatum: "Go to church, pay more attention to the family, or I'm out of here." Amazingly, he did everything I asked. Soon he surrendered to God and accepted Jesus as his Savior.

But the problems didn't end. I harbored bitterness. We had financial problems that seemed insurmountable. Though I was attending Bible study and trying to be a godly wife and mother, I was despondent. One night I told Kerry "I don't trust this change in you. I'm completely unhappy." He replied, "I'm committed to making things work. I don't know how we'll get out of this mess, but I love you and the kids."

Our evening devotion had been, "Humble yourselves under the mighty hand of God, that He may exalt you in due time, casting all your care upon Him, for He cares for you" (1 Peter 5:6-7). In desperation I said, "Maybe we haven't really humbled ourselves before God. Let's confess our fears and doubts." And we did. We cried tears of sorrow and confessed the ways we had failed God and one another. I don't know how long we lay there praying and crying. Finally we rose and looked deep into each other's eyes. I knew then that we would make it. We had surrendered our lives unconditionally to God. I trusted Him to work things out. And He has.

exploration

We have found that submitting to God brings true repentance. Now we discover that submitting to God also means humbling ourselves before Him.

Review James 4, then focus on verses 9b-10.

> **Let your laughter be turned to mourning and your joy to gloom.** James 4:9b

1. Compare and contrast the difference between the Christian and non-Christian response to sin.

. . . .

. . . .

2. Read Proverbs 14:9, 12-13. Explain the difference between the foolish and upright person.

. . . .

. . . .

3. James encouraged us to mourn over our sin. Fill in the following chart to discover how God blesses those who mourn and weep.

SCRIPTURE	BLESSINGS OF MOURNING
Ps. 6:8	
Ps. 30:5	
Ps. 126:6	

> **Humble yourselves in the sight of the Lord, and He will lift you up.** James 4:10

4. Instead of laughing, what should we do? Before whom?

. . . .

. . . .

5. What does God promise those who humble themselves?

. . . .

. . . .

1
LAUGH OR CRY?
There is a time to weep and a time to laugh. The wise woman knows the appropriate time for each. Sinners should cry; repenters can celebrate. "Sorrow is better than laughter. . . . The heart of the wise is in the house of mourning" (Ecclesiastes 7:3-4).

3
NOW OR LATER?
Laugh now, and you'll cry later: "The angels will come . . . and cast [the wicked] into the furnace of fire. There will be wailing and gnashing of teeth" (Matthew 13:49-50). Cry now and you'll laugh later: "Blessed are you who weep now, for you shall laugh" (Luke 6:21).

5
UP OR DOWN?
The way down is the way up. Humble yourself and let God lift you up, or lift yourself up and let God take you down. "For the day of the Lord of hosts shall come upon everything proud and lofty, upon everything lifted up— and it shall be brought low" (Isaiah 2:12).

SYMPATHETIC
It has been said, "Laugh and the world laughs with you; cry and you cry alone." A Christian will laugh *and* cry with others. We are to be sympathetic. "When others are happy, be happy with them. If they are sad, share their sorrow" (Romans 12:15, NLT).

COMFORT
God comforts us with motherly tenderness and fatherly compassion. Motherly? "As a mother comforts her child, so will I comfort you" (Isaiah 66:13, NIV). Fatherly? "The Father of compassion and the God of all comfort, who comforts us in all our troubles" (2 Corinthians 1:3-4, NIV).

6. Today we learned that laughter can be good or bad, depending on what you think is funny. Check off the following situations that make you laugh.

— At a dirty joke
— The calamity of others
— Answered prayer
— My husband's sense of humor
— With my friends
— Because I was nervous
— When I was tickled
— Behind someone's back
— At a funny movie
— At my friends

Journal about a time when you laughed at an inappropriate situation. How did it make you or others feel later?

. . . .

. . . .

. . . .

. . . .

7. God comforts those who mourn over sin. Isaiah 61:1-3 reveals God's exchange program for the truly repentant. Read this passage and list the evidence of godly sorrow and God's response.

GODLY SORROW	GOD'S RESPONSE
(Example: poor in spirit)	(Example: preach glad tidings)

. . . .

. . . .

. . . .

. . . .

8. This week the message of humility has been repeated. When Scripture repeats something, it is intended to get our attention and is God's way of emphasizing a point. Peter closely repeats James's exhortation about humility.

> Using 1 Peter 5:5 as a template, journal a prayer to God asking Him to strip you of pride and then clothe you with humility: "Be clothed with humility, for 'God resists the proud, but gives grace to the humble.'"

. . . .

. . . .

. . . .

. . . .

A cocky seminary graduate was given the opportunity to try out for the pastorate in a simple country church. The week before his big debut, he purchased a new suit to dazzle the congregation and had his hair styled in the latest fashion. The day of his first sermon, he strutted up to the pulpit full of self-confidence. He pulled out his copious notes full of wit and wisdom and began to deliver his message. But suddenly he was struck with stage fright and began to stutter. The words simply would not come out. Finally, he burst into tears and rushed off the platform in utter humiliation.

There sitting in the front row were two elderly, no-nonsense, farm wives. They had watched in silence as the young man made his grand entrance. But when he slunk from the stage, one remarked to the other, "If he would have come in the way he went out, he would have gone out the way he came in." It was her way of saying two very profound things. First, "Pride comes before the fall," and second, "The humble will be exalted."

Each of us faces the same opportunity as this young preacher: Humble ourselves or be humiliated. If we trust in ourselves, our talents, or our abilities, we're headed downhill fast. But when we humbly offer ourselves to God, acknowledging our utter dependence upon Him, and give Him credit for the gifts He has given, we are on our way up.

8
HUMILIATION
There's a difference between *humility* and *humiliation*. The humble person *willingly* lowers herself to positions of service, like Jesus who became a man that He might serve. *Humiliation* means to be reduced to a lower position in others' eyes. You have a choice: Be humble or be humiliated?

contemplation

Humility is a necessary prerequisite for grace. When you are humiliated, grace is on the way. It is only the one who can see the value of being humbled that is completely righteous. The humble person has changed humiliation into humility.
Bernard of Clairvaux

What You Don't Know Can Hurt You

*S*ome clichés make sense. "A place for everything, and everything in its place" is a great way of saying get organized. "Absence makes the heart grow fonder" means what it says: We miss those who are out of sight but not out of mind.

But some catch phrases just don't ring true. The 1960s movie *Love Story* propagated the most lame sentiment ever uttered: "Love means never having to say you're sorry." Picture actress Ali MacGraw batting her eyelashes as she spoke those heartfelt but completely absurd words. If, as the saying goes, "You always hurt the ones you love," then you probably need to tell them you're sorry.

Another untrue adage is "What you don't know can't hurt you." Really? If you don't know you've got cancer, does that mean you won't die? Does not knowing your bank account is empty stop the checks from bouncing? Ignorance is *not* bliss.

James wants his readers to know that what you don't know *can* hurt you! Some members of the early church judged one another, assuming they knew the motives of others. Some were making grand plans for a future they could not predict. Still others assumed they knew God's will when, in fact, they had no clue. We will learn that the worst ignorance is a lack of knowing ourselves—thinking we're something we are not. This week discover that "What you don't know really *can* hurt you."

DAY 1
You Don't Know Another's Heart

DAY 2
You Don't Know What's Good for You

DAY 3
You Don't Know God's Will

DAY 4
You Don't Know Yourself

DAY 5
You Do Know Right from Wrong

YOU DON'T KNOW ANOTHER'S HEART

preparation

Father, I am glad that You alone can judge because You alone are just. Thank You for combining mercy with judgment. Help me to extend mercy instead of judging others. Amen.

JUSTICE
The humble He guides in justice, and the humble He teaches His way. Psalm 25:9

explanation

1

EVIL SPEAKING
Speaking evil means to slander another person. This sin of the tongue includes thoughtless, critical, derogatory, or untrue speech against others. "Let your speech always be with grace, seasoned with salt, that you may know how you ought to answer each one" (Colossians 4:6).

exploration

In last week's lesson, we learned how to make peace with God by humbling ourselves and repenting of sin. As James continues his faithful teaching on Living Faith, he focuses on some things we really need to know about how we speak and think of our brothers and sisters in Christ.

Read James 4, then focus on verses 11-12.

> *Do not speak evil of one another, brethren. He who speaks evil of a brother and judges his brother, speaks evil of the law and judges the law. But if you judge the law, you are not a doer of the law but a judge.*
> James 4:11

1. What did James warn the brethren against? . . . .

. . . .

2. Explain what is at the root of badmouthing fellow Christians.

. . . .

. . . .

3. One who speaks evil of and judges a believer also speaks against what?

. . . .

. . . .

4. Read Matthew 22:36-39. According to this passage, what two commands reveal the heart of God's law?

. . . .

. . . .

5. What indictment did James make against those who judge the law?

. . . .

> *There is one Lawgiver, who is able to save and to destroy. Who are you to judge another?* James 4:12

6. Who is the only One who has the right to judge? . . . .

. . . .

7. What power does the Lawgiver wield?. . . . .

. . . .

8. Write your answer to James's ironic concluding question.

. . . .

transformation

9. James warned us against speaking evil of others. Ephesians 4:31-32 describes the various forms of evil speaking and then gives a remedy. Record something you've said that reflects each form of evil speech.

Bitterness: (Example: She's such a backstabber; I'm glad she finally got what she deserved.). . . . .

. . . .

Anger:. . . . .

Harsh Words:. . . . .

Slander: . . . .

Malice:. . . . .

2

JUDGE
The word *judge* does not refer to evaluation but to condemnation. Thus, when we judge others, we are really saying they deserve to be condemned. Jesus said that judging others has consequences: "With what judgment you judge, you will be judged" (Matthew 7:2).

6

LAWGIVER
John said the Law was given through Moses, but Moses merely transcribed God's words. "For the Lord is our Judge, the Lord is our Lawgiver" (Isaiah 33:22). To criticize the Law is to usurp God's authority, presuming to enact a better law.

9

SLANDER
Slander means "to make false charges; to misrepresent in order to damage another's reputation." Slander is like dirt thrown against a clean wall: it may not stick, but it will leave a mark. Once you have dirtied someone else's reputation, it takes God's love to clean it up.

EDIFICATION

Edification means "to build up"; therefore a building is called an edifice. Strengthening believers in the faith is appropriately expressed edification. Christians are built up by good speech. "Encourage each other and build each other up, just as you are already doing" (1 Thessalonians 5:11, NLT).

LAW REJECTED

God's laws make humans aware of their sinfulness: "Through the law we become conscious of sin" (Romans 3:20, NIV). Without speed limits it would not be wrong to drive 150 mph. The law is the great equalizer— we're all guilty. "All have sinned; all fall short of God's glorious standard" (Romans 3:23, NLT).

Journal a prayer asking God to replace your evil speech with a tender heart by rewriting the following verse: "Be kind to each other, tenderhearted, forgiving one another, just as God through Christ has forgiven you" (Ephesians 4:32, NLT).

. . . .

. . . .

. . . .

10. Instead of evil speech, Paul exhorts, "Let no corrupt word proceed out of your mouth, but what is good for necessary edification" (Ephesians 4:29). Transform your five hurtful statements in question 9 into words of edification by using the word *EDIFY* as an acrostic.

E (Example: Even though she did wrong, I pray God will forgive her and make things right.) . . . .

. . . .

D . . . .

I . . . .

F . . . .

Y . . . .

11. Today we learned that God is the ultimate lawgiver. Fill in the following chart to discover some of the reasons God has given us His laws.

SCRIPTURE   REASON FOR LAW

Rom. 7:7 . . . .

Gal. 3:24 . . . .

Gal. 5:14 . . . .

1 Tim. 1:8-9 . . . .

Heb. 9:28–10:1 . . . .

My mother always said, "If you can't say something nice, don't say anything at all." It takes just one rumor to devastate someone's life. In high school a dirty secret spread throughout my school: "Rachel Rodriquez was raped." No one could verify it, but nobody denied it either. That summer Rachel went from all-American girl to pot-smoking hippie chick. She was so humiliated by the gossip mill that she just checked out. I wish my classmates could have attended the following summer camp.

At this church camp, an ugly rumor about two counselors quickly became the talk of the camp. At morning prayer the youth leader retold the story of how Jesus refused to condemn the woman caught in adultery, saying, "If any one of you is without sin, let him be the first to throw a stone at her" (John 8:7, NIV). So one by one the accusers walked away. Then the leader passed around a bucket of stones, insisting each person carry one in his or her pocket until camp ended. Any time the campers felt like criticizing someone else, talking behind another's back, or passing on an ugly rumor, they were told, "Reach into your pocket, touch the stone, and ask yourselves if you are without sin."

It's so easy to judge others, but only God knows a person's heart. Let's try an experiment. Find a small stone to carry in your pocket or purse as a reminder that we are not to judge others, and pray, "Lord, keep me from casting stones."

2 YOU DON'T KNOW WHAT'S GOOD FOR YOU

Left to our own devices, most of us would be living in a world of hurt. What seems good to us now isn't necessarily good later. The all-you-can-eat buffet on Sunday means an extra two pounds on Monday. Smoking cigarettes may make you look cool now, but you'll look pitiful later pulling an oxygen tank behind you. Short-term gratifications rarely have long-term benefits. That's why for generations parents have been warning their children, "You don't know what's good for you!"

For instance, my son Nathan doesn't understand that a penny saved is a penny earned. Each Friday as we hand him his allowance, it begins burning a hole in his pocket. On the way home from the bank, if we stop at the gas station, he'll go in and squander his money on junk food. Inevitably, Saturday morning as we're shopping in Target, he doesn't have enough money to buy the latest music CD. As he gazes longingly at the display case, the words I said Friday echo in his ears: "You just don't know what's good for you!"

God's children can be clueless, too. They often think they are in control of their futures. Sometimes they squander the resources God has given them on the stock market, the lottery, or shady business deals. James reminds us that when we make our plans without asking God about His plans, we will inevitably come up short. While we may not know what's good for us, our heavenly Father really does know best.

exploration

We have found that we must not slander or judge others because we don't know their hearts. Now we learn that sometimes we make plans without knowing what God has in store for us.

Review James 4, then focus on verses 13-14.

> *Come now, you who say, "Today or tomorrow we will go to such and such a city, spend a year there, buy and sell, and make a profit, . . . "* James 4:13

1. What two words did James use to get their attention?

   . . . .

2. Who was James addressing here?. . . . .

   . . . .

3. The business people James addressed made five presumptions that excluded God. What five plans did they make for themselves apart from God?

   Time:. . . . .

   Location:. . . . .

   Duration of business:. . . . .

   Purpose of travel/enterprise: . . . .

   Objective or goal: . . . .

> *. . . whereas you do not know what will happen tomorrow. For what is your life? It is even a vapor that appears for a little time and then vanishes away.* James 4:14

4. In making their plans, what could they not know? . . . .

   . . . .

5. What rhetorical question did James ask here? . . . .

   . . . .

6. Restate in your own words the answer James gave about the brevity of life.

   . . . .

   . . . .

explanation

2

GODLESS PLANS
In business and life, it is wise to plan and have a strategy for future goals. Planning is not sinful. The problem occurs when God is left out and His will is not considered. When God is not part of the agenda, planning is foolish and sinful.

3

PRESUMPTUOUS
To *be presumptuous* is to overstep your bounds or take liber-ties; to expect or assume an outcome. The psalmist prayed, "Keep back Your servant also from presumptuous sins; let them not have dominion over me. Then I . . . shall be innocent of great transgression" (Psalm 19:13).

6

UNPREDICTABLE
When James describes life as unpredictable and a vapor, he reveals two reasons why it's foolish to plan without God: 1) ignorance of the future and 2) the brevity of life. "An entire lifetime is just a moment to You [God]; human existence is but a breath" (Psalm 39:5, NLT).

transformation

SUCCESS
Failing to consult God ultimately leads to failure. Humbly submitting your plans to God will lead to success, if not here, then in the hereafter. "Commit your work to the Lord, and then your plans will succeed" (Proverbs 16:3, NLT). Include God in all your plans.

SEEK GOD FIRST
It has been said, "Keep the main thing, the main thing." To believe in God, yet not consult Him, reveals that He is not *your* main thing. Instead, "Seek first the kingdom of God and His righteousness, and all these things shall be added to you" (Matthew 6:33).

GOD'S PLANS
It is utter folly to make your own plans apart from God because ultimately He will supersede them. God is the sovereign ruler of the universe and the master of your fate. "In his heart a man plans his course, but the Lord determines his steps" (Proverbs 16:9, NIV).

7. Jesus told a parable about a man who sinned presumptuously. Read Luke 12:16-21, then answer the following questions:

   a. Explain how this man had prospered (v. 16). . . . .

   . . . .

   b. Describe what he planned to do with his profits (vv. 17-19).

   . . . .

   . . . .

   c. What was really in his future (v. 20)? . . . .

   . . . .

   d. What is the main message of this parable (v. 21)?

   . . . .

   . . . .

8. Examine your own life. Do you have your own agenda? Do you pray before you make decisions, or do you assume that it is your choice? When making business decisions, does the goal of making a profit take precedence over pleasing God?

   Journal about the areas in your life where you do not consult God. Then journal a prayer asking Him for His advice.

   . . . .

   . . . .

   . . . .

   . . . .

   . . . .

9. As Christians, we have the privilege of making our plans according to God's will and for His glory. God gives us the resources that we need in order to please Him. Fill in the chart to discover what benefits there are in consulting God.

Ps. 37:3-6 . . . .

Prov. 3:5-6 . . . .

Jer. 29:11-13 . . . .

Rom. 8:28 . . . .

Isn't it amazing the time and money people spend on plans that may never come true? I've always loved thinking about future space flight. My favorite childhood cartoon was *The Jetsons,* about a family that traveled by spacecraft, had robots clean their home, and with the push of a button received piping hot meals. I thought that living on the moon or even Mars would be possible in my lifetime.

I found out that I wasn't alone. There was a planetarium that needed money so its director dreamed up a gimmick that preyed upon future-oriented, hopeful yet gullible people like me. He printed brochures that offered one-thousand-acre lots on the planet Mars for only twenty dollars. "This land still features pink skies, unlimited rock gardens, and not one but two moons. So peaceful, quiet, and romantic—even the natives are friendly," the literature promised. "At one-sixth the gravity of Earth, your golf game will improve immensely—drives will be six times longer. Mars will provide a world of adventure for the entire family." The gag was surprisingly successful. People across the country sent in their money for a deed.

James reminds us that making life plans without praying and seeking God is just as foolish as buying land on Mars. I may not know what the future holds, but I know Who holds my future. Because God holds eternity in His hands, isn't it a good idea to trust Him with all your tomorrows?

contemplation

The future has a habit of suddenly and dramatically becoming the present.
Roger Ward Babson

YOU DON'T KNOW GOD'S WILL

GOD'S PLANS
The counsel of the Lord stands forever, the plans of His heart to all generations. Psalm 33:11

The million-dollar question is, "What is God's will for my life?" If I possessed a miraculous way of discerning God's exact plans for individuals on a personal basis, I'd put every psychic on this planet out of business. There is a market out there for inquiring minds who desperately need to know, "What is God's will?"

My friend Kent Bagdasar is a public relations and marketing genius whose career has tapped into the pulse of what Americans want. Several years ago Kent, then on a church staff, was asked to fill in for their pastor who had a thriving tape ministry. Kent was concerned that tape sales would plummet once people saw his name on the package instead of the beloved pastor's name. So when the secretary asked for the title of his message he said, "'Knowing God's Will,'" insisting, "I'd spend two dollars to find out what God's will is, wouldn't you?" But when it came to preparing his message, Kent realized that discovering God's will is much more complicated than buying a two-dollar tape. He decided to teach on something else, but unfortunately the labels had already been printed. The tape became a best-seller at the time, even though it did not reveal how to know God's will.

James realized the necessity of not only discovering the will of God but also obeying it. He assumes that God's will is not that difficult to discern. Today we will gain insight into what Scripture has to say about knowing the will of God.

exploration

We have found that it is unwise to make plans without asking God to reveal His plan to us. Now we discover the blessings of acknowledging God and obeying His will.

Review James 4, then focus on verse 15.

Instead you ought to say, "If the Lord wills, we shall live and do this or that." James 4:15

1. What did James encourage believers to say when making plans?

. . . .

2. How does this differ from what they said before (see James 4:13)?

. . . .

3. What do you think the word "if" implies here? . . . .

. . . .

4. What things were included in God's will? . . . .

. . . .

5. What do you think is meant by "this or that"? . . . .

. . . .

6. Read Colossians 1:9-12 to discover more about God's will.

   a. What was Paul's prayer for the Colossians (v. 9)?

. . . .

. . . .

   b. List four ways you can fulfill God's will (v. 10).

. . . .

. . . .

   c. Describe the results of walking in God's will (v. 11).

. . . .

. . . .

   d. How should you respond (v. 12)? . . . .

. . . .

explanation

1
GOD'S WILL
God's will is found in God's Word. Understanding God's *general will* leads to knowing His *specific will*. For instance, Scripture teaches that God hates divorce. Unless your spouse is unfaithful, it's not God's will for you to separate. "Do not be unwise, but understand what the will of the Lord is" (Ephesians 5:17).

4
DO HIS WILL
It's one thing to know God's will and another thing to do it. "Do the will of God with all your heart" (Ephesians 6:6, NLT). And we should do *good*! "It is God's will that by doing good you should silence . . . foolish men." (1 Peter 2:15, NIV).

6
IN HIS WILL?
What is the proof of knowing God's will? Ceasing to copy the world and starting to imitate God. "Do not be conformed to this world, but be transformed by the renewing of your mind, that you may prove what is that . . . perfect will of God" (Romans 12:2).

WILLFUL?

God promises eternal life to those who do His will and loss for those who don't. "This world is fading away. . . . But if you do the will of God, you will live forever" (1 John 2:17, NLT). Your will determines how He will respond to you!

IN HIS WILL?

When Christians conform to the will of God, they reveal that they are part of His family. Jesus taught, "Anyone who does God's will is my brother and sister and mother" (Mark 3:35, NLT). Obedience strengthens relationship. The more we do the will of God, the more we resemble Him.

WILLING?

Some don't do God's will because they don't know what it is. Others don't obey because they're not willing. If you are unwilling to obey, ask God to help make you willing. "It is God who works in you both to will and to do for His good pleasure" (Philippians 2:13).

7. Today we learned that God's will is discovered in God's Word. Fill in the chart to discover some aspects of God's will for you.

SCRIPTURE   GOD'S WILL

John 7:17. . . . .

Rom. 12:2 . . . .

Eph. 6:6-8 . . . .

Heb. 10:6-7 . . . .

8. We have a choice: To accept or reject God's will as revealed in His Word. Luke 7:30 reveals that the "Pharisees and lawyers rejected the will of God for themselves, not having been baptized by him." With this in mind, check off the ways you are not living up to God's known will in these areas.

— Receive salvation   — Be thankful in all things
— Be separate from the world   — Be a worshipper of God
— Be baptized   — Stay sexually pure
— Do good works   — Develop a transformed mind
— Pray according to His will   — Tithe

9. The writer of Hebrews says that not only does God want you *to know* His will, but He also completely equips you *to do* His will.

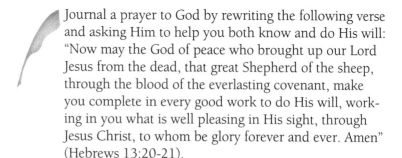

Journal a prayer to God by rewriting the following verse and asking Him to help you both know and do His will: "Now may the God of peace who brought up our Lord Jesus from the dead, that great Shepherd of the sheep, through the blood of the everlasting covenant, make you complete in every good work to do His will, working in you what is well pleasing in His sight, through Jesus Christ, to whom be glory forever and ever. Amen" (Hebrews 13:20-21).

. . . .

. . . .

. . . .

. . . .

. . . .

A girlfriend once confided in me (Penny), "I'm scared to pray 'Thy will be done' because I am afraid God will want me to go to Africa. Or maybe my husband or daughter will get cancer!" I hugged her and said, "Imagine your daughter telling you, 'I want to do whatever you want today, Mommy.' You wouldn't think, *Now's my chance to make her do all the chores I hate to do. I'll make things hard for her and won't allow her to play!*" "Of course not," said the lady. "I'd try to give her the best day ever." "So why would you think that God is less loving than you?" I asked.

I reminded her of a time when Jesus corrected his disciples' wrong thinking about their heavenly Father. In the book of Matthew, we read, "What man is there among you who, if his son asks for bread, will give him a stone? Or if he asks for a fish, will he give him a serpent? If you then, being evil, know how to give good gifts to your children, how much more will your Father who is in heaven give good things to those who ask Him!" (Matthew 7:9-11).

Although we may not always know God's specific will, we can always know His heart. "'For I know the plans I have for you,' says the Lord. 'They are plans for good and not for disaster, to give you a future and a hope'" (Jeremiah 29:11, NLT).

contemplation

I find the doing of the will of God leaves me no time for disputing about His plans.
George MacDonald

DAY 4 — YOU DON'T KNOW YOURSELF

preparation

Lord, give me wisdom and insight into the areas of my heart that do not please You. Help me to be humble and not proud. If I boast, let it be in You and Your goodness. Amen.

GODLY WISDOM
For the Lord gives wisdom; from His mouth come knowledge and understanding; He stores up sound wisdom for the upright; He is a shield to those who walk uprightly. Proverbs 2:6-7

"I am the master of my fate: I am the captain of my soul." These chilling words were quoted as part of Timothy McVeigh's last statement before dying by lethal injection June 11, 2001. McVeigh was executed for the 1995 Oklahoma City bombing that killed 168 people and injured more than five hundred. It was one of the largest terrorist acts ever committed on U.S. soil.

McVeigh's biographer said, "If you didn't know his history and you began chatting with him, . . . you'd find him a very affable, knowledgeable young man." Yet his downfall appeared to be his arrogance. McVeigh not only confessed to the crime, but he also took pride in being responsible for the bombing. He put himself in the position of judge, jury, and executioner for the alleged crimes of the U.S. government. Convincing himself that he was on a soldier's mission, Timothy described the civilian deaths as "collateral damage."

A self-described agnostic, he appeared to be unrepentant to the end. Paul Howell, who lost his daughter, Karan Howell Shepherd, in the vicious attack said, "I was hoping . . . we could see some kind of, maybe, 'I'm sorry,' something like that," Howell recalled. "We didn't get anything from his face."

Timothy McVeigh's boastful and arrogant attitude led him to commit acts of incredible evil. Today we discover that those who arrogantly follow their own self-serving agenda are, in fact, rejecting God's authority. Because they don't know God, they don't really know themselves either.

exploration

James has taught us that seeking God's will is wise. Now we discover that it is not God's will for us to be boastful or arrogant.

Review James 4, then focus on verse 16.

> **But now you boast in your arrogance. All such boasting is evil.** James 4:16

1. What type of speech did James consider here?. . . . .

   . . . .

2. What underlying attitude did this speech reveal?. . . . .

   . . . .

3. How did James classify boasting?. . . . .

   . . . .

4. Why do you think arrogant boasting is evil? . . . .

   . . . .

5. Fill in the following chart to discover more about evil boasting.

   SCRIPTURE   EVIL BOASTING
   _____

   Ps. 5:5-6 . . . .

   Ps. 49:5-6 . . . .

   Ps. 94:4 . . . .

   Ps. 97:7 . . . .

6. While boasting in our pride and arrogance is evil, the apostle Paul speaks of proper boasting. Fill in the chart to learn more.

   SCRIPTURE   PROPER BOASTING
   _____

   2 Cor. 1:12 . . . .

   2 Cor. 7:4 . . . .

   2 Cor. 10:13 . . . .

   2 Cor. 11:30 . . . .

explanation

1

BOASTING
Boasting can mean to speak loudly in valid rejoicing or in parading one's own accomplishments. Boasting in this text refers to pretentious or presumptuous bragging. Solomon warned, "Do not boast about tomorrow, for you do not know what a day may bring forth" (Proverbs 27:1).

2

ARROGANCE
Arrogance is a feeling of superiority shown in presumptuous claims. Hannah proclaimed, "Talk no more so very proudly; let no arrogance come from your mouth, for the Lord is the God of knowledge; and by Him actions are weighed" (1 Samuel 2:3).

6

OUR BOAST
Not all boasting is wrong. Boasting in the Lord is very right. "My soul shall make its boast in the Lord; the humble shall hear of it and be glad. Oh, magnify the Lord with me, and let us exalt His name together" (Psalm 34:2-3).

transformation

7.
GIVING CREDIT
How does it feel when someone takes credit for something you did? Give credit where credit is due. "But now, O Lord, You are our Father; we are the clay, and You our potter; and all we are the work of Your hand" (Isaiah 64:8).

8.
HAUGHTY
Murder? Sin! Stealing? Sin! Lookin' cool? Sin! Did you realize that a haughty look, "looking cool" in modern vernacular, is a sin? The next time teenagers try to strut their stuff remind them, "A haughty look, a proud heart, and the plowing of the wicked are sin" (Proverbs 21:4).

9.
BOAST NOT
The mark of a true believer is to hate what God hates. Since God hates boasting, you should too. If you hate it, you won't do it. "All who fear the Lord will hate evil. That is why I hate pride, arrogance, corruption, and perverted speech" (Proverbs 8:13, NLT).

7. Arrogant boasting takes personal credit for what God has done. The prophet Isaiah revealed the absurdity of this by using the imagery of the potter and the clay. Read Isaiah 29:16.

> With this verse in mind, journal about a time when you, the clay, took credit when it should have been given to God, the potter.

. . . .

. . . .

. . . .

. . . .

8. List the seven things from Proverbs 6:16 that the Lord hates. What tops His list?

1). . . . .

2). . . . .

3). . . . .

4). . . . .

5). . . . .

6). . . . .

7). . . . .

9. Rather than being boastful, believers are to be humble. Place an (**H**) beside the humble attributes and a (**B**) beside the boastful attitudes.

—— Admits when wrong

—— Says "I'm sorry"

—— Name drops

—— Serves others without recognition

—— Proclaims his or her good deeds loudly

—— Dominates conversations

— Looks down on others

— Gives God the glory

— Always seeks the limelight

— Thinks he or she is always right

— Elevates others

— Team player

Journal about which of the humble attributes you will develop in your life.

. . . .

. . . .

. . . .

. . . .

Mongolian folklore recounts this little tale of a boastful frog. Two geese were headed south on their annual autumn migration when they were entreated by a frog to take him along. The geese were willing to carry him if a means of transportation could be devised. The quick-witted frog produced a long stalk of grass and told the two geese to hold one end while he clung to the middle with his mouth. The three friends were soaring along enjoying their journey when some men noticed them from below.

The men shouted their admiration for the device and called out, "Who was clever enough to figure that out?" When the vainglorious frog opened his mouth to say, "It was I!" he lost his hold, fell to the earth, and was dashed to pieces.

Uncle! I don't know about you, but we're feeling a bit bruised by all this ego bashing. Time and again, James has reminded us: Humility—Good! Pride—Bad! But James is not the only harbinger of this message. The entire Bible is rife with Scriptures that warn against pride and promote humility. Moses taught it, the Old Testament prophets proclaimed it, the psalmists sang it, Jesus exemplified it, and the apostles preached it. If by now you haven't humbled yourself before God, you must have a will of iron. Isn't it time to give your pride the final deathblow and humbly say "Uncle!" to the Lord?

contemplation

Arrogance has its own built-in misery. The arrogant person may offend others, but he hurts himself more.
Billy Graham

5 YOU *DO* KNOW RIGHT FROM WRONG

In the middle of a recurring nightmare, I (Penny) awoke in a cold sweat. The apocalypse had come. The world was in utter chaos—fires raging, sirens screaming, people running around in panic. Suddenly a bright light shone from heaven. The arms of God reached out to rescue His children. Looking up I watched my family rising to meet Him in the clouds. I was left behind.

I was raised in the buckle of the "Bible belt"—the southern part of America where conservative Christianity is part of the culture. I attended church every Sunday and asked Jesus into my heart in the fourth grade. I was a good Christian girl until high school. I turned from reading the Bible to reading trashy novels; from partaking of the Living Water to drinking beer; from fellowship with believers to party hopping. Knowing better, I had the same bad dream night after night.

This week's lesson has revealed three kinds of people: 1) Those who presumptuously ignore God's will, living as if God and his will do not exist; 2) Those who acknowledge that God exists but arrogantly reject God's will in favor of their own goals; 3) Those who believe God exists, acknowledge that His will is best, then proceed to disobey it. Today we discover that the third type of person is the worst of all. Doing what's wrong when you know what is right reveals that "You *Do* Know Right from Wrong."

exploration

James has exhorted us to not boast about tomorrow. As we come to the end of James 4, he warns us again that a Living Faith is a doing faith.

Review James 4, then focus on verse 17.

Therefore, to him who knows to do good and does not do it, to him it is sin. James 4:17

1. James links what he has said with what he is about to say. What do you think the "therefore" is there for?

   . . . .

2. Did those being addressed know what was good and right? How do you know?

   . . . .

3. How did the people respond to this knowledge? . . . .

   . . . .

4. What did James conclude in verse 17?. . . . .

   . . . .

5. Jesus told the chief priests and elders a parable contrasting what two sons did with what they knew. Read Matthew 21:28-31, then answer the following questions.

   a. Explain what the father asked the first son and the son's response (vv. 28-29).

   . . . .

   b. Explain what the father requested of the second son and his response (vv. 30).

   . . . .

   c. Explain what the religious leaders learned from this parable (v. 31).

   . . . .

6. James said it is sinful to know the truth and not do it. Look up each passage and briefly explain the consequence of willful disobedience.

   Romans 1:21-22:. . . . .

   Hebrews 10:26-27: . . . .

   2 Peter 2:20-21: . . . .

2

KNOWING GOOD
Knowing and doing good should go together in a persistent lifestyle. God "will give eternal life to those who *persist* in doing what is good" (Romans 2:7, NLT, emphasis added). If helping the poor is good today, it will be good tomorrow. Doing good is the gift that keeps on giving.

4

DOING WRONG
Knowing God's will but choosing to disobey expresses the sin of willful pride. It's saying, "I know what You want, God, but you can't make me do it." "The words of his mouth are wickedness and deceit; he has ceased to be wise and to do good" (Psalm 36:3).

JUST DO IT!
God's will is not a "take it or leave it" proposition. We are obligated to just do it! With knowledge comes responsibility. "People who are not aware that they are doing wrong will be punished only lightly. Much is required from those to whom much is given" (Luke 12:48, NLT).

PERSISTENCE
Persist means "to resolutely continue despite opposition." "At Joppa there was a certain disciple named . . . Dorcas. This woman was full of good works and charitable deeds which she did" (Acts 9:36). For Dorcas to be "full of good works," she must have continued them throughout her lifetime.

NO EXCUSE
The Bible clearly shows what we should and should not do, so there's really no excuse for failing to do good. Jesus said, "They would not be guilty if I had not come and spoken to them. But now they have no excuse for their sin" (John 15:22, NLT).

7. Based on James 4:17, what did James imply we should do in order to avoid sin?

. . . .

. . . .

transformation

8. We have found that doing good means persisting in a lifestyle of good deeds.

Journal about something good you have done in the past. How will you continue to repeat it in the future?

. . . .

. . . .

. . . .

. . . .

9. We can usually find excuses for not doing something we know is right. Check the spaces that indicate something you've failed to do, and then write the excuse beside it.

Good Deed   **Bad Excuse**

— Help the oppressed (Isaiah 1:17) . . . .

. . . .

— Pray for enemies (Matthew 5:44) . . . .

. . . .

— Help other believers (Galatians 6:10) . . . .

. . . .

— Be willing to share (1 Timothy 6:18). . . . .

. . . .

— Pursue peace (1 Peter 3:11) . . . .

. . . .

10. An obedient believer both knows and does what God asks. From the following list, circle the ways God has let you know what He wants you to do.

Prayer   Bible reading

Sound biblical teaching   Conversations with believers

Godly counsel   Providential circumstances

Now journal about a time you failed to do what God asked even though you knew better. What was the result?

. . . .

. . . .

. . . .

. . . .

10
DISOBEDIENCE
Disobedient means "to refuse to hear; to be insubordinate." Passively avoiding doing what's right is as disobedient as actively doing something wrong. "They profess to know God, but in works they deny Him, being abominable, disobedient, and disqualified for every good work" (Titus 1:16).

Before sixteen-year-olds can drive, they must get a license, and my son Nathan was no exception. We enrolled him in The McGinnis School of Driving, where he had to fulfill certain requirements before receiving his license: thirty-three hours of classroom instruction, including a written test and eye exam; seven hours driving with a certified instructor; forty-three hours driving with a licensed adult; passing the state driving test. With all of this preparation, Nathan and all drivers should know the rules of the road. But knowing and obeying are two different things. People who detour from the law make excuses like this list, provided by a car insurance company:

"The other car collided with mine without giving warning of its intentions."

"A pedestrian hit me and went under my car."

"Coming home I drove into the wrong house and collided with a tree I don't have."

"I glanced at my mother-in-law and headed over the embankment."

"The pedestrian had no idea which direction to run, so I ran over him."

While these excuses are humorous, they show how prone we are to evade responsibility for our wrong actions. James tells us that, like errant drivers, Christians who do not obey the Bible are full of excuses. But there is really no good excuse for doing something wrong when you know what is right.

contemplation

Our human nature is pulled in two directions with more or less equal force. Whether it is for evil or for good, our actions are made with our consent.
Pseudo-Macarius

While You Wait

In 1942 during World War II, General Douglas MacArthur was ordered to leave the Philippines prior to the takeover by the invading Japanese army. Before General MacArthur left the islands, he spoke the famous words, "I will return." Two years later, as supreme commander of the Southwest Pacific for the Allies, he stood again on the Philippine Islands and said, "This is the voice of freedom. People of the Philippines, I have returned."

As we have learned throughout the book of James, Christians live in a state of emotional, physical, and spiritual warfare. What, then, is our hope amidst the suffering, persecution, trials, and tribulations of life? Our hope is this: *The* Supreme Commander, Jesus Christ, will return to establish His perfect kingdom. Biblical prophecy confirms this steadfast hope in Christ's return. Both the Old and New Testaments overflow with references to the second coming of Christ. It has been estimated that in the Old Testament there are nearly two thousand references to Christ's second coming. In the New Testament there are over three hundred references to the second advent of Christ—one out of thirty verses.

General MacArthur was a trustworthy man who kept his promise to return. How much more is Jesus Christ, the perfect God-man, able to keep His promise to return and put an end to the wars that rage within and without? This week James gives us insight into what you should do "While You Wait" for His return.

DAY 1 I WILL RETURN

preparation

Father, the more I experience the sorrow in the world, the more I long for Your return. Please give me patience to live faithfully and confidence to wait expectantly until You come. Amen.

PATIENT
The end of a thing is better than its beginning; the patient in spirit is better than the proud in spirit. Ecclesiastes 7:8

explanation

1

PATIENCE
Patience is the ability to endure pain and hardship without complaint; the ability to persevere without losing heart. James used patience as bookends to his letter. He began by encouraging the persecuted believers to be patient in trials. Now he encourages them to wait patiently for the Lord's return.

exploration

In Lesson 2 we studied the first part of James 5, which spoke against the corruption of the wicked rich, and how much better it is to trust God than gold. As we move forward in chapter 5, James continues his no-nonsense teaching to believers in the early church. Remember that they were suffering persecution for their faith and had been scattered to different places throughout the Roman world. James reminds them, and us, to trust in God's promise that Christ will come again. Until then, we must be patient.

Read James 5, then focus on verse 7.

> ***Therefore be patient, brethren, until the coming of the Lord. See how the farmer waits for the precious fruit of the earth, waiting patiently for it until it receives the early and latter rain.*** James 5:7

1. James was drawing his letter to a close; "therefore," what did he exhort the brethren to be?

. . . .

2. What did James urge them to patiently await? . . . .

. . . .

3. Like Jesus, James often used natural illustrations to make spiritual applications. Who did James use as an example of patience?

. . . .

4. For what does the farmer wait? . . . .

. . . .

5. What must the fruit of the earth receive in order to grow properly?

. . . .

6. James's readers would have been familiar with farming illustrations. Read Deuteronomy 11:10-14 and answer the following questions about the climate and weather in Israel.

a. How were the crops in Egypt watered (v. 10)?. . . . .

. . . .

b. Explain how the crops in the Promised Land were watered and why (vv. 11-12).

. . . .

. . . .

c. What spiritual conditions did the Lord set for cultivating a fruitful harvest (v. 13)?

. . . .

. . . .

d. What physical blessings did God provide (v. 14)?

. . . .

. . . .

7. Read Hosea 6:3. How did Hosea symbolically connect the coming of the Lord with the rains?

. . . .

. . . .

transformation

8. *Patience* is the ability to endure pain, difficulties, and hardship without complaining or losing heart.

2

HIS COMING
"The coming of the Lord" speaks of Christ's future return to the earth. This next historical event on God's calendar is the climax of His plan to redeem humanity. "They will see the Son of Man coming on the clouds of heaven with power and great glory" (Matthew 24:30).

5

HEAVENLY RAIN
Early rains were the first autumn showers and latter rains were the last spring showers. Early rains prepared the soil for seed; latter rains prepared the crops for the harvest. "He will cause the rain to come down for you; the former rain, and the latter rain" (Joel 2:23).

8

NO COMPLAINT
No matter what situation God places you in, one thing you must never do is complain. "Do everything without complaining or arguing, so that you may become blameless and pure, children of God" (Philippians 2:14-15, NIV). Complaining Christians are a bad witness.

9

CAN'T WAIT
In today's world of instant gratification, patience is not always seen as a virtue. But there are some things worth waiting for: dessert after a meal, sex in marriage, God's perfect timing. The one thing most worth waiting for is Jesus Christ's return. Can't wait!

10

PROMISED RAIN
The Old Testament speaks often of the Messiah coming to rule and reign on the earth. Solomon said of the Lord's coming: "He shall come down like rain upon the grass before mowing, like showers that water the earth. In His days the righteous shall flourish" (Psalm 72:6-7).

Journal about three situations that have tried your patience and indicate whether or not you complained or lost heart.

SITUATION	COMPLAINED?	LOST HEART?
Painful:	__ yes __ no	__ yes __ no
. . . .		
. . . .		
Difficult:	__ yes __ no	__ yes __ no
. . . .		
. . . .		
Hardship:	__ yes __ no	__ yes __ no
. . . .		
. . . .		

9. James exhorted us to be like spiritual farmers who patiently wait for a fruitful harvest. In the columns list something you have waited for, how long you waited, and whether the wait was worth it.

WAITED FOR	HOW LONG?	WORTH IT?
. . . .		
. . . .		
. . . .		
. . . .		
. . . .		

10. Today we learned that the early and latter rain could refer to the two advents of Jesus Christ.

Journal about how you have responded to Christ's first coming. How does that make you feel about His second coming?

. . . .

. . . .

. . . .

. . . .

An atheist farmer ridiculed people who believed in God. He wrote this letter to the local newspaper: "I plowed on Sunday, planted on Sunday, cultivated on Sunday, hauled in my crops on Sunday; but I never went to church on Sunday. Yet I harvested more bushels than any of those God-fearing Christians." The editor printed the letter and then added this remark: "God doesn't always settle His accounts in October."

The psalmist has a name for someone who lives as though God doesn't exist—fool! "Only fools say in their hearts, 'There is no God'" (Psalm 14:1, NLT). Foolish suppositions lead to foolish lifestyles. The foolish farmer did not believe that God existed; hence there would not be any consequences for ignoring Him. But the wise editor knew that the story isn't over until Jesus returns. At that time many people will be surprised by what happens.

In Matthew 24 Jesus revealed that when he comes, it will be "as the days of Noah" (v. 37). People will be going about their normal business, eating meals and getting married. But when He comes, "two men will be in the field: one will be taken and the other left" (v. 40). While no one knows the day or time of Christ's return, the truly wise will go about their business with an attitude of patient expectancy, waiting for their Savior to take them to their heavenly home.

DAY 2 — YOU'D BETTER WATCH OUT

ESTABLISHED
May the God of all
grace, who called us
to His eternal glory by
Christ Jesus, after you
have suffered a while,
perfect, establish,
strengthen, and settle
you. 1 Peter 5:10

The word *Christmas* fills my heart with anticipation that something special is about to happen. As a child, after Thanksgiving I'd count the days, hours, minutes until Christmas. Every store window, twinkling light, and song on the radio reminded me that "Santa Claus is coming to town." The song said, "You'd better watch out," so I knew I should be on my best behavior. I can still remember hanging my stocking on the mantle with care, "in hopes that St. Nicolas soon would be there." I could hardly sleep and would wake long before everyone else.

Now as a mother, I'm still the first one up. I turn on Christmas carols really loud, so Skip and Nathan will get up. Nathan walks down the stairs saying, "Mom, it's Christmas!"

The tragedy of Christmas is that some people teach their children to anticipate the return of the jolly man in the red suit, not the babe in the manger. We ascribe to Santa the attributes of Christ: he sees all, knows all, keeps track of bad and good, and rewards accordingly. If children can exude such enthusiasm over the return of a mythical character, shouldn't Christians be ecstatic over the reality of Jesus Christ's return? Perhaps we could use some childlike faith. Jesus said, "Unless you . . . become as little children, you will by no means enter the kingdom of heaven" (Matthew 18:3). We mature Christians could use a dose of wonder, excitement and anticipation as we await the Lord's coming.

exploration

We have learned that as believers we must patiently wait for Jesus to return. Now we explore another attribute we should adopt as we wait.

Review James 5, then focus on verse 8.

You also be patient. Establish your hearts, for the coming of the Lord is at hand. James 5:8

1. In addition to being patient, what else did James encourage the believers to do?

   . . . .

2. Psalm 27:14 says "Wait on the Lord; be of good courage, and He shall strengthen your heart." From this, explain how you can cultivate a strong heart and how God promises to help.

   . . . .

   . . . .

3. Why should we establish our hearts, according to James?

   . . . .

   . . . .

4. What phrase leads you to believe that Christ could return at any moment?

   . . . .

5. Since Christ's death, believers have gained strength in the imminence, or nearness, of His return. Fill in the table with phrases that describe Christ's imminent return and how we should live in light of His return.

SCRIPTURE	CHRIST'S RETURN	HOW TO LIVE
Rom. 13:12		
Heb. 10:25		
1 Pet. 4:7		
Rev. 22:7		

---

explanation

1

ESTABLISH
Establish means "to strengthen, cause to stand, prop up." James urged those ready to collapse under trials and persecution to be bolstered by the hope of Christ's return. "Now to Him who is able to establish you according to my gospel and the preaching of Jesus Christ" (Romans 16:25).

3

COMING
Coming carries the dual idea of arrival and presence. "The coming of the Lord" means Christ will arrive and bless us with His presence. "For what is our hope? . . . Is it not even you in the presence of our Lord Jesus Christ at His coming?" (1 Thessalonians 2:19).

5

WHILE WAITING
Patience is not just passive; it is also active. While you wait for the Lord's return, don't just twiddle your thumbs, but get busy doing those things that will establish your heart. "Do not become sluggish, but imitate those who through faith and patience inherit the promises" (Hebrews 6:12).

6. According to 2 Peter 3:9, why is Christ patiently waiting to return?

. . . .

7. Today James exhorts us to establish our hearts. The psalmist said trust strengthens hearts while fear weakens them: "His heart is steadfast, trusting in the Lord. His heart is established; he will not be afraid" (Psalm 112:7-8). Using the words *FEARS* and *TRUST* as acrostics, list the things you fear, then explain how to trust God instead.

F . . . . T . . . .

E . . . . R . . . .

A . . . . U . . . .

R . . . . S . . . .

S . . . . T . . . .

8. The coming of the Lord offers the promise of His physical presence. Until then Jesus has left us with the promise of His spiritual presence: "Be sure of this: I am with you always, even to the end of the age" (Matthew 28:20, NLT).

Journal about a time you felt very alone. How would someone's company have brought you comfort at that time?

. . . .

. . . .

. . . .

Now imagine Jesus being with you during that time of need. How does that make you feel? Journal a prayer thanking God for being "a very present help in trouble" (Psalm 46:1).

. . . .

. . . .

9. We've gained valuable insight into *how* to live while we wait. Review the chart in question 5 concerning "How to Live."

Which of these areas needs to be strengthened or established in your life? What will you do to grow stronger in this area?

. . . .

. . . .

. . . .

. . . .

9
AT HAND
At hand means "approaching imminently, drawing near, or coming soon." Believers in every age should live with the hope that Jesus could come at any moment, in the twinkling of an eye. " 'Surely I am coming quickly.' Amen. Even so, come, Lord Jesus!" (Revelation 22:20).

For nearly two centuries the poem *'Twas The Night Before Christmas* has told of the wondrous visit of Saint Nick. For nearly two millennia, the church has been waiting for the second coming of Jesus Christ. Here's what that night might look like:

'Twas the night before Jesus came and all through the house
    Not a creature was praying, not even this louse.
    Our Bibles were laying on the shelf without care
    In hopes that Christ Jesus would not come there.
The children were dressing to crawl into bed,
    Not once ever kneeling or bowing a head.
    And Mom in her rocker with babe on her lap
    Was watching the *Late Show* while I took a nap.
When out of the east there arose such a clatter,
    I sprang to my feet to see what was the matter.
    Away to the window I flew like a flash
    Tore open the shutters and threw up the sash!
When what to my wondering eyes should appear
    But angels proclaiming that Jesus was here.
    With a light like the sun sending forth a bright ray
    I knew in a moment this must be THE DAY!
I fell to my knees, but it was too late;
    I had waited too long and thus sealed my fate.
    I stood and I cried as saints rose out of sight;
    Oh, if only I had been ready tonight!

(Author unknown)

contemplation

The only way to wait for the Second Coming is to watch that you do what you should do, so that when he comes is a matter of indifference. It is the attitude of a child, certain that God knows what he is about.
Oswald Chambers

DAY 3 WAIT 'TIL YOUR FATHER GETS HOME

I (Penny) grew up with two brothers, so life could be miserable sometimes. They were "snips and snails and puppy dog tails," while I was "sugar and spice and everything nice." Sometimes their adventures got way out of hand, like the time they snuck into my room and stole my Barbies. First they cut off the dolls' hair. Then they dressed them in G.I. Joe combat gear and took them out to the mesa to play war. Finally they buried them where I could never find them. I was sitting in my room crying my eyes out while my brothers taunted me with the information that my Barbies had been taken as prisoners of war. Then Mom walked in. "What's wrong, honey?" "The boys are being mean to me!" I answered with my standard whine. Chris and Pat weren't laughing anymore. They knew they were in *big* trouble. My mom sent them to their rooms and said, "Just wait 'til your father gets home!"

Apparently in James's day, God's children were having some trouble getting along too. We've learned that they were treating some of the rich members with partiality, there were fights occurring among the congregations, and they were talking trash about one another. As he draws his letter to a close, James reminds the brethren that they should be one big happy family. But if they continued to contend with one another, he warned, "Wait until your heavenly Father gets home!"

exploration

Yesterday we discovered that by strengthening our hearts, we gain patience. Today we discover that we must live with contentment rather than contention until Christ comes.

Review James 5, then focus on verse 9.

Do not grumble against one another, brethren, lest you be condemned. Behold, the Judge is standing at the door!
James 5:9

1. What sin of the tongue did James warn the brethren against?

. . . .

2. The King James Version reads slightly differently: "Grudge not one against another." We've learned that the tongue only speaks what is in the heart. Based on this translation, what sin do you think a grumbler harbors in his heart?

. . . .

3. Against whom were the brethren sinning in this manner?

. . . .

4. What is the consequence of the sin of grumbling against one another?

. . . .

5. What title did James give Jesus?. . . . .

. . . .

6. What phrase reminds believers that Christ's return is imminent?

. . . .

7. In His first appearance, Jesus said, "I did not come to judge the world but to save the world" (John 12:47). However, today we discover that when Jesus returns, He will come in judgment. What qualities and characteristics do you think Christ possesses that make Him qualified to judge the world?

. . . .

. . . .

. . . .

explanation

GRUMBLE
Grumble means "to bear a grudge; to mutter or mumble something in a low or hushed tone." It can sound like a growl or a rumble. "Never seek revenge or bear a grudge against anyone, but love your neighbor as yourself. I am the Lord" (Leviticus 19:18, NLT).

CONDEMNED
Condemn means "to declare to be wrong; to pronounce judgment; or to convict." James warns believers that if they hold grudges against others, they themselves will be judged as wrongdoers. "For by your words you will be justified, and by your words you will be condemned" (Matthew 12:37).

JUDGE
A *judge* is one who weighs and pronounces a verdict after questioning and deliberation. He is a public official that gives an authoritative opinion. God has given all authority to the Son: "For the Father judges no one, but has committed all judgment to the Son" (John 5:22).

DISCONTENT

Grumbling is usually a sign of a deeper problem—discontentment with our lot in life. When others receive more attention, possessions, friendships, or honors, we hold it against them or against God, thinking He gives more to others. "Be hospitable to one another without grumbling" (1 Peter 4:9).

JEALOUSY

A jealous person is hostile, suspicious, or envious of one believed to enjoy an advantage. Jealous people constantly compare themselves to others, especially those who seemingly enjoy a privileged life. "Who can survive the destructiveness of jealousy?" (Proverbs 27:4, NLT).

transformation

8. Instead of grumbling we are to love one another. With this in mind, complete the following steps.

> **Step One:** Name someone you've grumbled about or are holding a grudge against:

. . . .

. . . .

> **Step Two:** Trace the cause of your grudge. Journal about how it began. (Example: Perhaps the person has more than you; hasn't paid attention to you.)

. . . .

. . . .

> **Step Three:** Journal a prayer of forgiveness for the person you hold a grudge against. Ask Christ to help you speak words of love rather than complaint.

. . . .

. . . .

9. Murmuring has its roots in jealousy and discontentment. In Matthew 20:1-16 Jesus tells the parable of the workers in the vineyard. Read these verses and answer the following questions:

    a. At what times of day did the landowner hire workers, and what did he promise them (vv. 1-7)?

    . . . .

    b. In what order did the landowner pay the workers, and how much did each receive (vv. 8-10)?

    . . . .

    c. How did the "first" respond to this process (vv. 11-12), and how did the landowner answer (vv. 13-15)?

    . . . .

d. What is the moral to this story (v. 16)?

. . . .

. . . .

10. James reminded us that the Judge is standing at the door.
This imagery almost makes one feel that God is eavesdropping
on our lives.

> Journal about how you might live differently knowing
> that God is listening in on your conversations, the music
> you play, and the shows you watch.

. . . .

. . . .

. . . .

. . . .

10

EAVESDROPPING
When God eavesdrops
at your door, does He
hear grumbling or glori-
fying? "Those who
feared the Lord spoke
with each other, and
the Lord listened to
what they said. In his
presence, a scroll of
remembrance was
written to record the
names of those who
feared him" (Malachi
3:16, NLT).

"You kids be quiet and go to sleep now," Dad called from the
living room where he was watching the news. But my sister
and I just couldn't keep silent. We were telling each other stories
and had gotten ourselves into a laughing jag. The more we tried
to shut up, the more we started to crack up. That's when Dad
snuck down the hall and silently stood outside our room. As
we were quietly whispering, he placed his ear against the door,
eavesdropping on us. After several minutes of whispers and
giggles, he burst into the room with a shout that scared us half
to death! If we had known the judge was standing at the door,
we would have done what he said.

Jesus told John, the revelator, "Behold, I stand at the door"
(Revelation 3:20). Jesus is watching and waiting to return for
His own and to judge the unfaithful. Sometimes we live as though
He is far away and unaware of what we're doing and saying. But
the truth is He is AT THE DOOR! When He bursts through the
clouds like lightning out of the east, will you be caught in the act
or caught-up in the air? Jesus warned that when He returns,
"Two men will be in the field: one will be taken and the other
left. . . . Watch, . . . for you do not know what hour your Lord
is coming" (Matthew 24:40, 42).

contemplation

*Some people are
always grumbling
because roses have
thorns; I am thankful
that thorns have roses.*
Alphonse Karr

DAY 4 — IN THE WAITING ROOM

INSPIRATION

All Scripture is given by inspiration of God, and is profitable for doctrine, for reproof, for correction, for instruction in righteousness, that the [wo]man of God may be complete, thoroughly equipped for every good work. 2 Timothy 3:16-17

I (Penny) sat looking through a magazine, but none of the words made any sense. I restlessly shifted in the uncomfortable chair and looked over at my mother. She was staring into space. Every few minutes I'd look at my watch. *How long have we been sitting in this waiting room?* An hour passed, then two. *The surgery shouldn't take this long, should it?* Finally, I looked down the sterile hallway and saw the doctor walking toward us with his head down. *This can't be good news.* We gathered as he said in a somber voice, "It was malignant. I got as much as I could, but she has a long road ahead of her." I realized then that I would be in the waiting room many more times in the future.

Though my grandmother suffered a great deal in her final days on earth, I now realize that our waiting room was her birthing room. In God's mercy and compassion, she was delivered into a kingdom where He will wipe away every tear.

In one sense all of life is a waiting room. Earth isn't our final destination; it's the place where we sojourn for a time. Sometimes in the waiting room of life, there's birth with all its joy and other times, death with all its sorrow. The early church was in the waiting room of sorrow, suffering intense persecution and experiencing great trials. But James wanted them to know that this isn't all there is. There's a better world coming.

exploration

Thus far we have learned to be patient, strong-hearted, and content until Christ returns. Now we discover that another key to Living Faith is to be comforted by Scripture.

Review James 5, then focus on verses 10-11.

My brethren, take the prophets, who spoke in the name of the Lord, as an example of suffering and patience. James 5:10

1. James asks us to look to the prophets for inspiration. What was their job description?

. . . .

2. What were the prophets examples of?. . . . .

. . . .

3. Read Luke 13:34. What did biblical prophets often have to suffer and endure?

. . . .

Indeed we count them blessed who endure. You have heard of the perseverance of Job and seen the end intended by the Lord—that the Lord is very compassionate and merciful. James 5:11

4. How did James view the prophets who endured? . . . .

. . . .

5. James moved from the prophets in general to Job in particular. How was Job described?

. . . .

6. What phrase lets you know that God had a purpose in allowing Job's suffering?

. . . .

7. In what two ways will God show His love to those who are undergoing trials?

. . . .

. . . .

explanation

3
PROPHET'S CALL
A *prophet* was a person who spoke for God and who communicated His message courageously to the nation of Israel. Since James was writing to the twelve tribes, they would understand this simple reference. "Remember, the ancient prophets were persecuted, too" (Matthew 5:12, NLT).

5
PERSEVERANCE
Persevere means "to persist steadfastly despite counter influences, opposition, or discouragement." You cannot persevere unless you face difficulties; you can't experience triumph without tragedy. To receive the blessing, you must bear the burden.

6
JOB
You've heard the expression "He (or she) has the patience of Job." Job lost his children, his property, and his health; yet, "in all this Job did not sin nor charge God with wrong" (Job 1:22). He was truly an example of perseverance amidst trials.

8

PROPHET'S PAIN
Biblical prophets inspire us as we endure suffering: 1) They prove that we can be in the will of God and still suffer; 2) They show us that sometimes we suffer *because* we are in God's will; 3) They remind us that God cares for us when we suffer.

9

SUFFERING
It's not just prophets who suffer. If you're human, you'll suffer too. Take heart from Jesus, our suffering Savior. "He was despised and rejected—a man of sorrows, acquainted with bitterest grief. We turned our backs on him and looked the other way" (Isaiah 53:3, NLT).

10

SO BLESSED!
Blessed can mean "to bestow prosperity or happiness, or to protect and preserve." Though Job lost much, God preserved his life for future blessing. If you're in a season of suffering, patiently endure until the springtime of blessing.

8. James reminded us that the prophets were examples of those who endured suffering. Fill in the chart to discover who some of the prophets were and how they suffered.

SCRIPTURE	PROPHET	HOW SUFFERED
1 Kings 18:4		
. . . .		
Jer. 37:15-16		
. . . .		
Dan. 6:16-17		
. . . .		
Heb. 11:36-38		
. . . .		

9. We saw that the prophets received God's blessing because they patiently suffered.

Journal about a situation you are facing or have faced in which God is using suffering to teach you patience.

. . . .

. . . .

. . . .

. . . .

10. Read Job 42:12-17. How did God show His mercy and compassion to Job in his "latter days"?

. . . .

. . . .

Journal about how this gives you hope in your situation of suffering.

. . . .

. . . .

. . . .

. . . .

Everyone thinks they would rather have sunshine than showers. But what would the earth look like if it never rained again? Franklin Elmer, Jr. found the answer in northern Chile. He described the desolate region where rain never falls lodged between the Andes Mountains and the Pacific Ocean. He wrote, "Morning after morning the sun rises brilliantly over the tall mountains to the east; each noon it shines brightly down from overhead; evening brings a picturesque sunset. Although storms are often seen raging high in the mountains, and heavy fog banks are observed far out over the sea, the sun continues to shine on this favored and protected strip of land. . . . It is a sterile and desolate desert. There are no streams of water, and nothing grows there."

When the storm clouds darken our path, we long for sunshine and joy. We plead with God to bring a halt to the downpour of suffering. A wise Arabian proverb says, "All sunshine makes the desert." Deserts, like this sunny part of Chile, are infertile and desolate places. So, too, life without trials leads to life void of depth, beauty, and character. God knows we need both sunshine and showers to make us fruitful. The prophets realized that the blessings found in suffering far outweighed their temporal pain. We, too, must recognize that in God's wise design and under His sovereign control, times of sorrow actually bring showers of blessing.

contemplation

Suffering is the very best gift God has to give us. He gives it only to his chosen friends.
Therese of Lisieux

DAY 5 WAITING WITH INTEGRITY

preparation

Father, I know that You desire truth in my inner heart. I also know that You require my words and deeds to match. Help me to walk with inward and outward integrity until You come. Amen.

INTEGRITY

Better is the poor who walks in his integrity than one who is perverse in his lips, and is a fool.
Proverbs 19:1

"God, if you get me through tonight, I promise at dawn I'll give all my money to the poor." These kind of bargains made with God during desperate situations are called "foxhole confessions."

Jephthah, an Old Testament warrior, made a hasty vow to God and lived to regret it. Before engaging in battle with the Ammonites, Jephthah pledged, "If you give me victory over the Ammonites, I will give to the Lord the first thing coming out of my house to greet me when I return in triumph. I will sacrifice it as a burnt offering" (Judges 11:30-31, NLT). Victoriously returning from battle, Jephthah looked up to see his only daughter emerging from the house, dancing to celebrate his triumph. "When he saw her, he tore his clothes in anguish. 'My daughter!' he cried out. 'My heart is breaking! What a tragedy that you came out to greet me. For I have made a vow to the Lord and cannot take it back'" (Judges 11:35, NLT). Right or wrong, Jephthah fulfilled his vow.

James warns against making such foolish vows, especially if we have no intention of keeping them. While we may not make vows like Jephthah today, we have a modern equivalent: the New Year's Resolution. In January, we resolve to give up sugar. By Easter, we're caught eating chocolate bunnies and regretting our weakness. James reminds us that instead of making promises, we should let our yes be yes and our no be no.

exploration

We have learned some valuable lessons concerning how to live until Christ comes. Now we discover the importance of living with integrity.

Review James 5, then focus on verse 12.

But above all, my brethren, do not swear, either by heaven or by earth or with any other oath. But let your "Yes" be "Yes," and your "No," "No," lest you fall into judgment. James 5:12

1. What phrase tells you that this is the most important lesson James wanted the brethren to learn?

. . . .

2. Name the two kinds of proclamations we are warned against.

. . . .

. . . .

3. What phrase lets you know that no oath is appropriate?

. . . .

4. Rather than taking an oath, what did James instruct believers to do?

. . . .

5. What is the result of failing to keep our word? . . . .

. . . .

6. James took this instruction directly from Jesus' teaching in the Sermon on the Mount. Read Matthew 5:33-37 and answer the following questions.

   a. Why should we not swear by heaven (v. 34)? . . . .

   . . . .

   b. Why should we not swear by earth (v. 35)?. . . . .

   . . . .

   c. What other things did Jesus warn against swearing by? What reasons did He give (v. 35-36)?

   . . . .

   . . . .

2

"I SWEAR"
To *swear* is to take an oath. Herod swore foolishly to Salome when her dancing pleased him. "He also swore to her, 'Whatever you ask me, I will give you' " (Mark 6:23). Salome's mother took advantage of the situation and told her to request the head of John the Baptist.

3

AN OATH
Oaths were promises to fulfill verbal agreements. To make an oath testified that one's word was true and invoked consequences for not fulfilling it. We might say "Cross my heart and hope to die" to prove our sincerity.

4

YES! OR NO!
Instead of swearing, promising, or making an oath, we are told to be true to our word. We don't need to swear by any created thing to prove our sincerity; we prove our sincerity by acting with integrity. Actions *do* speak louder than words!

"I PROMISE"
A *promise* is a declaration that you will or will not do something. In other words, a promise is simply keeping your word. It means that you will say it, mean it, and do it. People who keep their word don't have to make promises.

LIARS
There's no such thing as a little white lie. When we say we'll do something and fail to do it, we are liars. We live in a world of lies promoted by Satan, "for he is a liar and the father of lies" (John 8:44, NIV).

d. Who is the power behind unnecessary, untruthful oaths (v. 37)?

. . . .

transformation

7. James tells us to say what we mean, mean what we say, and do what we say we'll do. In which of the following ways have you failed to keep your word?

— Said to a friend, "I'll pray for you" then neglected to pray
— Said to a child, "I'll play in a minute" then never found the time
— Said to God, "I won't ever do that again" but did it anyway
— Said to my boss, "I'll get it done" then neglected my duty
— Said to myself, "I'll stop that bad habit" but couldn't kick it
— Said to God, "I'll make time for you" then got distracted by life

8. We often lie to others and to ourselves by saying one thing and doing another. Sometimes we say yes when we should have said no, and end up breaking a promise.

Journal about something you've said yes to this week that you should have said no to. (Perhaps you said yes to a phone call when you should have been doing Bible study.)

. . . .

. . . .

Journal about how this action prevented you from keeping your word. (Perhaps you didn't get your lesson done and were unable to keep your promise to participate in your small group.)

. . . .

. . . .

9. In order to keep our word we must prioritize. Looking at your calendar, write a list of things you'll say yes or no to this week to maintain integrity.

Yes | **No**

(Example: Quiet time with the Lord) | (Example: Watching morning TV shows)

. . . .

. . . .

. . . .

. . . .

BEST THINGS
If you are a "yes" person, remember that no can be a positive word. It's alright to say no to one thing so that you can say yes to a better thing. A good thing can be bad if it keeps you from the *best thing.*

The Festival of Lying began at The Grizedale Theatre in Cumbria, England, where lying in all its forms is celebrated and debated. The festival offers a diverse curriculum including courses offered by professionals and professors on Internet hoaxes, techniques used by magicians and fake psychics, and discussions on lying, behavior, and conspiracy theories. Each year in November, a contest awards the title of "The Biggest Liar in the World" to the person worthy of following in Will Ritson's footsteps.

Will Ritson was a famous Cumbrian nineteenth-century tax collector, who lived in the English Lake District. Will always kept his customers enthralled with stories of regional folklore. Of course, he insisted that all his tall tales were true. Like the story about his foxhound who mated with a golden eagle: the hound's pups sprouted wings for leaping over the Lake District's dry stone walls more easily. Since that time there has been little trouble with foxes in the region.

If someone examined your life and your words, could you be invited to this festival? Do you tell distorted details to cover up promises you haven't kept, such as blaming traffic for being late when really you lingered too long in the mall? A half truth is a whole lie.

contemplation

A [wo]man of words and not of deeds is like a garden full of weeds.
English Proverb

Powerful Prayers

As a new Christian, the only "prayer" I knew was, "Now I lay me down to sleep. . . ." I had no idea that prayer was simply talking to God, nor did I understand the power unleashed when a believer practices intercessory prayer. My first pastor, Chuck Smith, taught that intercessory prayer is real labor and real battle against Satan.

"Suppose that someone attacked you on a dark street and started wrestling with you," Chuck suggested. "If he were to pull a knife, the whole battle would suddenly be centered on one thing—control of the knife. All of a sudden, you'd forget about punching him in the nose. You'd be grabbing for his wrist and trying to knock that knife, the deciding factor in this battle, out of his hand. Satan knows that prayer brings victory and spells his defeat. He knows it's the deciding factor in this spiritual warfare. That's why he concentrates all his efforts against prayer. He'll do all he can to upset you and keep you from praying."

No matter what situation we face, praying is the most important thing we can do. Our "Powerful Prayers" may be the deciding factor in an unseen battle. As we come to the end of the book of James, we are encouraged again to put feet on our faith and act on what we believe. James knew the power of prayer, and he reminds us to pray for the suffering, the sick, the sinner, the saint, and the straying.

DAY 1
Prayer for the Suffering

DAY 2
Prayer for the Sick

DAY 3
Prayer for the Sinner

DAY 4
Prayer of a Saint

DAY 5
Prayer for the Straying

explanation

THEY SUFFERED
The word for *suffering* here refers to ill treatment from others. James addresses those who are persecuted, abused, or treated unfairly, not those who are sick. "This is commendable, if because of conscience toward God one endures grief, suffering wrongfully" (1 Peter 2:19).

exploration

We've been challenged to be doers of the Word, not to be partial to the rich, to tame our tongues, to humbly submit to God, and to patiently wait for the Lord's return. Now James concludes his teaching on Living Faith with a firm call to prayer.

Read James 5, then focus on verse 13.

> *Is anyone among you suffering? Let him pray. Is anyone cheerful? Let him sing psalms.* James 5:13

1. What did James first ask the scattered Jewish believers?

. . . .

2. Read 1 Peter 4:12-16 to learn more about suffering in the early church, then answer the following questions.

   a. How did some believers in the early church view suffering (v. 12)?

   . . . .

   b. How did Peter want them to respond to suffering and why (vv. 13-14)?

   . . . .

   . . . .

   c. What kind of suffering were they exhorted to avoid (v. 15)?

   . . . .

d. What type of suffering was commended and why (v. 16)?

. . . .

3. According to James 5:13, what action should the suffering believer take?

. . . .

4. What was the second question James asked? . . . .

. . . .

5. What should the cheerful believer do? . . . .

. . . .

6. Review James 1:17. Why should we sing songs of praise to God?

. . . .

. . . .

transformation

7. From earlier lessons we know that the believers were persecuted because of their faith. Listed below are some of the ways the early believers suffered. Check the ways that parallel how believers suffer today.

— Job discrimination
— Family division
— Government persecution
— Dissension among believers
— Persecution from other religions
— Other_____

Think of some ways you have experienced similar suffering. Journal a prayer telling your heavenly Father about your pain by rewriting the following psalm: "O God, listen to my cry! Hear my prayer! From the

---

2

HE SUFFERED
We follow a suffering Savior. Jesus never promised Christians life without sorrow; He did offer peace along the way! "You may have peace in me. Here on earth you will have many trials and sorrows. But take heart, because I have over-come the world" (John 16:33, NLT).

3

KEEP PRAYING
The word James used for *prayer* suggests an ongoing pleading. It could be translated, "keep on praying." Suffering can last for more than a moment; therefore, prayer must be continuous. "Keep on praying. No matter what happens, always be thankful, for this is God's will for you" (1 Thessalonians 5:17-18, NLT).

7

WE SUFFER
Suffering means "afflic-tion or distress that includes intense pain or sorrow." Suffering has been part of the human experience since the Fall. Some suffering is the result of sin; some suffering serves to refine God's children. It can demonstrate God's power and help believ-ers identify with Christ.

PRESENT HELP
God does not always
choose to remove our
suffering, but He does
promise to hear our
prayers and help us
through our suffering.
Without suffering we
tend to become self-
sufficient and think we
don't need God. Suffer-
ing reminds us that God
is "a very present help
in trouble" (Psalm 46:1).

9

PRAISE
We don't always praise
God *for* our circum-
stances, but we can
always praise Him for
who He is in the midst
of suffering. That takes
Living Faith! Though
beaten and imprisoned,
"at midnight Paul and
Silas were praying and
singing hymns to God"
(Acts 16:25).

ends of the earth, I will cry to you for help, for my heart
is overwhelmed. Lead me to the towering rock of safety,
for you are my safe refuge, a fortress where my enemies
cannot reach me" (Psalm 61:1-3, NLT).

. . . .

. . . .

. . . .

. . . .

8. Fill in the chart to discover some of the ways God helps us in
our suffering when we come to Him in prayer.

SCRIPTURE	GOD'S HELP
Ps. 118:5-7	
Ps. 138:3	
2 Cor. 12:7-9	
Phil. 4:6-7	

9. Throughout the book of James, we've learned that we can be
cheerful despite our suffering. Write a list of things you can
praise God for despite your circumstances.

. . . .

. . . .

. . . .

You've heard it said, "Prayer changes things." In this beautiful
poem written by an unknown Confederate soldier, we unearth
the truth behind the old adage:

I asked God for strength that I might achieve.
I was made weak that I might learn humbly to obey.
I asked God for health that I might do greater things.
I was given infirmity that I might do better things.
I asked for riches that I might be happy.

I was given poverty that I might be wise.
I asked for power that I might have the praise of men.
I was given weakness that I might feel the need of God.
I asked for all things that I might enjoy life.
I was given life that I might enjoy all things.
I got nothing that I asked for—but everything I had hoped
    for . . .
Almost despite myself, my unspoken prayers were answered.
I am among all men most richly blessed.

It is natural to ask and hope for things from God, especially
when we are suffering. Yet we've learned from James that we
often "ask amiss." Thankfully, God doesn't always give us what
we want; He gives us what we need to grow in spiritual maturity.
Does this mean we shouldn't pray because God gives us what
He wants anyway? Absolutely not! God wants us to pray with
power, with purpose, and in His will—He delights to answer
the prayers of His people. Whether we're going through a rough
time or feeling especially joyful, it's always the right time to pray.

contemplation

*Don't ask God for what
you think is good; ask
him for what he thinks
is good for you.*
Anonymous

DAY 2 PRAYER FOR
THE SICK

preparation

*Father, my greatest
need is forgiveness.
I ask that You forgive
me of my sins. I ask You
to heal me according
to Your will: body, mind,
and spirit. Amen.*

FORGIVENESS
*If You, Lord, should
mark iniquities, O Lord,
who could stand? But
there is forgiveness with
You, that You may be
feared. Psalm 130:3-4*

According to a study published in the 1982-83 *Journal of the American Medical Association,* prayer for recovery may help the healing process. This scientific study found that hospitalized heart patients had fewer complications when born-again Christians prayed for them. The study found that patients in the group being prayed for were less likely to need antibiotics, diuretics, or the insertion of tubes for feeding or breathing.

Sir Thomas Browne, a seventeenth-century physician, dedicated his life to prayer: "I have resolved to pray more and pray always, to pray in all places where quietness inviteth: in the house, on the highway and on the street; and to know no street or passage in this city that may not witness that I have not forgotten God. I purpose . . . to pray for my sick patients and for the patients of other physicians; at my entrance into any home to say, 'May the peace of God abide here' . . . to pray God to give them wholeness of soul, and by and by to give them the beauty of the resurrection."

James instructs believers to pray for the sick, not just for their physical healing but, more importantly, for their spiritual healing. Again we must remember that all prayers should be prayed in God's will. It may not be God's will to physically heal an ailing brother or sister in Christ; but it is *always* His will to bring spiritual healing and wholeness. Is anyone sick? Pray for them—body, mind, and spirit!

exploration

We have learned that we should pray when suffering and praise when cheerful. We also found that true Living Faith praises even in pain. Now we learn to ask others to pray for us.

Review James 5, then focus on verses 14-15.

Is anyone among you sick? Let him call for the elders of the church, and let them pray over him, anointing him with oil in the name of the Lord. James 5:14

1. What was James's next question?. . . . .

. . . .

2. What action should the sick person take? . . . .

. . . .

3. Describe what the elders of the church should do for the sick person?

. . . .

4. In whose name are the elders to pray? . . . .

. . . .

And the prayer of faith will save the sick, and the Lord will raise him up. And if he has committed sins, he will be forgiven. James 5:15

5. Describe how the elders should pray, and what will result.

. . . .

6. Who receives the credit for this? . . . .

. . . .

7. James first focused on the physical condition of the sick. Next he focused on their spiritual condition. Besides healing, what can you infer the sick person and the elders should ask for in prayer?

. . . .

. . . .

8. What does God promise concerning sin?. . . . .

. . . .

explanation

ELDER
An *elder* is an overseer. The term literally means "aged person," not necessarily referring to years but rather to one's experience of walking with the Lord in prayer and study of the Word. Elders are to rule, teach, guard the truth from perversion and error, and shepherd the flock.

ANOINTING
Anointing is a medicinal term that literally means "massaging." In the New Testament, anointing was frequently used in connection with healing. It was often therapeutic—applying oil to soothe wounds, refresh tired bodies, and stimulate muscles. James may be suggesting that we use all available means for healing.

WHOSE FAITH?
Notice that it is not the faith of the sick person but the faith of the elders that brings healing. Today many "faith healers" lay blame for sickness at the feet of the victim. Instead, the burden sits squarely on the shoulders of the one doing the praying.

9

HONORABLE
Elders have the job of recognizing the gifted, helping the struggling, rebuking the rebellious, and praying for the weak. They deserve to be honored. "Let the elders who rule well be counted worthy of double honor, especially those who labor in the word and doctrine" (1 Timothy 5:17).

10

SET APART
In ancient Israel anointing was performed to set apart a person for a particular work or service. Anointing symbolized that the person belonged to God in a special sense. Prophets, priests, and kings were anointed when oil was poured on their heads.

11

FORGIVEN
Sin can cause physical sickness: Promiscuous sex causes STDs; a guilty conscience triggers ulcers. When the Corinthians partook of the Lord's Supper unworthily, Paul said, "For this reason many are weak and sick among you" (1 Corinthians 11:30). Since humanity's greatest disease is sin, the greatest cure is forgiveness.

9. The elders should provide spiritual maturity and leadership. In which of the following ways have you sought help from the elders or deacons of your church?

___ Dealing with a sinning Christian (Matthew 18:15-16)
___ Resolving a dispute (Acts 15:2)
___ Commissioning for ministry (Acts 15:22)
___ Giving updates on ministry (Acts 21:18-19)
___ Learning sound doctrine (Titus 1:9)
___ Prayer and anointing for illness (James 5:14)

10. James encouraged the sick to go to the elders and be anointed for healing. Fill in the following chart to discover other types of anointing and the reason for them.

SCRIPTURE	ANOINTED & WHY?
Exod. 40:12-15	
Num. 7:1	
1 Sam. 10:1, 24	
Luke 4:18	

11. More important than physical healing is spiritual healing. James taught that *all* who pray to be healed from the disease of sin will be forgiven.

Journal a personal prayer by rewording Psalm 25:16-18, asking God to forgive you of your sins: "Turn Yourself to me, and have mercy on me, for I am desolate and afflicted. The troubles of my heart have enlarged; bring me out of my distresses! Look on my affliction and my pain, and forgive all my sins."

Some people blame God for not answering prayers the way they desire. Ted Turner, self-made millionaire and founder of CNN broadcasting network, once received the *Humanist of the Year* award. In his acceptance speech, he shared a very emotional story revealing that he had been raised in a God-fearing family. His sister became ill, and as her illness progressed, she became critical. Ted desperately prayed to the Lord to heal her and spare her life. She died. From that time on, Ted chose to believe there is no God. He would not believe in a loving God who allowed his sister to suffer and die. Turner insisted that he would live his life depending on himself, not on an unfeeling, phantom-being who did not exist. The audience applauded wildly.

Simply because God does not answer our prayers for physical healing does not mean we should give up on our faith. I (Penny) have suffered from severe migraines for fourteen years. I've gone to the elders for prayer and anointing. I've asked God to heal me. I've confessed my sins. I've consulted doctors. Yet I still have headaches. Through it all I have learned, with Paul, that God's grace is sufficient for me. I've experienced God's love and power in amazing ways through my suffering. I know with absolute certainty that God will answer my prayer for healing either on earth or in heaven, and I trust Him to know which is the right choice for me.

contemplation

I have prayed hundreds, if not thousands, of times for the Lord to heal me—and he finally healed me of the need to be healed.
Tim Hansel

preparation

Father, thank You for the intimate relationships You have given me. Thank You for my sisters and brothers in the Lord who pray for me and hold me accountable. Amen.

ONE ANOTHER

This is My commandment, that you love one another as I have loved you. John 15:12

You've heard it said that confession is good for the soul. Dietrich Bonhoeffer agreed: "A man who confesses his sins in the presence of a brother knows that he is no longer alone with himself; he experiences the presence of God in the reality of the other person. As long as I am by myself in the confession of my sins everything remains in the dark, but in the presence of a brother the sin has to be brought into the light."

Satan had found a foothold in my past that was hindering the present. Although I had recited "the sinner's prayer," I still felt ashamed of certain sins I had committed and unworthy to be used by God. I was convinced that if any of my Christian friends knew how *bad* I really was, they'd avoid me. At a summer retreat, the youth pastor taught on this text in James, saying, "If Satan is continually reminding you of sins you've already confessed, if you feel stuck in the past, then confessing your sins to another could break the cycle." I was terrified but felt compelled to confess the untold story of my past to my friends. Instead of condemnation, they offered compassion. Instead of pointing fingers, they laid hands on me and asked God to heal my wounds. From that time on, the cycle of guilt and shame was broken, and the light of God flooded my soul.

Today James offers hope to all believers: Confessing our sins to one another and praying for each other brings God's healing touch.

exploration

This week we have learned to pray for the suffering and the sick. Now James discusses the value of intimate, confessional prayer between brothers and sisters in Christ.

Review James 5, then focus on verse 16.

Confess your trespasses to one another, and pray for one another, that you may be healed. The effective, fervent prayer of a righteous man avails much. James 5:16

1. What is the first thing we are commanded to do with one another?

....

2. Read Galatians 6:1-3. How should we deal with another person's trespasses?

....

3. According to James, what should we do for one another after confession?

....

4. What does God promise will result from prayer and confession?

....

....

5. Describe the attitude with which we should pray. . . . .

....

6. What kind of person offers dynamic prayers? . . . .

....

7. What is the effect of fervent prayers? . . . .

....

transformation

8. James admonishes us to confess our sins to one another. Have you ever obeyed this command?

Yes!   No!

explanation

1

CONFESS
Confess means "to say the same thing." Confession openly admits sin, declaring oneself guilty of what one is accused (adapted, *Unger's*). We must confess our sins to the Lord and to those who've been affected by them. James doesn't say confess to a priest but to one another.

2

TRESPASS
Trespass means "a violation of a law." The Old Testament calls it "a stepping aside from the (correct) path." The New Testament translates it as "a falling aside." The apostle Paul wrote: "And you He made alive, who were dead in trespasses and sins" (Ephesians 2:1).

4

HEALED
Healing is not necessarily physical—it also includes spiritual restoration. James used the word *healed* in the context of a repentant believer becoming spiritually whole again. Confessing our sins to fellow believers will cure the sin-sick soul and bring restoration.

PRAYER PARTNER
Everyone needs a prayer partner or confidante. Choose a person of the same sex whom you trust. Things shared in these relationships: 1) should be completely confidential; 2) should be prayed over, not just talked about; 3) should never be held up for ridicule or scorn.

9

RIGHTEOUS
Righteousness is the action that promotes the peace and well-being of people in their relationships to one another and to God. "The mouth of the righteous speaks wisdom. . . . The law of his God is in his heart; none of his steps shall slide." (Psalm 37:30-31).

10

GOOD COMPANY
Powerless prayers turn passionate when others join in. "If two of you agree on earth concerning anything that they ask, it will be done for them. . . . Where two or three are gathered together in My name, I am there" (Matthew 18:19-20). When you pray with others, God participates too.

If your answer is yes, journal about a time you confessed a sin, whom you confessed it to, and how you were healed.

. . . .

. . . .

. . . .

If your answer is no, journal about whom you'll ask to become your accountability/prayer partner and what you'd like to confess to that person.

. . . .

. . . .

. . . .

. . . .

9. James says the prayers of a righteous person will be effective. Read Matthew 5:23-24, then answer the following questions to discover why some prayers are rendered ineffective.

a. Describe the situation that interrupted prayer here (v. 23).

. . . .

b. List the three steps required to restore the effectiveness of your prayers (v. 24).

. . . .

10. A righteous person's prayers will be both fervent and effective. Based on the definitions provided, evaluate your own prayer life.

Effective comes from the word meaning *energy* and speaks of "putting forth power or putting into action." Effective prayers are full of energy and get the job done.

1	2	3	4	5	6	7	8	9	10

powerless   **powerful**

Fervent means "to be hot or boil; to have zeal." Fervent prayers are so passionate they heat things up.

1	2	3	4	5	6	7	8	9	10

ice cold   **red hot**

Two dangers threaten confession: too little and too much. Richard Owen Roberts said, "Beware lest your concern for propriety and pride keep you from confessing those sins the public deserves to hear about. Likewise, beware that your earnestness in making all things right before God does not play into the hands of the great deceiver who would love to turn your confession of sin into an inducement for another to sin."

Joy Dawson told a story about confessing too much that rings like a warning signal. A pastor was struggling in his flesh, consumed with lust for his beautiful secretary. As the two worked side by side, his desire grew. One day the pastor foolishly confessed his attraction to his young assistant. This opened the door for Satan to gain a foothold. The secretary was harboring the same feelings. They began an extramarital affair that divided two families and an entire church. Instead of confessing to one another, they could have consulted their spouse, their accountability partner, or a spiritual advisor from another church.

Before confessing your sins to another, ask yourself:

Why am I confessing? To make myself *feel* better or to ruthlessly deal with sin?

What am I confessing? My own sins and not someone else's shortcomings?

Who is the right person to confess the sin to? Will it cause the hearer to stumble, or will this person help stabilize my walk with the Lord?

How should I confess? Publicly or privately? If you sinned publicly, confess in public; if you sinned in private, confess privately.

contemplation

For him who confesses,
shams are over and
realities have begun.
William James

DAY 4 PRAYER OF A SAINT

preparation

Father, I thank You for listening and responding to my prayers. Amen.

ANSWERED PRAYER
In the day of my trouble I will call upon You, for You will answer me.
Psalm 86:7

Miracles in Black by John C. Wengatz tells of an African convert named Joao Mbaxi who became a missionary to a cannibal tribe. He came to the village during a drought, but the tribe was sure tropical rains would come soon. However, months passed without a cloud in the sky. Everyone was suffering, and many were on the brink of starvation. They complained to Joao that in the years they had worshipped their idols, it had always rained. They urged Joao to leave the country and take "the white man's God" with him. When the brave missionary refused to leave, the angry chief warned, "If your God is as good as you say and so powerful that He rules the sky, why doesn't He send rain? If it doesn't rain by sunrise tomorrow, we will drink your blood and eat your flesh!"

Remembering the prophet Elijah, Joao went to his hut and prayed for divine help with great urgency. Throughout the night, the members of the tribe waited for the dawn when the Christian would become their victim. Just before daylight, thunder roared in the distance, lightning flashed across the sky, and rain poured across the entire region. The fervent prayer warrior was able to continue his work for Christ for many years.

James brings Elijah to our attention as an example of a righteous man with a powerful prayer life. As we examine the prayers of this saint, ask yourself if you have the Living Faith to pray as he did.

exploration

Yesterday we discovered that fervent prayer yields results. Now we look at an example of one righteous man's effective prayer.

Review James 5, then focus on verses 17-18.

Elijah was a man with a nature like ours, and he prayed earnestly that it would not rain; and it did not rain on the land for three years and six months. James 5:17

1. What Old Testament figure did James refer to, and how was he described?

. . . .

2. How did Elijah pray, and what were the results? . . . .

. . . .

3. To better understand the basis for Elijah's prayers, read Deuteronomy 11:13-17, and discover how God used the weather to reward or punish his people.

Blessed with rain because (vv. 13-14): . . . .

. . . .

Cursed with drought because (vv. 16-17): . . . .

. . . .

And he prayed again, and the heaven gave rain, and the earth produced its fruit. James 5:18

4. Describe how God responded to Elijah's next prayer and how it blessed others.

. . . .

. . . .

5. Look up the following passages to discover why Elijah prayed the way he did.

a. 1 Kings 16:33: Describe the condition of the nation of Israel based on Ahab's leadership.

. . . .

b. 1 Kings 17:1: How did Elijah predict God would respond?

. . . .

explanation

1

ELIJAH
Elijah was an influential prophet during the ninth century B.C. Emphasizing the need for unconditional loyalty to God, he opposed accepted standards of his day, which included belief in many gods. He served as God's instrument of judgment on wayward Israel because of the people's widespread idolatry.

3

PRAY THE WORD
God honors the prayers of those who are obedient to His Word. Elijah interceded earnestly because he prayed according to the Word of God and the will of God. The Word of God and prayer must go hand in hand, for His Word gives us the promises to claim when we pray.

5

INTERCEDE
Elijah interceded for Israel, first for drought so they would return to God: "A drought on her waters! . . . For it is a land of idols" (Jeremiah 50:38, NIV). Next he prayed for rain so God would shower blessings on His repentant people: "There shall be showers of blessing" (Ezekiel 34:26).

c. 1 Kings 18:17-18: Contrast whom Ahab and Elijah blamed for the drought.

. . . .

d. 1 Kings 18:36-37: What did Elijah pray for the nation?

. . . .

e. 1 Kings 18:38-39, 45: How did God answer Elijah's prayer?

. . . .

transformation

6. James said that Elijah was a man with a nature just like the rest of us. From a study of Elijah's life, check off the ways you are like Elijah.

___ Self-righteous	___ Obedient to God
___ Fearful	___ Spoke God's Word
___ Complained to God	___ Depressed
___ Hungry	___ Prayed for others
___ Thirsty	___ Discipled others

7. James encouraged us to pray earnestly. Fill in the chart to learn about some biblical figures who prayed and what they prayed for.

SCRIPTURE   EARNEST PRAYER

1 Sam. 1:9-11 . . . .

Mark 5:22-23 . . . .

Luke 22:42-44 . . . .

Col. 4:12 . . . .

8. Today we learned through Elijah's example to pray for our nation. With this in mind, write out some things you earnestly believe your nation needs prayer for.

. . . .

. . . .

6

ORDINARY?
God empowers ordinary people to do extraordinary tasks. Moses, a murderer with a speech impediment, was used to deliver the children of Israel from bondage. Mary, a teenager pregnant out of wedlock, delivered the Savior to the world. When common people surrender to an uncommon God, miracles happen.

7

EARNEST
Earnest prayer refers to prayer that is immediate, intense, and continuous. This type of prayer recognizes a need and turns to God for the solution. It does not give up but continues to pray intently. "Continue earnestly in prayer, being vigilant in it with thanksgiving" (Colossians 4:2).

8

INTERCESSION
Intercession is the "act of petitioning God or praying on behalf of another person or group." The sinful nature of this world separates human beings from God. However, it is the privilege and duty of all Christians to pray for others to be reconciled to God (adapted, *Nelson's* and *Vine's*).

Journal an intercessory prayer for your nation to God using the following verse: "If My people who are called by My name will humble themselves, and pray and seek My face, and turn from their wicked ways, then I will hear from heaven, and will forgive their sin and heal their land" (2 Chronicles 7:14).

. . . .

. . . .

. . . .

. . . .

Elijah's prayers brought spiritual revival to the nation of Israel during the wicked King Ahab's reign. God's miraculous answers to Elijah's prayers caused the people to take notice and return to worshiping the one true God. It's astounding to realize that the prayers of one person can impact an entire nation.

President Abraham Lincoln asked an entire nation to join him in prayer, proclaiming April 30, 1863, a National Day of Fasting, Humiliation, and Prayer: "We have been the recipients of the choicest bounties of heaven. We have been preserved, the many years, in peace and prosperity. We have grown in numbers, wealth and power, as no other nation has ever grown. But we have forgotten God. We have forgotten the gracious hand which preserved us in peace and multiplied and enriched and strengthened us; and we have vainly imagined, in the deceitfulness of our hearts that all these blessings were produced by some superior wisdom and virtue of our own.

"Intoxicated with unbroken success, we have become too self-sufficient to feel the necessity of redeeming and preserving grace, too proud to pray to God that made us! It behooves us, then to humble ourselves before the offended Power, to confess our national sins, and to pray for clemency and forgiveness."

Abraham Lincoln saw the abolition of slavery and the reuniting of a nation. Perhaps God is waiting for *you* to intercede for your country so the nation will return to Him.

contemplation

An intercessor means one who is in such vital contact with God and with his fellowmen that he is like a live wire closing the gap between the saving power of God and the sinful men who have been cut off from that power.
Hannah Hurnard

DAY 5 PRAYER FOR THE STRAYING

preparation

Father, when I stray, thank You for always bringing me back to the right path. Give me eyes to see those who are wandering and help me to turn them back toward You. Amen.

REPENTANCE

Or do you despise the riches of His goodness, forbearance, and longsuffering, not knowing that the goodness of God leads you to repentance?
Romans 2:4

Some Christians have been known to shoot their wounded. When a believer falls into sin, it's easy to criticize and condemn the offender. However, God offers a better approach to restoring those who have strayed from the path: comfort and consolation.

A pastor's child learned this valuable lesson from an experience that made a deep impression upon him. His father received a call saying a well-known Christian had been found drunk on the sidewalk. Immediately his father sent his chauffeured limousine to pick the man up, while his mother prepared the best guest room. The boy watched wide-eyed as the beautiful comforter was turned down on the exquisite, four-poster bed, revealing the finest monogrammed sheets.

"But mother," the young man protested, "he's drunk. He might even get sick!" His mother replied kindly, "I know. But this man has slipped and fallen. When he comes to, he will be so ashamed. He will need all the prayer and loving encouragement we can give him." It was a lesson the son never forgot.

In his closing words, James offers a similar lesson of compassion that we must never forget. As believers we must come alongside those who have wandered from the truth. We are admonished to restore them by revealing to them the error of their ways and concealing from others the way they have erred.

exploration

As James concludes his letter, he reminds those who have Living Faith to pray for those who have wandered from the faith.

Review James 5, then focus on verses 19-20.

Brethren, if anyone among you wanders from the truth, and someone turns him back, let him know that he who turns a sinner from the error of his way will save a soul from death and cover a multitude of sins. James 5:19-20

1. What final problem did James address among the brethren?

. . . .

2. Explain the responsibility of the believers to those among them who wander.

. . . .

3. Jesus talked about wandering "sheep." Read the parable in Matthew 18:12-14. Summarize how God responds to straying sheep and how He feels about sinners who return to Him.

. . . .

4. How did James describe the sin of the wanderer in verse 20?

. . . .

5. Where will the wrong path eventually end?. . . . .

. . . .

6. What two things will the brethren accomplish in their rescue operation?

. . . .

7. Read 1 Peter 4:8. What attitude should the brethren have when bringing people to repentance?

. . . .

transformation

8. James warned that some believers in the church had wandered from the truth to error. Using the words *TRUTH* and *ERROR* as

explanation

WANDER
Wander means "to roam from safety, truth, or virtue." In this instance it means to roam from obedience to God's Word, to gradually move away from the will of God. Wandering from the truth to sin can lead to chastening and premature death.

TURN BACK
Turn back means "to repent—turn away from sin and toward to God." The church helps the backslider by praying and promoting scriptural truth. "All Scripture is given by inspiration of God, and is profitable for doctrine, for reproof, for correction, for instruction in righteousness" (2 Timothy 3:16).

6

COVER
To *cover* means "to hide or veil." Once a sinner has repented of his backsliding, God promises to cover his or her sins. This does not mean that believers should sweep sin under a carpet; it does mean that once sin has been forgiven, it should also be forgotten.

ON TRACK
How to stay on track?
Pray for God's help and
ponder God's Word.
"Let me not wander
from Your command-
ments! Your word I have
hidden in my heart, that
I might not sin against
You!" (Psalm 119:10-
11). Trusting God helps
avoid detours. Medi-
tating on His truth
exposes errors.

acrostics, list some of the truths in God's Word and some ways people wander into error.

T (Ex.: Telling the truth)   E (Ex.: Exaggerating the situation)

T. . . . . E. . . . .

R. . . . . R. . . . .

U. . . . . R. . . . .

T. . . . . O . . . .

H . . . . R. . . . .

BACKSLIDING
What the New Testa-
ment calls *wandering*,
the Old Testament
defines as *backsliding*,
which means reverting
to sin or lapsing morally.
This term is found
mainly in Jeremiah (see
Jeremiah 3) and refers
to the lapse of the
nation of Israel into
paganism and idolatry.

9. We are told that when believers turn from the truth, it is our duty to pursue them that they might turn back to God.

Journal about someone you know who has backslidden from the truth. What lies does this person believe? What road is he or she on?

. . . .

. . . .

. . . .

RESTORATION
God is the God of
second chances. He
delights to restore
broken things. If you've
strayed from Him, resto-
ration is just a prayer
away. "When he prays
to God, he will be
accepted. And God
will receive him with
joy and restore him
to good standing"
(Job 33:26, NLT).

10

Journal a prayer asking God to bring this person back to the truth. Tell God you will be willing to be used by Him as a messenger of repentance and forgiveness.

. . . .

. . . .

. . . .

10. Even the most well-intentioned believers can find themselves straying from God, and the apostle Peter is no exception. Read the passages, then answer the questions.

Matthew 26:69-75: Describe how Peter strayed from the truth.

. . . .

John 21:15-17: How and by whom was Peter turned back to God?

. . . .

11. James has taught us what having Living Faith really means.

> In closing, journal about some of the ways you have been challenged to live out what you believe. How has your faith increased through this study?

. . . .

. . . .

. . . .

. . . .

Many of us stray from the truth when life gets hard. If God doesn't answer our prayers in the way or in the time we expected, we are tempted to take matters into our own hands and wander from the truth. However, James reminds us that Living Faith is a confident belief in God and an unwavering commitment to His promises.

Abraham trusted God's promise of fruitfulness despite infertility. He believed God could resurrect the dead while relinquishing his son Isaac on the altar of sacrifice. Paul said, "[Abraham] did not waver at the promise of God through unbelief, but was strengthened in faith, giving glory to God, and being fully convinced that what He had promised He was also able to perform" (Romans 4:20-21). *Living Faith believes God's promises regardless of circumstances, and Living Faith acts on God's Word.*

Lost something or someone precious? Faith believes **God is good**!

Depressed, lonely, or afraid? Faith believes **God is light**!

Marriage falling apart? Faith believes **God is love**!

Health waning and you are weak? Faith believes **God is strong**!

During the holocaust, Jewish teenager Anne Frank wrote: "I believe in the sun even when it is not shining; I believe in love even when I do not feel it; I believe in God even when He is silent." Whether you are sick or straying, a sinner or a saint, will you turn to God in Living Faith and believe that His promises are true?

contemplation

Fold the arms of your faith and wait in quietness until the light goes up in your darkness. Fold the arms of your faith, I say, but not of your action. Think of something you ought to do, and go do it. Heed not your feelings. Do your work.

George MacDonald

Bibliography

The authors have used the following books and electronic sources in preparing the illustrations and sidebar material for this book.

Bible Illustrator 3 Deluxe for Windows. Version 3.0f. Copyright © 1990-1998 by Parsons Technology, Inc.

Farrar, Steve. *Family Survival in the American Jungle.* Sisters, Oreg.: Multnomah Press, 1991.

Henry, Matthew. *Matthew Henry's Commentary on the Whole Bible: One Volume Edition, Complete and Unabridged.* Peabody, Mass.: Hendrickson, 1991.

Hewett, James S. *Illustrations Unlimited.* Wheaton, Ill.: Tyndale House, 1988.

INFOsearch™. *Version 4.11d. Illustrations data and database.* The Communicator's Companion™, P.O. Box 171749, Arlington, Tex. 76003. Web site: <www.infosearch.com>.

International Standard Bible Encyclopaedia. Electronic Database. Copyright © 1995-1996 by Biblesoft. From *The PC Study Bible for Windows.*

Lockyer, Herbert. *All the Doctrines of the Bible.* Grand Rapids, Mich.: Zondervan Books, 1964.

Lockyer, Herbert, ed. *Nelson's Illustrated Bible Dictionary.* Nashville, Tenn.: Nelson, 1986. (Out of print, but appears in *The PC Study Bible for Windows.*)

MacArthur, John. *The MacArthur New Testament Commentary: James.* Chicago: Moody Press, 1998.

MacArthur, John, ed. *The MacArthur Study Bible, NKJV.* Nashville, Tenn.: Word Publishing and Thomas Nelson, 1997.

Moody Monthly. Chicago: Moody Press, June 1988.

The PC Study Bible for Windows. Biblesoft, Version 3.0. Seattle: Jim Gilbertson, 1999.

www.sermonIllustrations.com.

Smith, Chuck. *Effective Prayer Life.* Costa Mesa, Calif.: Maranatha House Publishers, 1979.

Strong, James H., ed. *Strong's Concordance of the Bible.* Grand Rapids, Mich.: Baker, 1992. From *The PC Study Bible for Windows.*

Unger, Merrill F., and R. K. Harrison, eds. *New Unger's Bible Dictionary.* Chicago: Moody Press, 1998. From *The PC Study Bible for Windows.*

Vine, W. E. *Vine's Complete Expository Dictionary of Old and New Testament Words.* Merrill F. Unger and William White, Jr., eds. Nashville, Tenn.: Nelson, 1985. From *The PC Study Bible for Windows.*

Webster's New Collegiate Dictionary, 7th ed. Springfield, Mass.: Merriam-Webster, 1996.

With Gratitude

Lenya—I am forever indebted to the inspiring saints who have boldly displayed their Living Faith to me and the world around them: Tamara Nuttle, who had the courage in high school to share her faith with me at the risk of being labeled a "Jesus Freak." Dave and Debbie Gustaveson, who were willing to sacrifice property, plans, and their professions to become life-long ministers with Youth With A Mission, leaving me an example to follow. Kim Ackerman, who is the godliest woman I know, displaying her faith with a meek and quiet spirit. She's the kind of woman I want to be when I grow up. Lastly, I dedicate this book in loving memory of my friend Patty Davis. She was the feistiest and most fervent prayer warrior ever to stand by my side. Her heart for the world, her friends, and her family motivated her to do good works that continue to shine like the stars.

Penny—I dedicate this book to the memory of my grandparents. I am so grateful that they exhibited Living Faith and passed it on to their children and grandchildren. On my maternal side: to "Mima," Lillian Maloy Whitlock, whose faith was the hallmark of her life and who gently touched the heart of everyone who crossed her path, and to "Granddaddy," Frank Whitlock, who never met a stranger and was always willing to lend a helping hand. On my paternal side: to "Mom," Beulah Pierce, who loved Bible study and prayed diligently for her family, and to "Pop," Chrys Pierce, who assisted anyone in need and whose dinnertime prayers we remember to this day.

Lenya Heitzig was headed for a promising career in fashion merchandising when God changed her direction. After a lifetime steeped in agnosticism, Lenya was converted in 1978 and then was thrust into the explosive days of the Jesus Movement in southern California.

Her early training for ministry was forged on the anvil of servant leadership. Lenya's "job description" as a counselor for new believers included vacuuming the church sanctuary and cleaning rest rooms. After joining Youth With A Mission (YWAM) in 1980 as a single women's counselor, she once again discovered that ministry is not just telling people how to act but serving them as cook and school secretary.

These days of small beginnings were preparation for a wider scope of service. After her term with YWAM, Lenya met a determined California surfer who was undergoing his own spiritual groundwork for great things ahead. After marrying in 1981, Skip and Lenya Heitzig headed to the Rocky Mountain Southwest and settled in Albuquerque, New Mexico. Soon their home Bible study blossomed into Calvary of Albuquerque, a church exceeding 12,000 in weekly attendance.

Lenya's gift in teaching and communicating truth paved the way for a thriving women's ministry that has had a strong impact on the Southwest. Lenya has served on the executive board for a Billy and Franklin Graham Crusade and currently chairs and directs the Southwest Women's Festival, which hosts yearly conferences and where Lenya has shared the podium with such speakers as Kay Arthur, Florence Littauer, and Anne Graham Lotz. Lenya is the founder of Mercy B.A.N.D. (Bearing Another's Name Daily), a nonprofit organization that remembers the victims of the September 11 terrorist attacks and encourages prayer for their loved ones.

Lenya speaks regularly to the Women at Calvary and is in demand as a conference speaker for retreats and seminars throughout the United States and Europe. Lenya is the author of two other books in Tyndale's Women's Bible Journal Series—*Discovering the Path to God's Treasures: Ephesians* and *Pathway to God's Plan: Ruth and Esther.* She was featured in Tyndale's *Finding God's Peace in Perilous Times.*

Skip, Lenya, and their son, Nathan, live in Albuquerque and continue this exciting pathway that God has set them on.

Penny Pierce Rose was raised in a loving Christian home and heard God call her by name while attending church camp at the age of nine. During high school and college she wandered off God's pathway and followed the ways of the world. Soon after marriage and motherhood she became discontented with her life and grudgingly attended a Bible Study Fellowship meeting with her mother. God's Word inspired her to renew her relationship with Him. Her husband, Kerry, soon followed in the footsteps of faith, bringing salvation to their household.

Penny graduated from Texas Tech University with a degree in political science. After seven years in Bible Study Fellowship, Penny joined the leadership team of the Women at Calvary. She also serves on the board of directors of Southwest Women's Festival. Reflecting her heart to minister to women and children, she has participated as Kid's Crusade coordinator for Harvest Crusade with Greg Laurie and as secretary for the Women's Committee of New Mexico Festival '98 with Franklin Graham.

Penny is the author of two other books in Tyndale's Women's Bible Journal Series—*Discovering the Path to God's Treasures: Ephesians* and *Pathway to God's Plan: Ruth and Esther.* She continues to write for the Women at Calvary Bible study and speak at conferences and retreats. Her fervent desire is to minister to women by teaching them to study God's Word, apply the truths to their daily lives, and embrace the Christian life as a grand adventure. Penny and Kerry live in Albuquerque with their three great kids: Erin, Kristian, and Ryan.